Applications and Innovations in Intelligent Systems XI

Applications and Innovations in
Intelligent Systems XI

Springer
London
Berlin
Heidelberg
New York
Hong Kong
Milan
Paris
Tokyo

Max Bramer, Richard Ellis and
Ann Macintosh (Eds)

Applications and Innovations in Intelligent Systems XI

Proceedings of AI2003, the Twenty-third SGAI
International Conference on Innovative Techniques
and Applications of Artificial Intelligence

Springer

Professor Max Bramer, BSc, PhD, CEng, FBCS, FIEE, FRSA
Faculty of Technology, University of Portsmouth, Portsmouth, UK

Richard Ellis, BSc, MSc
Crew Services Ltd, Portsmouth, UK

Dr Ann Macintosh, BSc, CEng
Napier University, International Teledemocracy Centre, Edinburgh, EH10 5DT, UK

British Library Cataloguing in Publication Data
A catalogue record for this book is available from the British Library

Library of Congress Cataloging-in-Publication Data
A catalog record for this book is available from the Library of Congress

Apart from any fair dealing for the purposes of research or private study, or criticism or review, as permitted under the Copyright, Designs and Patents Act 1988, this publication may only be reproduced, stored or transmitted, in any form or by any means, with the prior permission in writing of the publishers, or in the case of reprographic reproduction in accordance with the terms of licences issued by the Copyright Licensing Agency. Enquiries concerning reproduction outside those terms should be sent to the publishers.

ISBN-13: 978-1-85233-779-7   e-ISBN-13: 978-1-4471-0643-2

DOI: 10.1007/978-1-4471-0643-2

Springer-Verlag is part of Springer Science+Business Media GmbH
springeronline.com

© Springer-Verlag London Limited 2004
Softcover reprint of the hardcover 1st edition 2004

The use of registered names, trademarks, etc. in this publication does not imply, even in the absence of a specific statement, that such names are exempt from the relevant laws and regulations and therefore free for general use.

The publisher makes no representation, express or implied, with regard to the accuracy of the information contained in this book and cannot accept any legal responsibility or liability for any errors or omissions that may be made.

Typesetting: Camera-ready by editors

34/3830-543210 Printed on acid-free paper SPIN 10951514

APPLICATION PROGRAMME CHAIR'S INTRODUCTION

M.A.Bramer
University of Portsmouth, UK

This volume comprises the refereed application papers presented at AI-2003, the Twenty-third SGAI International Conference on Innovative Techniques and Applications of Artificial Intelligence, held in Cambridge in December 2003. The conference was organised by SGAI, the British Computer Society Specialist Group on Artificial Intelligence.

The papers present new and innovative developments in the field, divided into sections on Personalisation, E-Commerce and Resource Management, Hazard Prediction, Fault Diagnosis and Design, Medical and Social Services and Image Recognition, Knowledge Bases and Attribute Selection.

This year's prize for the best refereed application paper, which was sponsored by the Department of Trade and Industry, was won by a paper entitled *Design-a-Trial: A Rule-Based Decision Support System for Clinical Trial Design*, which has no fewer than nine authors: K Nammuni, C Pickering (InferMed Ltd), S Modgil (University College, London), A Montgomery (InferMed Ltd), P Hammond (University College, London), JC Wyatt (National Institute for Clinical Excellence), DG Altman (Centre for Statistics in Medicine), R Dunlop (InferMed Ltd) and H Potts (Kings College, London).

This is the eleventh volume in the *Applications and Innovations* series. The Technical Stream papers are published as a companion volume under the title *Research and Development in Intelligent Systems XX*.

On behalf of the conference organising committee I should like to thank all those who contributed to the organisation of this year's application programme, in particular the programme committee members, the referees and our administrators Fiona Hartree and Linsay Turbert.

Max Bramer
Application Programme Chair, AI-2003

ACKNOWLEDGEMENTS

AI-2003 CONFERENCE COMMITTEE

Prof. Ann Macintosh, Napier University (Conference Chair)
Dr Robert Milne, Sermatech Intelligent Applications Ltd. (Deputy Conference Chair, Finance and Publicity)
Dr Nirmalie Wirantunga, Robert Gordon University (Deputy Conference Chair, Poster Session)
Professor Max Bramer, University of Portsmouth (Application Programme Chair)
Richard Ellis, Stratum Management Ltd. (Deputy Application Programme Chair)
Dr Frans Coenen, University of Liverpool (Technical Programme Chair)
Dr Alun Preece, University of Aberdeen (Deputy Technical Programme Chair)
Prof. Adrian Hopgood, Nottingham Trent University (Tutorial Organiser)
Dr. Bob Howlett, University of Brighton (Exhibition Organiser)
Rosemary Gilligan, University of Herfordshire (Research Student Liaison)

APPLICATION PROGRAMME COMMITTEE

Prof. Max Bramer, University of Portsmouth (Chair)
Mr. Richard Ellis, Stratum Management Ltd (Vice-Chair)
Dr. Rob Milne, Sermatech Intelligent Applications
Mr. Richard Wheeler, University of Edinburgh

APPLICATION PROGRAMME REFEREES

Dr. Victor Alves, Universidade do Minho, Portugal
Dr. Andreas Abecker, DFKI GmbH
Prof. Max Bramer, University of Portsmouth
Professor Paul Chung, Loughborough University
Dr. Euan Davidson, University of Strathclyde
Richard Ellis, Stratum, UK
Dr. Florentino Fdez-Riverola, University of Vigo, Spain
Rosemary Gilligan, University of Hertfordshire
Dr John Gordon, Applied Knowledge Research Institute, Blackburn
Dr. Bob Howlett, University of Brighton
Runhe Huang, Japan
John Kingston, University of Edinburgh
Dr. Stewart Long, University of East Anglia
Prof. Ann Macintosh, Napier University

Dr Rob Milne, Sermatech Intelligent Applications, Scotland
Dr. Alan Montgomery, InferMed Ltd, UK
Mike Moulton, University of Portsmouth
Dr. Gilbert Owusu, BTExact Technologies, UK
Professor Derek Sleeman, University of Aberdeen
Dr. Somayajulu Sripada, University of Aberdeen
Sundar Varadarajan, Electronic Data Systems, USA
Dr Matthew West, Shell Services International, London
Dr. Ian Wilson, University of Glamorgan
Dr. Jin Yu, University of Aberdeen

CONTENTS

SESSION 4: MEDICAL AND SOCIAL SERVICES

SESSION 5: IMAGE RECOGNITION, KNOWLEDGE BASES, ATTRIBUTE SELECTION

BEST REFEREED APPLICATION PAPER

Design-a-Trial: A Rule-Based Decision Support System for Clinical Trial Design

K Nammuni[1], C Pickering[1], S Modgil[2], A Montgomery[1],
P Hammond[2], JC Wyatt[3], DG Altman[5], R Dunlop[1], H Potts[4]

[1]*Infer*Med Ltd, London, {kushan.nammuni, claire.pickering,
alan.montgomery, robert.dunlop}@infermed.com, www.infermed.com

[2]University College London, Eastman Dental Institute, {S.Modgil,
P.Hammond}@eastman.ucl.ac.uk , www.eastman.ucl.ac.uk

[3]National Institute for Clinical Excellence, London,
Jeremy.Wyatt@nice.nhs.uk, www.nice.org.uk

[4]Kings College London, henry.potts@kcl.ac.uk, www.kcl.ac.uk

[5]Centre for Statistics in Medicine, Oxford, doug.altman@cancer.org.uk,
www.ihs.ox.ac.uk/csm

Abstract

The complexity of clinical research has meant that clinical trial protocols are often scientifically and ethically unsound. Trial designers often have limited statistical skills and experience in clinical research. This problem is exacerbated in the academic arena, in which access to statistical expertise is limited. Design-a-Trial (DaT) is an expert system that assists trial designers in designing and planning clinical trials. The system is developed in Visual Basic.NET and Prolog, and is due for commercial release in September 2003. The main aim of DaT is to help trial designers with limited statistical and research experience to design scientifically and ethically sound trials. It also serves as a checklist for the more experienced designers and can potentially be used to assist in the training of new clinical researchers.

1. Introduction

Randomised controlled clinical trials are the preferred way to assess the effectiveness of medical interventions. Hence, clinical trial design is a core activity in the pharmaceutical industry and in clinical trial units in academic institutions.

3

The design of a clinical trial involves the production of a design document, called a 'Trial Protocol', which describes in detail the clinical trial being proposed. The protocol must be written and submitted to the appropriate regulatory authority for approval, before treatment can be administered to patients in clinical trials [1]. The protocol is also referenced by different people during the running of the trial and when writing up the trial for publication. Hence, the protocol must describe accurately and correctly the planned trial, and clinical trial activities must not deviate from those described in the protocol. As well as the protocol, an 'Ethics Application' must be submitted to the ethics committee responsible for the geographical area in which the research is being conducted.

There are strict guidelines [2, 3, 4, 5] that dictate what the protocol should contain. The protocol should include: 1) information relating to the medical (and possibly non-medical) interventions that are to be administered to the participants; 2) details about the population from which the participants will be drawn i.e. selection criteria; 3) how the different interventions will be allocated to the participants i.e. the method of randomisation [6]; 4) any measurements to be taken to assess the effect of the treatments on the participants, and details of monitoring and analysis of results (including a calculation of the required sample size); 5) information pertaining to how the trial will satisfy ethical requirements.

The complexity of trials from both a medical and statistical perspective makes protocol authoring both difficult (particularly in the case of larger multi-centre trials) and time consuming (protocols may take many months to write). Owing to the differing skills and substantial knowledge required to design a clinical trial, trial designers have to consult a wide variety of resources, including specialist (e.g., [7, 8]) and general medical texts, and statisticians, doctors and pharmacists. However, the inherent complexity together with the fact that trial designers often have limited research experience and statistical skills, and often limited access to statistical expertise (especially in the academic arena) has meant that trial protocols are often poorly designed and contain errors, with details often omitted and/or incorrect [9].

The financial and ethical costs of poorly designed trials are significant. Protocols rejected by regulatory authorities have to be re-submitted, thus requiring re-payment of fees. Trials that are re-submitted often take much longer to go through the approval process than those being approved for the first time (it is estimated that delay in approval by the US Food and Drug Administration costs pharmaceutical companies as much as 1 million dollars a week). Large sums of money can be wasted on trials that, subsequent to completion, prove to have been poorly designed with insufficient care taken to ensure rigour in the statistical analysis. Furthermore, inconsistencies and unclear information in the protocol can lead to problems interpreting what activities should be carried out and exactly when they should occur. From an ethical standpoint, poorly designed trials are unacceptable, since prejudiced studies lead to unnecessary exposure of participants to interventions.

2. The Design-a-Trial Concept

To overcome the problems of poor trial design, DaT makes use of rule-based decision support technology and a knowledge base of medical, statistical, ethical and trial design information, to provide guidance during the trial design process, and thus help produce more rigorous protocols more rapidly and easily.

Prototypes of DaT were originally developed as an output of academic research [10, 11, 12, 13, 14, 15, 16]. Concept testing and end-user evaluation with people in the field of clinical research suggested that DaT could add value to the trial design process, and ultimately benefit clinical research. At the end of 2001, work on commercialisation of DaT began, as part of a Teaching Company Scheme project (TCS) run by University College London and the medical software company *Infer*Med Ltd. DaT Version 3.0 (beta release) was released for evaluation earlier this year.

The current version – DaT4.0 - is the focus of this paper. Design of a trial requires the user to enter details about their planned trial in data-entry forms, while receiving advice on a range of statistical, medical, trial design and ethical issues. Due to the large scope, inter-connectivity and complexity of knowledge required in planning a well-designed trial, Artificial Intelligence (AI) techniques were used to both validate data entered, and subsequently generate advice. The DaT system uses expert rules (constraints) and multiple knowledge bases to provide a logical, intelligent, coherent guidance system that not only provides advice to the user but also lets them know the reasoning that led to that advice. The advice is in the form of natural language critiques generated by Prolog encoded definite clause grammars [17], in response to violation of Prolog encoded constraints. Users can choose the amount of advice DaT provides and the available context-sensitive help can be turned on or off depending on user preferences. Note that as far as possible, the knowledge encoded in constraints is employed to pre-emptively suggest possible problems with the design, rather than letting the user enter data, which is subsequently critiqued, thus prompting data revision and the attendant problems of reason maintenance. The advice facility also serves as a memory tool / checklist for more experienced designers who may not require full advice.

The key outputs of DaT are an automatically generated trial protocol document and ethics application form, generated in both text and HTML format. These are both generated by Prolog encoded definite clause grammars. DaT contains information on guidelines [2, 3, 4, 5] that dictate what should be included in the required documentation therefore helping to ensure that users design trials that are compliant with them. Figure 1 on the following page shows a typical user-system interaction with DaT.

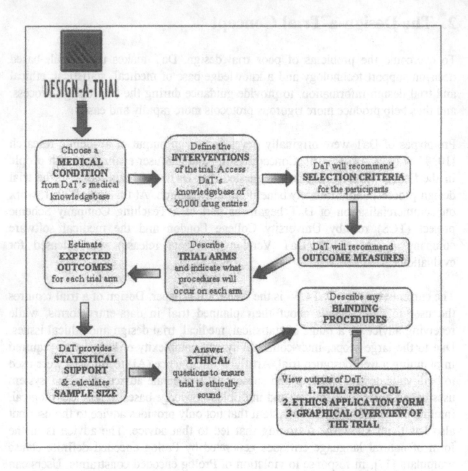

Figure 1: A typical user interaction with the Design-a-Trial system

In the following section, we describe the design architecture of DaT4.0. The project team involved in the development of DaT4.0 consisted of two full-time TCS associates with backgrounds in AI and human-computer interaction. Two day-to-day project managers, with research experience in AI applications, supervised the development of DaT. In addition, project collaborators included experts in statistics, medicine and medical informatics.

3. Design-a-Trial 4.0 – Design Architecture

The DaT user interface is programmed in the Microsoft Visual Basic.NET programming environment [18], and WinProlog [19] has been used to code the expert system core. DaT4.0 has all the functionalities of its predecessors as well as an improved user interface and expanded knowledgebase including a commercial drug database [20]. It also generates a graphical overview of a trial design for inclusion in the protocol. Here, we outline some design issues and strategies used to develop DaT4.0.

In order to maximise the potential for future development, the design takes a modular approach with each module having minimum knowledge of other modules. All the required communication is via module specific interfaces. This is in keeping with modern object-oriented design methodologies, so that in future, new developers can take responsibility for individual modules without having an extensive understanding of the overall design of the software.

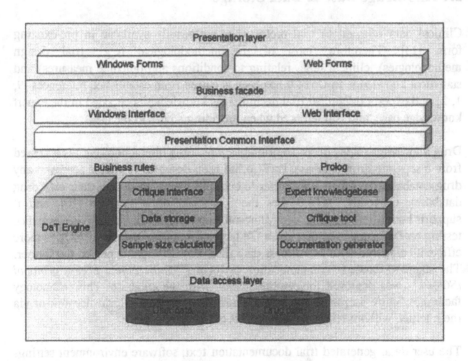

Figure 2: Architectural overview of Design-a-Trial 4.0

Figure 2 shows an overview of the DaT4.0 architecture. It consists of a presentation layer, business façade, business rules, data access layer and a Prolog module. All platform specific user interface coding (i.e. windows forms and web forms) are in the presentation layer. The Business façade has a common interface that can communicate to the presentation layer classes. This gives DaT4.0 the flexibility to extend its presentation layer devices (e.g. having access through handled devices). The presentation common interface is the common module that is extended by the windows interface for windows specific communication. In DaT4.0, business rules consist of all the core modules, including engine, critique interface, data storage and sample size calculator. WinProlog 4.0 was use to encode the knowledge base, expert rules (constraints) and definite clause grammars for critique text and protocol/ethics application text generation [14]. We have also included a commercial drug database referenced when generating drug related advice. All the user data, including generated protocols, are stored in a database to enable future development of multi-user access and to maintain protocol libraries. The following section briefly describes several important modules in DaT4.0.

3.1 Knowledge Base & Data Storage

Clinical data relevant to trial protocols is not readily available in pre-existing form [13]. Therefore, most of the methodological (e.g., trial design methodologies), clinical (e.g., relating to conditions and outcome measures) and statistical knowledge in DaT4.0 has been acquired from established references [9, 1, 2] and experts in clinical trial design. This knowledge is encoded in the expert knowledge base, and is referenced when providing advice to the user.

Drug knowledge (side effects, contraindications, drug interactions etc.) is accessed from a separate drug database. DaT4.0 has been designed to enable access to any drug database (customers may prefer to customise for inclusion of their own drug database). Currently DaT4.0 uses the SafeScript drug database [20], and it supports both Microsoft SQL and Microsoft Access database formats. Performance testing on DaT suggested that given the large size of drug databases, SQL is more efficient compared with MS Access data files. We therefore deployed the former. The standard database communication protocol - *Simple object access protocol (SOAP)* - was deployed for communication with the database. This technology facilitates future user access to a single database either on a local network or via the internet, without requiring local copies of the database.

The user data, generated trial documentation text, software environment settings and user preferences are stored in a local file system in extensible mark-up language (XML) file format. Therefore, the data files are interoperable between different versions of the software and can be exported to other software packages that are capable of reading the specific XML schema used in DaT. An immediate goal is to work on exporting DaT data to the clinical trial data management tool MACRO [21] to automatically generate the case report forms used to collect patient data when running the trial. In addition, DaT should be adaptable to Clinical Data Interchange Standards Consortium (CDISC) standards [22]; a standardisation of clinical data storage and transfer. Figure 3 on the following page shows a snapshot of the XML schema that is used in Design-a-Trial 4.0.

```
<DaT_4.0 Trial_Name>
        <UserInterfaceRecord>
          <FormName> Trial Summary </FormName>
          <FormID> frm_trial_summary </FormID>

          <WidgetRecord>
            <WidgetID> wig_trial_creation_date </WidgetID>
            <WidgetValue> 10/11/01 </WidgetValue>

          </WidgetRecord>

          <WidgetRecord>
            <WidgetID> wig_pi_name </WidgetID>
            <WidgetValue> Prof. J Smith </WidgetValue>

          </WidgetRecord>

        </UserInterfaceRecord>

</DaT_4.0_Trial_Name>
```

Figure 3: XML Schema

3.2 User Interface Design - Dynamic Initialisation

Software user interfaces should be flexible enough to adapt to ever-changing user requirements. Hence, DaT4.0 provides a dynamic initialisation of interface components (i.e., allowing the developer to add or remove components without having to change the core modules of the software). This requirement is particularly important when different developers develop the user interface and the core modules.

Figure 4 shows the pseudo code for the dynamic user interface initialisation. Note that the method explained in this section has been tested for windows platforms. The initialisation begins when loading window forms (i.e. onLoad method). Interface data (i.e. widget values) are stored in a dataset [23] (this is similar to data records in VB 6). If the widget information is not stored in the dataset, it should initialise the new widget information in the dataset. The advantage of this method is that the developer then could add or remove widgets from the interface, but it would not effect the saved trials of previous versions, since it dynamically identifies the new widgets in the user interface. Finally, DaT updates the widget values form the dataset to the user interface for display.

```
For each form
1.   Get associated knowledge base widgets
2.   For each widget in the form
     2.1.  If widget not in the dataset
           2.1.1. Create an instance of the widget in the
                  dataset
     2.2.  Updates data from KB (only if it is a KB widget)
     2.3.  Update user entered/selected data
3.   Repeat
```

Figure 4: Pseudo code for dynamic user interface initialisation

3.3 Advice system

To guide the user in the design of an ethically and scientifically sound trial, advisory critiques are generated in response to violation of pre-defined "hard" and "soft" constraints [15]. Where possible, usability is enhanced by pre-empting such critiquing, so avoiding the "reason maintenance" problem of revision of a data item in response to a critique and subsequently having to change data dependent on this revised item of data. To illustrate, a critique in the ethics section requires the user to justify their choice of a control drug (e.g. Prednisolone), given that there are other drugs that have fewer side effects. This critique might prompt the user to change the choice of control drug, which might subsequently require changes to other data previously entered based on this chosen drug. This problem is avoided by prioritising (on the basis of side effect) the list of control drugs from which to choose. Hence, the user is encouraged to comply with the ethical constraint from the outset.

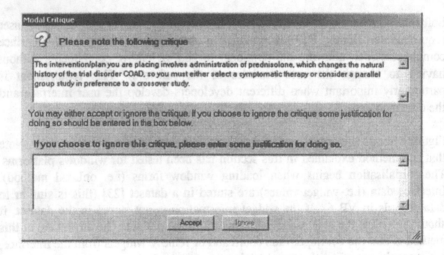

Figure 5: Modal critique window

There are three types of advisory critiques generated by DaT: those based on hard constraint violation; those based on soft constraint violation; and those resulting from data validation errors. If the user violates a hard constraint then DaT will flag a definite clause grammar (DCG) [17] generated modal critique, which the user must respond to before proceeding further (see Figure 5). Should the user choose to ignore such a critique (i.e., by not revising the culpable data entered) then they are encouraged to provide a justification as to why the critique has been ignored. This justification is exported for inclusion in the protocol document and can play an important role in gaining ethical approval. Critiques generated due to violation of the less critical soft constraints are recorded separately in a different section of the software in which the user can view all critiques applicable to the current state of the trial being designed.

3.4 Navigation

From a human-computer interaction perspective, a key requirement is that applications enable expert users to use shortcuts in the system, whilst still supporting new users [24, 25]. In DaT4.0, there are two modes of navigation (see Figure 6). The browser mode is designed for expert users, whereas guided navigation has been provided for those users new to DaT and/or clinical trial design. In the guided mode, the user is led through the collection of data-entry forms in a pre-defined order using back and forward buttons. With the browser navigation, the user can see all of the forms in a tree hierarchy, and can access any form at any time. However, access to some forms is dependent upon data entered elsewhere in DaT. The user is notified of these access restrictions and their dependencies when attempting such access.

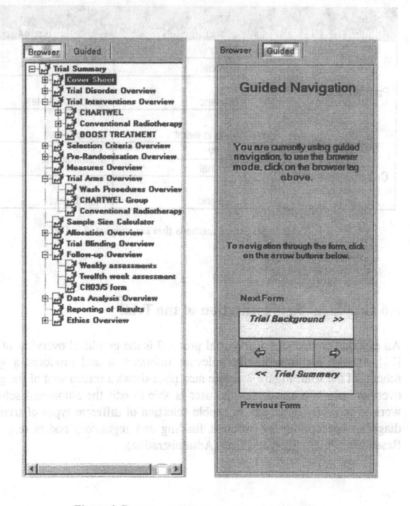

Figure 6: Browser and Guided navigation modes

3.5 Statistical Support

Statistical analysis is an essential aspect of randomised controlled clinical trials (RCT). Detailed discussions of statistical methods used in clinical trials are given in [6]. The DaT statistical tool supports various statistical methods for different types of trial design. Based on data entered by the user, statistical algorithms for power calculations are used to compute a recommended sample size for the trial (i.e. the number of patients required for the trial to ensure confidence in the statistical validity of the results). DaT also suggests to the user an appropriate statistical test to use. Table 1 shows the design and variable types supported by DaT, along with the statistical tests recommended.

Clinical Trial Design Type	Variable Type	Statistical Tests
Parallel group trials	Binary	Chi-square test
	Nominal	
	Numeric	Independent t-test
	Time to event	Log rank test
Crossover trials	Binary	McNemar test
	Nominal	
	Numeric	Paired t-test

Table 1: Statistical methods that are supported in DaT

3.6 Graphical Representation of the Trial

An essential component of any trial protocol is the graphical overview of the trial [26]. DaT4.0 captures all the relevant information and produces a graphical schema of the trial. Figure 7 on the next page shows a screen shot of the graphical overview of a two-arm trial. The user is able to edit the automated schema and work is currently underway to enable selection of different types of trial schema diagrams appropriate for different funding and regulatory bodies (e.g. Medical Research Council, Food and Drug Administration).

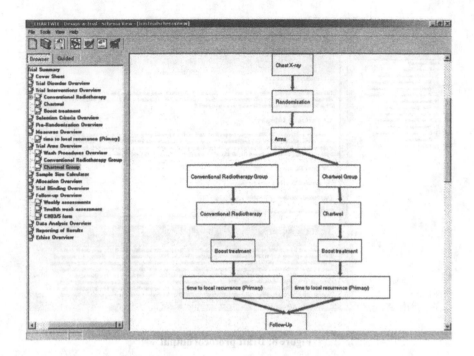

Figure 7: Graphical representation of the trial

3.7 Protocol and Ethics Application Documents

The key outputs of DaT are the trial protocol (see Figure 8 on the next page) and ethics application form, each of which are automatically generated in plain text or HTML format. In the HTML format, hyperlinks are provided, which when clicked on navigate the user back to the data-entry form associated with the hyperlinked text. Missing data in the protocol is hyperlinked and parenthesised by question marks; the user can thus gain immediate access to where the required data can be entered. In the text format, the documents can be edited in a traditional word processing environment. Definite clause grammars are used to generate the protocol text (see [15] for a more detailed explanation). We are currently working on exporting the graphical trial representation for inclusion in the protocol document generated by DaT4.0.

Recently, there has been standardisation of ethics application forms, resulting in the National Health Service (NHS) format. DaT automatically generates a populated form in this format.

14

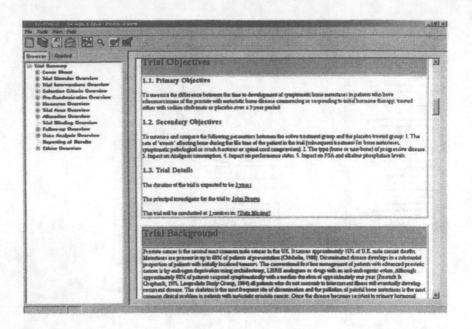

Figure 8: Draft protocol output

Conclusions

The main aim of DaT is to improve standards in the ethical and scientific soundness of designed trials, and to aid more rapid and easy authoring of clinical trial protocols and ethics application forms. As well as the scientific and ethical benefits arising from use of DaT, we also anticipate financial benefits. Indeed, in a report by the Ernst and Young Life Sciences Group [27], protocol design is identified as an area in clinical research where e-opportunities could be employed to reduce the time taken to complete a clinical trial. It is estimated that for a £1 billion product, reducing the timeline by 70-100 days translates to an extra £190-275 million in sales.

Currently, the main target audience for DaT are users who lack the required expertise. These include researchers in academic institutions who are required to design trials on an occasional basis. We also intend targeting researchers in clinical trial units in public sector institutions. With regard to pharmaceutical companies, we believe that with further development, DaT can serve as a useful checklist for supplementing in-house expertise. It remains an open question as to whether DaT will be taken up as a primary tool for trial design, given the already existing dedicated resources and expertise available in pharmaceutical companies. Finally, we believe that DaT can serve a useful didactic purpose in training clinical trial designers.

Work related to DaT includes software developed by [28], which allows aspects of a trial to be described, but does not provide critiques of medical and ethical aspects. Neither is there support for the generation of documentation. However, [28] does provide considerable support for optimising the statistical aspects of a trial, by allowing participants to test multiple 'what if' assumptions. The aims of the PaTriCIa project [29] are similar to those of DaT. However, support for statistical calculation and extensive critiquing is not provided. Finally, [30] describes early development of a protocol-critiquing tool. The critiques cover medical and procedural content, such as patient treatments, monitoring tests, and drug toxicity, but do not address the statistical, design and ethical content of a trial.

While a more comprehensive evaluation is still to be conducted, the results of preliminary evaluation suggest that DaT succeeds in the aims set out above. The preliminary evaluation involved researchers in public sector institutions (including the clinical trial unit at the Royal Free Hospital, London [31]), private companies [32], the BMJ Clinical Evidence [33], and statisticians at [34, 35]. Initial feedback has also suggested directions for future work.

In particular, we aim to provide editing facilities for expert rules. An identified user (e.g., the head of a clinical trial unit) should be able to link (possibly newly introduced) widgets to user-composed critiques (specifically required for the types of trial being designed) which can be automatically translated to Prolog constraints. A similar functionality has been implemented in the clinical guideline-authoring tool, AREZZO [21].

At present, DaT4.0 includes a local copy of a commercial drug database. However, we plan for a more efficient means of maintaining access to drug information, by hosting the drug database on a central *Infer*Med server, accessible over the internet. In this way, updates can be centrally implemented rather than having to post CDs or requesting the users to download updates. An auto update mechanism would then ensure that the user's local system and knowledgebase be kept up to date with software fixes and updates.

Regarding linkage to other systems, the need for expanding the clinical knowledge used in DaT4.0, suggests linkage to knowledge repositories maintained by medical institutions such as Clinical Evidence [33]. Potential also exists for linkage to clinical trial register databases such as Cochrane [36]. As mentioned in previous sections, work has already begun on linkage to the commercial electronic data collection tool MACRO [21]. Such linkages are feasible because of DaT's flexible architecture facilitating export of data to other systems. In addition, we intend expanding the range of trial design types which DaT can support (e.g., equivalence trials require specification of randomisation procedures not currently covered in DaT4.0).

16

References

1. Raven A. Consider it Pure Joy. An Introduction to Clinical Trials. Cambridge Healthcare Research Ltd, Cambridge, 3rd Edition, 1997

2. US Food & Drug Administration, ICH E6: Good Clinical Practice: Consolidated Guideline 1996. Date accessed: 13th June 2003, www.fda.gov/cder/guidance/959fnl.pdf

3. Medical Research Council, MRC Guidelines for Good Clinical Practice in Clinical Trials 1998. Date accessed: 13th June 2003, www.mrc.ac.uk/pdf-ctg.pdf

4. Department of Health, Research Governance Framework for England. Date accessed: 13th June 2003, www.doh.gov.uk/research/rd3/nhsrandd/researchgovernance.htm

5. The World Medical Association, Declaration of Helsinki: Ethical Principles for Medical Research Involving Human Subjects. Date accessed: 13th June 2003, www.wma.net/e/policy/b3.htm

6. Altman DG. Practical Statistics for Medical Research. Chapman & Hall, London, 1991

7. Wyatt JC. Clinical Knowledge and Practice in the Information Age: A Handbook for Health Professionals. The Royal Society of Medicine Press Limited, London, 2001

8. CONSORT Homepage. Date accessed: 15th June 2003, www.consort-statement.org/

9. Altman DG, & Dore CJ. Randomisation and Baseline Comparisons in Clinical Trials, Lancet, 1990: 335: 149-153

10. Wyatt JC, Altman DG, Pantin C et al. Design-a-Trial: A Knowledge-Based Aid for Writers of Clinical Trial Protocols. In: Reichert A, Sadan B, Bengtsson S et al. (eds), Proceedings of Medical Informatics Europe '93, Jerusalem (ISBN 965-294-091-7). London: Freund Ltd, 1993: 68-73

11. Wyatt JC, Altman DG, Heathfield H et al. Development of Design-a-Trial: A Knowledge-based Critiquing System for Authors of Clinical Trial Protocols. Computer Methods and Programs in Biomedicine 1994: 43: 283-91

12. Potts HWW, Wyatt JC, Modgil S et al. Design-a-Trial: A Knowledge-based System to Support Clinical Trial Designers. Sept 1999: ISCB-GMDS-99 Abstract Volume, 339. Abstract of presentation at ISCB-GMDS-99, Heidelberg

13. Modgil S, Hammond P, Wyatt JC et al. (2001). The Design-a-Trial project: Developing a knowledge-based tool for authoring clinical trial protocols. In: Computer-Based Support for Clinical Guidelines and Protocols: In Proceedings of EWGLP-2000 (Studies in Health Technology and Informatics, Vol. 83), Heller B, Löffler H, Musen M et al. (ed.s), IOS Press, Amsterdam, p. 71-85.

14. Modgil S, & Hammond P. Generating Symbolic and Natural Language Partial Solutions for Inclusion in Medical Plans. In Proceedings of 8th Conference on Artificial Intelligence in Medicine in Europe, AIME2001, Cascais Portugal, July 2001, (eds. Quaglini S, Barahona P, Andreassen S.) LNAI 2101, pp 239-248.

15. Modgil S, & Hammond P. Decision Support Tools for Clinical Trial Design, Artificial Intelligence in Medicine, 2003: 27:181-200

16. Potts HWW, Wyatt JC, & Altman DG. (2001) "Challenges in Evaluating Complex Decision Support Systems: Lessons from Design-a-Trial." In: Artificial Intelligence in Medicine, Quaglini S, Barahona P, & Andreassen S. (ed.s), Springer, Heidelberg. p. 453-6

17. Sterling L, Shapiro E. The Art of Prolog, Second Edition: Advanced Programming Techniques. MIT Press; 2nd edition (March 10, 1994), ISBN: 0262691639

18. Microsoft, Microsoft .NET. Date accessed: 13th June 2003, www.microsoft.com/net/

19. LPA, Win-Prolog 4.3. Date accessed: 13th June 2003, www.lpa.co.uk/win.htm

20. SafeScript Ltd - The World Standard Drug Database. Date accessed: 13th June 2003, //admin.safescript.com/

21. *Infer*Med Ltd, Homepage. Date accessed: 13th June, www.infermed.com

22. CDISC, Homepage. Date accessed: 16th June 2003, www.cdisc.org/

23. Balena F. Programming Microsoft® Visual Basic® .NET (Core Reference). (1st Edition) 2002 Microsoft Press., ISBN: 0-7356-1375-3

24. Shneiderman B. Eight Golden Rules of Interface Design. In Designing the User Interface. Addison-Wesley, 3rd Edition, 1997

25. Smith SL, & Mosier JN. Design guidelines for user-system interface software. Technical Report ESD-TR-84-190, The Mitre Corporation, Bedford, MA, 1984

26. Egger M, Jüni P, & Bartlett C. Value of Flow Diagrams in Reports of Randomized Controlled Trials, American Medical Association, 2001: 285:1996 - 1999

27. Ernst & Young, Eighth Annual European Life Sciences Report. Date accessed:16th June 2003, www.ey.com/global/Content.nsf/UK/HS_-_Library_-_Integration

28. Pharsight, Solutions for Clinical Development: The Need for Computer-Assisted Trial Design (CATD). Date accessed: 13th June 2003, www.pharsight.com/solutions/soln_catd_need.php

29. Haag U. Knowledge representation for computer-aided planning of controlled clinical trials: the PaTriCIa project. Methods of Information in Medicine, 1997: 36(3): 172-178

30. Rubin DL, Gennari J, Musen MA. Knowledge representation and tool support for critiquing clinical trial protocols. SMI Report Number: SMI-2000-0844

31. The Royal Free Clinical Trials Centre, Homepage. Date accessed: 16th June 2003, www.clinical-trials-centre.org

32. Scirex Corporation, Homepage. Date accessed: 16th June 2003, www.scirex.com

33. Clinical Evidence, Homepage. Date accessed: 16th June 2003, www.clinicalevidence.com/lpBinCE/lpext.dll?f=templates&fn=main-h.htm&2.0

34. Centre for Statistics in Medicine, HomePage. Date accessed: 16th June 2003, http://www.ihs.ox.ac.uk/csm/

35. University College London Department of Statistical Science. Date accessed: 16th June 2003, http://www.ucl.ac.uk/Stats/

36. Cochrane Collaboration, Homepage. Date accessed: 16th June 2003, www.cochrane.org

SESSION 1:

PERSONALISATION

Smart 4G Mobiles: A User Centric Approach

D.J. Allsopp, T. Kalus
University of Portsmouth, Department of Creative Technologies,
Buckingham Building, Lion Terrace, Portsmouth PO1 3HE

Abstract

The new developments in 4G mobile technology and Software
Defined Radio will bring with them increased complexity in using
such devices in the face of multiple network choices, location-based
information, varying Quality of Service, and a range of software
applications. In order for the user to be able to easily manage such
complexity, adaptive user profiles are offered as one solution. This
paper describes the work being done to develop such profiles, and
details current thinking about these profiles and associated research
areas within the IST-SCOUT project. Artificial Intelligence
techniques are investigated in the implementation of the user profiles
as a possible means of reducing the complexity for the user.

1 Introduction

No sooner have mobile telecom companies had a chance to recover part of the
money they invested in UK 3rd Generation (3G) licences, then talk of 4th
Generation (4G) services begins to appear in the computer press [1]. As 3G phone
and service packages begin to retail in the UK, research teams turn their attention
to 4G and its planned debut for the end of this decade.

3G services offer higher bandwidth communications than current 2nd Generation
(2G) and enhanced 2.5G services, allowing for example the use of multimedia
software on mobiles, software downloads, video streaming, and internet access [1].
But with the increase in complexity of 3G mobiles and their supporting software
and infrastructure, costs are set well above those of current 2G services. Some 2G
network operators have even adapted services to provide 3G-like content [2, 3, 4].

While 4G services are a fair way off, the current thinking on 4G sees the next
generation of mobile services as having features such as:

- The use of Internet Protocol (IP) as a basis for all communications - voice,
  data, and video – 'IP in everything' [5].

- Services 'that provide effortless access to other people's spheres and devices
  around us' [6].

21

- Access to a whole range of heterogeneous networks; Global System for Mobile Communications (GSM), Universal Mobile Telecommunications Service (UMTS), Wireless LAN (WLAN) and Ad-Hoc[1] networks [7].

- Moving intelligence out to the users – 'smart technology' encapsulated in software agents and applets cited on mobiles [5].

- High data transfer rates, upwards to 100Mbits/s and possibly beyond – compared to 3G transfer rates of around 3Mbits/s [8].

Manufacturers and service providers will obviously have to get the product/service costing right [3]. Moreover, it seems the industry is searching for the next 'killer application,' a fashionable application that uses the new generation of services. In the UK, the Short Message Service (SMS) was just such an application for 2G, made all the more popular by its low cost.

4G terminals are likely to be highly interoperable, connectable, delivering user task and location specific services, with up-to-the-minute information content tailored to user requirements and interests[2] [8]. Research teams and research programmes such as the IST-TRUST project – continued by IST-SCOUT – have started developing concepts for 4G mobiles, which they describe as 'Reconfigurable Terminals' [9, 10]. In a research study conducted by IST-TRUST, a panel of would-be users was questioned about what they would like to see in future terminals [11].

In terms of usability, participants were asked about what kind of information they would expect to be stored in a user profile. They were also asked what kind of information/user behaviour the terminal might track and how it might adapt to this information while being used for such things as accessing files remotely and making group multimedia calls. Potential users put a premium on ease-of-use and cost saving features. They also agreed that adaptive user specificity – automatically detecting, storing, and eliciting user's interests and goals to make the terminal more user life-style oriented – would be useful feature if handled correctly [11, 12].

This paper describes how some of the recommendations derived from these studies are being developed in a prototype. In particular, we describe the research being undertaken to produce an adaptive (i.e. non-static, changeable) user profile for 4G mobiles to facilitate usability, user specificity and cost savings. We are currently prototyping and evaluating terminal user monitoring software that uses AI techniques (a case-based reasoner) to elicit and store user preferences in the

---

[1] 'An ad-hoc network (or spontaneous) network is a local area network or other small network, especially one with wireless or temporary plug-in connections, in which some of the network devices are part of the network only for the duration of a communications session or, in the case of mobile or portable devices, while in some close proximity to the rest of the network' [13].

[2] 'Mobile Augmented Reality based services may become the killer services for 4G' [8]. These user location based mobile 'augmented reality' services involve precision positioning and orientation, accessed via futuristic mediaphone terminal equipment (including a tracking device worn by the user) that provides service discovery, navigation, secretarial service agents and mcommerce tailored to the user's location and current task/interests.

adaptive user profile. We also describe a decision making component which uses this profile data to handle calls, filters, reconfiguration, software downloads and other 4G terminal network interactions.

There is an associated SCOUT project research team which is looking closely at terminal human-computer interaction (HCI) issues. Their work is closely related to our own, although it is not documented in this paper and is not yet available outside the SCOUT consortium. Their work includes an extensive review of HCI for adaptive systems, examining for example the YOUNGSTER project on PDA user interface personalisation and content filtering [14].

1.1 The 4G 'Reconfigurable' Terminal

4G terminals are likely to handle all high bandwidth 3G services such as video and audio streaming, software downloads and advanced distributed games e.g. 'Samurai Romanesque' [15]. Future mobile internet services will increasingly offer 'personalised content' via customised web portals, e.g. with access to specific user-groups, chat rooms and smart e-mail filtering. 4G terminals will be highly customisable – offering the ability to select and use a variety of media 'modes' for communication [16]. For example, voice-only economy calls may be used on a budget, whereas video-calls might be made for company-use, and call filters may switch on or off automatically according to the user's context – location and activity. For more information on monitoring mobile phone user location and activity see [17, 18].

4G terminals will also be able to reconfigure to another network operator/network type 'on-the-fly' [16] i.e. will allow users to select one from a range of many service providers as and when needed. For example, a telecom provider P1 might be selected for video streaming, whereas provider P2 might be used for making voice calls. The IST SCOUT vision is for a reconfigurable terminal that operates over a heterogeneous network, although this raises a series of problems including the need for revised security, service interoperability standards, and revised terminal hardware and software [10, 16, 19, 20, 21].

1.2 Research Aims – Terminal User Management, Automation and the Adaptive User Profile

Because 4G terminals will be more complex than today's mobiles, efforts are being made to ensure that they will be usable and intuitive. Although we focus on user profile automation in this paper, we acknowledge that this technology is not a panacea. This research will be evaluated by further user trials, and recommendations from these evaluations should help highlight the strengths and weaknesses of this approach.

This paper focuses on two specific goals:

- To automate or semi-automate user terminal interactions, so that users will not have to constantly manipulate or interact with the terminal. E.g. the process of reconfiguration could be automated if the terminal knows which telecom provider the user prefers for each given service.

- To observe user terminal behaviour and recommend courses of action based upon these observations. E.g. for reconfiguration, the terminal software could recommend saving a particular network operator/service combination within the user profile after observing that the user selects a particular combination at frequent intervals over a period of time.

In the rest of this paper we discuss the following issues:

- The types of user terminal transactions that may be automated.

- The role of the user's context (activity and location) in defining user preferences.

- The nature of the user preference data stored in the adaptive user profile required to automate terminal transactions.

- The 'terminal user architecture', which describes, as well as the user's interaction with the terminal, all relevant interactions between the adaptive user profile and the network, network data, and terminal hardware resources (e.g. battery life).

- The components that we are prototyping to test the terminal user architecture.

2 Monitoring User Terminal Transactions

The SCOUT terminal may monitor the following user transactions from which user preferences could be defined [11, 12]:

- The user's terminal multimedia preferences. An example of a multimedia preference is the quality of a video image on the terminal's screen. A user might select high quality image resolution only when viewing downloaded video-clips, and be content with lower resolution image quality for video calls.

- The user's call filtering preferences. A user might prefer to filter calls from friends and family members during a business meeting, for example. By referring to terminal diary entries, it should be possible to determine when a filter for a particular caller-group should be switched on or off.

- The user's call modality preferences. Call modality defines the call format (video-call, voice-only) that the user selects in dialogue with a particular caller or caller group. Call modality preferences may be monitored and stored for a particular contact or contact group, e.g. the use of voice-only calls with friends.

- The user's reconfiguration preferences. These preferences might, for instance, describe when a user adopts, selects, and switches to a particular network operator to use a particular service, and may incorporate Quality of Service ratings and/or cost-saving preferences.

3 User Context

For user preferences to be of practical use, the user's context needs to be associated with relevant preferences as they are being elicited. The role of user context in tailoring services to users is recognised elsewhere [22, 23, 24]. The prototype systems MERCURY and CONCHAT 'demonstrate the usefulness of augmenting device mediated communication with contextual information' [23]. A good review of context modelling is also given [24] which describes the LISTEN project - an application that deals with the audio augmentation of real and virtual environments. In [24], case based reasoning is being used to describe user contexts within the environment, from which emergent system properties (e.g. audio descriptions of the user's location) are evaluated.

For our purposes, as in [24], a user's context describes 'when', 'with whom', and 'where' the preference option was made. The terminal has access to this information from the following sources:

When: The terminal clock, accessed using a function call, such as the Java 2 Micro Edition (J2ME) 'Date' class function 'getTime()' on Java-enabled mobiles may be used to determine when a particular preference was made [25].

With Whom: The terminal address book / list of contacts associated with the caller number can be used to determine the contact to whom the preference relates.

Where: The user's (c.f. terminal's) location (as a general value, e.g. home, work, travel) associated with the preference may be determined from a number of sources; the terminal diary, the user's location data stored on the terminal (i.e. the GPS position of home and office), and the location of the terminal via positioning data using a service such as GPS. In the terminal user architecture we are currently prototyping (see Figure 1), the user's location is being used to align the user's profile to the user's activity where possible. This is done using sub-profiles, which may be thought of as child profiles of the main user profile.

Sub-profile: A sub-profile stores user preferences relevant for a specific location/activity. For prototyping, we currently define the following sub-profiles:

- Home: User preferences for when the user is at home (not working).

- Work: User preferences for when the user is working.

- Meeting: User preferences applicable when a user is in a meeting, e.g. call filter preferences relevant to the meeting context.

- Travel: User preferences for when the user is travelling, e.g. travelling alert tones or modes and call filters.

4 Information Stored in the Adaptive User Profile

The user profile is commonly viewed as a set of information that describes the user of a system [26], which may be characterised by a set of attribute value pairs [27], and which may be used to tailor the behaviour of a system to a particular user [26].

Together with other IST-SCOUT partners, we have determined that the adaptive user profile and its constituent sub-profiles need to store the following user data:

- Cost preference data – e.g. use economical (lower cost) services for home use.

- Terminal GUI settings preferences – i.e. terminal background screen colour, font size and type.

- Multimedia preferences showing caller status – e.g. show caller terminal battery life and Quality of Service (QoS) data.

- Multimedia preferences for user – e.g. optimise video to show best picture quality.

- Modality preferences – e.g. use voice-only calls for friends and family, use video calls for business.

- Reconfiguration data – i.e. sets of tuples each of which comprise a network operator name, a service provided by that operator that the user prefers, and the Quality of Service rating values expected for that service.

- Call Filtering data – i.e. when to switch on or off a call filter for a specific caller or caller group.

5 Terminal User Side Architecture

The terminal user architecture is given in Figure 1 and shows the terminal in relation to its network environment, the user, and terminal hardware. The network interface forms the bridge between the network environment and the terminal, and the GUI forms a bridge between the user and the terminal software. The terminal interface provides a link between the user architecture software and the terminal hardware layers (these are not shown). Straddling these interfaces is the Adaptive User Profile (AUP) software with its user profile data (AUP data), and an additional software component called the Decision Maker (DM).

Within the terminal there is a division of labour between these components. The AUP monitors the user's operation of the terminal, such as the network services selected, and updates the user profile data accordingly. The DM performs general 'house-keeping' duties and relies in part upon user profile data for this. For example, the DM ensures that the correct network for a particular service is selected (where specified in the user profile). If battery power is low, the DM might suggest turning off an application that is resource intensive. Or it may advise that reconfiguration is needed on basis of the user preference values set in the AUP.

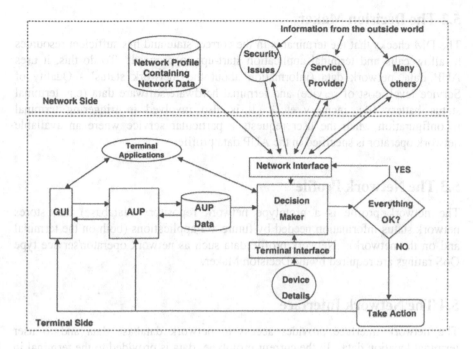

Figure 1: SCOUT Terminal User Architecture

5.1 The Adaptive User Profile

The AUP software comprises four components, each of which varies in size and complexity:

- The Profile Editor – which provides user access to the AUP profile data for editing preferences stored there.

- The terminal application favourites list definition module – which observes the user's selection of terminal applications and produces the terminal application favourites list, accessed from the main application menu.

- The AUP user monitoring and user preference evaluation module – which buffers user preference data and identifies trends within it in order to produce user preferences automatically[3]. This is the most complex part of the AUP, which involves monitoring GUI interactions in association with a range of terminal user data sources (not shown in Figure 1) such as the user's contacts address list and the terminal clock.

- The sub-profile selection module – which automatically selects the relevant sub-profile, to ensure that the appropriate user preferences are 'active' in the current user context.

---

[3] The user may be notified of a preference elicited by the AUP and asked whether the preference should be stored.

5.2 The Decision Maker

The DM checks that the terminal is in the correct state and has sufficient resources to allow calls and terminal application start-ups to proceed. To do this, it uses AUP data, network data (information about the 'network status' - Quality of Service level, cost of service) and terminal hardware/software data (e.g. terminal status battery life, memory etc). It is also involved in triggering terminal reconfiguration when the user requests a particular service where an available network operator is specified in the AUP data profile.

5.3 The Network Profile

The network profile is a prototype network repository (database) that stores network status information needed by future 4G applications (both on the terminal and on the network). Network profile data such as network operator/service type QoS ratings are required by the Decision Maker.

5.4 The Network Interface

The network interface provides access to network database data and to user terminal location data. In the current prototype, data is provided to the terminal in IP format.

5.5 The Terminal Interface

The terminal interface is a program that provides access to terminal hardware status information, and which relays messages from the DM to trigger a reconfiguration (this involves optimising terminal hardware and software to function using the new network).

6 Prototyping Adaptive User Profile and Decision Making Agent Components

There is a limited choice of programming languages suitable for coding applications on resource-constrained devices which includes the Binary Run-time Environment for Wireless (BREW) [28], and Sun's 'Java 2 Micro Edition' [25, 29]. We have chosen to use J2ME rather than BREW because J2ME is more freely available, is well supported via the Sun web-site and mailing lists, and the J2ME language may be influenced by the developer/user base through the Java Community Process and Java Specification Requests [30].

6.1 J2ME

A J2ME configuration and its profile define the relevant Java platform for a specific resource constrained device. A J2ME configuration is a minimum Java platform (comprising a JVM and class libraries) applicable to a set of devices that share similar memory and processing power requirements [25]. Sun supports two configurations, the Connected Limited Device Configuration (CLDC) and the Connected Device Configuration (CDC). We are using the CLDC, aimed at lower end (highly resource constrained) cell phones, PDAs and personal organisers, because it comes with a development suite and a range of terminal emulators for code testing on the PC. The CDC on other hand, although applicable to high end set top boxes, car navigation systems and smart phones, has no freely available tools for development on PC.

A reasonably well-supported GUI class library is also important for our work. CDC profiles have limited GUI support (CDC derived code is best tested upon an actual device). On the other hand, the CLDC Mobile Information Device Profile (MIDP) has a comprehensive GUI class library in addition to a range of other APIs e.g. for persistent storage and networking [25].

6.2 AUP Components

In this section we describe in more detail three of the four AUP software modules previously introduced; namely the terminal application favourites organizer module, the user monitoring / user preference evaluation module and the sub-profile selection module. These three AUP software modules each contain AI components. The profile editor is not described, as it is entirely GUI based.

6.2.1 Terminal Application Favourites List

This application allows terminal applications to be organised within a favourites list accessed from the main applications menu. This is carried out by an algorithm based on the standard naïve Bayes learner [31] which uses a very simple form of probability and incorporates a decay (or forgetting) factor.

Bayesian methods usually require initial knowledge of many probabilities [31], but we cannot foretell which applications will be used most often. So, when a user first starts to use the terminal, a simple uniform probability distribution is assumed consisting of a transition table of $1/n$ as its initial values (where n is the total number of applications). If the user selects application A, followed by application B, then the row corresponding to application A is multiplied by a decay, or forgetting, factor, and (1 – decay factor) is added to application B's column. The decay factor is needed to give weight to the more recently used applications. Transition table weightings are used to organise the favourites list, promoting frequently used applications into the list and/or up to the head of the queue.

6.2.2 User Monitoring and User Preference Evaluation

The general principle behind user transaction monitoring and user preference evaluation involves these main steps:

- Storing (buffering) user transactions.
- 'Mining' the buffered data to elicit trends in user transactions.
- Producing user preferences for storage in the adaptive user profile database.

In our initial prototype we are producing a case base [32, 33] of user transactions that are stored in a database founded upon the J2ME 'recordset' class [25]. As new transactions are added to the database, previously stored transactions are examined for similarity. In our current prototype we are pursuing a number of research issues, namely:

- Identifying the heuristics by which transactions may be deemed 'similar enough' to be earmarked as potential user preferences.

- Identifying how many times 'similar' transactions must be undertaken by the user (and buffered by the terminal) before they may be identified as bona-fide user preferences.

- Identifying whether or not and/or when to notify the user that a user preference has been elicited so that it can be committed to the adaptive user profile.

- Maintaining the case base to reduce redundancy, removing buffered transactions once they have been summarised as a user preference.

- Optimising the entire process of user transaction monitoring and preference elicitation, e.g. co-ordinating between preferences stored in the user profile and transactions buffered in the case base to ensure that the same preference is not stored multiple times.

- Optimising the program size and minimising the terminal resources used, as we assume that space saving will continue to be of major importance when devising applications for near-future generation mobiles.

Unfortunately, the development of the case base was not complete at the time this paper was prepared for publication and we cannot release specific implementation details at this stage. In a subsequent publication we aim to provide a full description of the case-based system and results of testing and user evaluation trials. Meanwhile, please refer to [24] for more specific details of the application of case-based reasoning to user contextual information.

6.2.3 Sub-Profile Selection

In order to ensure the terminal sub-profile is kept automatically in step with the user's current context (location and activity) the AUP software must rely on data from the following sources:

- The user's location derived from the network.

- The user's location information retained in a 'location' database on the terminal.

- The user's diary entries (we envisage that users will set an activity 'type' for each diary entry available from a drop down list).

The selection of the relevant sub profile is determined by associating the terminal's current location with the current activity (if available from the diary) and with data in the user's location database (which indicates the location co-ordinates of the user's work and home addresses). The selection decision is based upon a series of rules kept within a small rule-base. If no obvious selection can be made, a default profile may be selected – though we have yet to establish the optimum criteria for building the default profile (this may well be derived in 'real-time' from data stored in the other sub-profiles).

6.3 The Decision Maker

The DM must check the preferences set by the user and/or by the AUP (and stored in the user profile) for each user-initiated action or incoming call and check these against the network parameters obtained from the network interface, and terminal hardware/software parameters obtained from the terminal interface. On the basis of these parameters, the DM determines if the user-initiated action or incoming call can proceed.

The DM is being developed to contain sets of rules implemented as blocks of if .. then statements in J2ME. Each block of rules will correspond to a situation that must be checked, e.g. there will be a set of rules to check that conditions are met for sending e-mail, for making a video-call, for downloading video etc. Each individual rule within each block is simple, checking one single condition, so that if an operation is not possible, the specific cause of failure may be related to the user.

7 Evaluation

We expect to complete the first prototype of the terminal user architecture by the end of 2003 and to conduct an in-house evaluation of the AUP and the DM shortly afterwards, as independent user trials of this work are scheduled for spring 2004. Depending on future funding allocations and results of these trials, our terminal user architecture might then be prepared for up loading onto an actual device for more rigorous testing.

This research is on going at the time of writing and regretfully we cannot highlight critical areas of success (or failure) of the application of case base technology to the problem of creating an adaptive user profile. Once our work has been evaluated, we hope that we shall be in a position to publish the benefits and lessons of value learnt from our approach.

8 Summary

This paper has presented a brief look at 4G mobile technologies, and describes how our work is aimed at ensuring that these technologies remain user centric and intuitive. We have described a terminal user architecture that uses case-based reasoning for deducing, storing and manipulating user profile data within an adaptive user profile with the aim of tailoring a 4G terminal to a user's life style. This research described here is on-going at the time of publication and is due for evaluation in 2004.

9 Acknowledgements

This work has been performed in the framework of the IST project IST-2002-12070 SCOUT, which is partly funded by the European Union. The authors would like to acknowledge the contributions of their project partners from Siemens AG, France Telecom R&D, Centre Suisse d'Electronique et de Microtechnique S.A., King's College London, Motorola Ltd., Panasonic European Laboratories GmbH, Regulierungsbehorde fur Post und Telekommunikation, Telefonica Investigacion Y Desarrollo S.A. Unipersonal, Toshiba Research Europe Ltd., TTI Norte S.L., University of Bristol, University of Southampton, University of Portsmouth, 3G.com, DoCoMo Communications Laboratories Europe GmbH.

The authors would especially like to thank Genevieve Conaty and Paola Hobson for reviewing earlier drafts of this paper.

10 References

[1] Computing. Computing News. 5th June 2003, p. 4.

[2] Hewson, D. Too many gimmicks spoil the smart phone. 'Sounding Off' Article in The Sunday Times, 9th March, 2003.

[3] Dixit, S.D. Technology Advances for 3G and Beyond. Guest Editorial article in IEEE Communications Magazine, August 2002.

[4] Fox, B. 'You don't need a 3G phone to get video.' Communications article in New Scientist, 19th April, 2003. p. 13

[5] Wilkus, S. 'North American Perspective on 4G Wireless Networks.' In Proceedings of the International Forum 4th Generation Mobile Communications, 2002. Available from [21].

[6] Niebert, N. 'The Wireless World Research Forum and its Vision of Systems beyond 3G.' In Proceedings of the International Forum 4th Generation Mobile Communications, 2002. Available from [21].

[7] Wisely, D. 'The EU IST Project BRAIN/MIND - An IP solution for systems beyond 3G.' In Proceedings of the International Forum 4th Generation Mobile Communications, 2002. Available from [21].

[8] Pulli, P. 'Natural Interfaces/Augmented Reality.' In Proceedings of the International Forum 4th Generation Mobile Communications, 2002. Available from [21].

[9] Bourse, D., Dillinger, M., Farnham, T. et al. SDR Equipment in Future Mobile Networks. In Proceedings of the IST Summit 2002, Thessaloniki, Greece, June 2002.

[10] Dillinger, M., Madani, K., and Alonistioti, N. (Eds). Software Defined Radio: Architectures, Systems and Functions. Wiley Europe. April 2003. ISBN 0-470-85164-3

[11] Navarro-Prieto, R., Conaty, G., Cook, K. et al. Results from Work Package 2 (User Assessment and QoS Requirements) for 2001. Public Deliverable 2.5 from the TRUST Project, IST-1999-12070. December 2001.

[12] Navarro-Prieto, R., and Conaty, G. User Requirements for SDR Terminals. In Dillinger, M., Madani, K., and Alonistioti, N. (Eds). Software Defined Radio: Architectures, Systems and Functions. Wiley Europe. April 2003.

[13] Techtarget. Last accessed 5th June 2003 from:
http://searchmobilecomputing.techtarget.com/sDefinition/0,,sid40_gci213462,00.html

[14] William, M.H., Halvatzara, D., McIntosh, N., et al. Role of a Personal Assistant in Delivering Personalised Context-Aware Services to Young People. In Proceedings of IST Mobile and Wireless Telecommunications Summit. 2002. p. 667-671.

[15] Krikke, J. 'Samurai Romanesque.' IEEE Computer Graphics and Applications, Jan/Feb 2003, pp. 16-23.

[16] Bender, P., Ravasio, G., Cordier, P. et al. Initial Requirements for Regulator, Operators and Spectrum Management. IST-2001-34091 SCOUT Work Package 2 Deliverable D2.1. 31st October, 2002.

[17] Erbas, F., Steuer, J., Eggesieker, D. et al. A regular path recognition method and prediction of user movements in wireless networks. IEEE Vehicular Technology Conference. 2001. Vol 4, p. 2672 – 2676.

[18] Ribeiro, D., Jennifer, L., Jerrams-Smith, I., et al. An Empirical Study on the Usability of an Information Navigation Aid. Posters/Proceedings of the 2000 International Conference on Intelligent User Interfaces. 2000. p.151-152.

[19] Clemo, G., Seneclauze, M., Farnham, T. et al. Requirements for software methodologies for reconfigurability such as agents, middleware and adaptive protocols. IST-2001-34091 SCOUT Work Package 3 Deliverable D3.1.1. 2002. Last accessed 16th June 2003 from: http://www.ist-scout.org/

[20] Scout. The SCOUT homepage: Smart user-Centric cOmUnication environmenT. Last accessed 11th June 2003 from: http://www.ist-scout.org/

[21] International Forum 4th Generation Mobile Communications. Centre for Telecommunications Research web-site at King's College, London. Last accessed 5th June 2003 from http://www.ctr.kcl.ac.uk/Pages/4GForum

[22] Ravasio, G., Micocci, S., Berzosa, F., et al. Requirements on Network and Security Architecture and Traffic Management Schemes for Download Traffic based on IP Principles in Cellular and Ad Hoc Networks. IST-2001-34091 SCOUT Public Deliverable D4.1.1. 31st October, 2002.

[23] Ranganathan, A., and Lei, H. Context-Aware Communication. Computer. IEEE Computer Society. April 2003, pp. 90 - 92.

[24] Zimmermann, A. Context-Awareness in User Modelling: Requirements Analysis for a Case-Based Reasoning Application. In Ashley, K.D. and Bridge, D.G. (Eds): In Proceedings of the 5th ICCBR 2003, LNAI 2689, Springer-Verlag. pp. 718-732. For more information, see http://www.iccbr.org/iccbr03/

[25] Ortiz, C.E., and Giguere, E. Mobile Information Device Profile for Java 2 Micro Edition. John Wiley & Sons, Inc. 2001.

[26] Brusilovsky, P., and Maybury, M.T. Adaptive Interfaces for Ubiquitous Web. Communications of the ACM. 2002. 45 (5), pp. 34 - 38.

[27] Martin, T., and Azvine, B. Adaptive User Models in an Intelligent Telephone Assistant. AI Group, Advanced Computing Research, University of Bristol. Last accessed December 2002 from http://www.infc.ulst.ac.uk/informatics/events/soft-ware/slides/Monday/martin.ppt

[28] Qualcomm website. Last accessed 11th June 2003 from:
http://www.qualcomm.com/brew

34

[29] Sun website. Last accessed 11th June 2003 from: http://wireless.java.sun.com/

[30] JCP website. Last accessed 11th June 2003 from: http://jcp.org/en/home/index

[31] Poole, D., Mackworth, A. et al. Computational Intelligence. Oxford University Press. 1998.

[32] Kolodner, J.L. Case-Based Reasoning. Morgan-Kaufmann. 1993.

[33] Ai-cbr website. Case Based Reasoning (The AI CBR Homepage). Last accessed 11th June 2003 from: http://www.ai-cbr.org/theindex.html

Providing Advanced, Personalised Infomobility Services Using Agent Technology

Pavlos Moraïtis [1,2], Eleftheria Petraki[2], Nikolaos I. Spanoudakis[2]

[1]Dept. of Computer Science, University of Cyprus,
75 Kallipoleos Str., 1678-Nicosia, Cyprus
moraitis@ucy.ac.cy
www.cs.ucy.ac.cy/~moraitis

[2]Singular Software SA,
26th October 43, 54626, Thessaloniki, Greece
{epetraki, nspan}@si.gr

Abstract

This paper describes a real world application, the IMAGE system, proposing e-services for mobile users. We believe that such an application can be interesting for a large public taking into account that current developments in many areas (e.g. mobiles devices, wireless networks industries, GPS, GIS, routing) make possible the proposal of quite complex services for such kind of users. To this end, we precisely present how we integrated electronic services for mobile users (e.g. geo-reference, routing, mapping services) and introduced the personalized service feature, using agent technology in the context of the IST project IMAGE. The overall system architecture and business model are presented along with a particular focus on the Intelligent Module (IM), which is a multi-agent system. The IM is the core component of the IMAGE system. It is composed of several types of agents who realize through interaction, the IM functionalities within the overall IMAGE system.

1. Introduction

Recent developments in the areas of the mobile devices and wireless networks industries, geo-referencing systems and other relevant technologies (e.g. GPS, GIS, routing) motivate works in the areas of intelligently servicing mobile users and the combination of services in order to provide more complex ones [15]. In this context, a user might not only wish to find a route from one place to another (routing service) and see it in a map (mapping service), but also to be able to store the destination for future use. Furthermore, he/she might wish the system to be able to suggest a destination that best matches his/her interests and position. Another user might want to get information on specialized events that occur in his/her geographical area such as concerts or new theatre shows. Finally, the users want accurate, up-to-date information and ability to roam through other countries. All these user demands constitute a brand new area of services: the mobile, global, personalized, location based services. The new term "Infomobility" services [9] refers to services that allow the mobile citizen to have seamless access to, and interaction with, personalised - location dependent - rich content multimedia information, that are, at the same time, essential parts of the autonomous and self-configuring business structures emerging in electronic businesses.

These are the main challenges for the IMAGE system and mainly its Intelligent Module (IM) presented herein and which was proposed in the context of the IST project IMAGE. This paper aims to show, through the description of a real world application, how such services will be offered and the added value that emerges from agent technology use (see e.g. [18]). Systems that treat similar aspects with IMAGE system are the Kivera [10], Maporama [13], CRUMPET [14] and PTA [8]. However there exist many differences comparing to Kivera and Maporama, where no agent technology is used, as well as to CRUMPET and PTA that, as in the IMAGE case, also use agent technology.

The rest of the paper is organized as follows. Section 2 presents the problem description and Section 3 the application description. In Section 4 issues related to the application's building are discussed while in Section 5 we discuss about application benefits. Finally, Section 6 discusses related work and conclusions.

2. Problem Description

2.1 Advanced Infomobility Services

Let us now precisely define the new services that we wanted to offer and that are our requirements. The Image system must be able to provide transport solutions and tourist services from a various set of providers, according to the user needs, matched to his/her profile and habits. More specifically, the system must be able to:

- support different "types of users". The user him/herself will choose his/her type and preferences (i.e. tourist, public transport user, driver, etc.) and will receive services that take these parameters into account (e.g. inform the user on various extra locations to visit if he/she is a tourist, suggest a trip according to user preference and habits). Actions will be taken to secure user's sensitive personal information. Moreover the user can choose to edit more than one profiles (i.e. commuter, tourist, business traveler, etc) in order to have different modes of service.

- be able to adapt the service according to user's habitual patterns, by keeping and processing the history of service requests and profiles of the particular user. Also, supply any missing information based on the user's profile. Nevertheless, system initiated actions will always be subjected to user's permission, to avoid user frustration or surprise.

- receive the user request, as analyzed by the user interface, his/her position (through GPS co-ordinates if available) and suggest optimal transportation solutions, tourist events and nearby attractions.

- monitor the users route and automatically provide related events during the journey (i.e. info on traffic jams or emergencies on route), events, etc. and helping him to his trip.

The Image concept provides the ideas and business model for such a system [6]

2.2 Why use agent technology?

The agent-based approach has been selected for developing this system, since the following requirements posed by such an application:

- Timely and geographical distribution of users and services, have to be taken into account.
- Heterogeneity of services, devices and networks are provided by different sources; services can be tailored to users profiles.
- Coordination of elementary services in order to provide the user with a complex, personalized service.

The above requirements invoke characteristics as autonomy, pro-activeness, intelligence and cooperation, which relate to basic motivations that would make someone utilizing agent technology (see e.g. [18]). More precisely agents can have the sufficient intelligence to achieve more (e.g. personalized assistance) or less complex (e.g. travel information retrieval, user location, etc.) tasks in an autonomous way. Such tasks can be achieved either by agents equipped with the appropriate individual capabilities, or by efficient interaction among agents of different types that have complementary capabilities. In the application described in this paper, agents belong to different types (i.e. interface, travel guide, educator, event handler, services, assistant and personalized assistant), and fulfil different tasks associated to the functionalities of the Intelligent Module (IM). In some cases, as we will see later, agents due to their characteristic of pro-activeness will be able to take the initiative to provide users with information related to their profile. The IM is the core module of the IMAGE system that services mobile users through a variety of devices (i.e. mobile phones, PDAs, PCs). The IMAGE project foresees the use of several IMAGE platforms in order to assist mobile users around the world and thus interoperability is a crucial point, which can be also very well achieved through the use of agent technology. This technology can presently provide, in combination with other adopted technologies (e.g. XML [16], DAML-S [4], Web Services [17], etc), appropriate solutions for the interoperability issue among heterogeneous agents.

3. Application Description

3.1 The Image Concept

The IMAGE project aims to create an information system that will satisfy the requirements presented above and therefore will service mobile users through a variety of devices (mobile phones, PDAs, PCs). The service will be customisable and adaptive to user habits (personalized service). The service will be location-based and will usually entail showing the user where he/she is, letting him/her view different points of interest (POIs) around him/her such as theatres, banks, museums, etc. and helping him/her plan trips either inside his/her original city or throughout Europe. Specifically, a potential IMAGE customer is able to set an inquiry to the system either requesting a map of the geographical area of his/her location, or requesting the calculation and display of a map representing a journey between two geographical points, an origin and a destination.

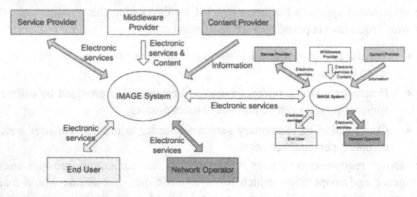

Figure 1 Image business model

These two points can be either defined by the user or calculated by the IMAGE system. Similarly, the types of the points of interest that will be embedded in the map can be either user defined or system defined. Additionally, each city or region will be served by its own IMAGE server and the system will have the ability to interoperate with other servers so that the user can arrange trips and get location based information for other European cities.

The overall Image concept/business model is presented in Figure 1. The Image concept is that the Image system will combine simple, possibly offered by third parties, services and content in order to provide a complex, personalized, global service. The term electronic service (e-service) refers to services that are offered in electronic form and are acquired through the use of electronic devices. Such services can be business-to-customer (through a web page or the mobile phone) or business-to-business (web services). The Image system main function is the interaction with the end users and thus can be operated by business entities that provide services to end-users (i.e. service providers). The relation between the Image system and the other business entities is one to many and involves a number of functions such as the provision of content, services or network infrastructure. The cooperative business entities can be:

- Content providers: entities that provide e-content (e.g. list of hotels for a city). They can have a direct link to the Image system or through a middle-ware provider.

- Service providers: entities that provide e-services to end-users. They can interact directly with the Image system (e.g. e-payment case) or through another middleware provider.

- Middleware providers: entities that provide e-content and e-services. They can operate as an integral part of the Image system or on an agreement basis.
- Network operators: entities that provide the network infrastructure and can operate as application service providers.

The system's main goals are:

- To successfully personalize the service.
- To seamlessly interoperate with other IMAGE systems in order to achieve a global service.
- To acquire services from different and possibly heterogeneous external – third party service providers.

The Image system bases its operation in several modules, namely the intelligent module (IM), the data management module (DM), the geo-reference services module (GS), the e-Payment module (PM) and the user interface module (UI).

Intelligent Module (IM) is the core of the IMAGE system. It manages, processes and monitors the user's requests and establishes the interconnection between the various IMAGE modules. Thus it can provide a complex service by aggregating geo-reference, mapping, routing and proximity search services, that originate either from DM, GS or from external to IMAGE electronic services and middleware providers. It is also responsible for the interoperability between the different IMAGE system installations. To that way it provides the complex, personalized IMAGE services based on individual profile and preferences model. In this paper we focus on the IM conception and implementation, which along with the DM module are the core Image modules (other modules are optional, can be any local service or middleware provider), because IM actually provides the IMAGE services. DM module is mainly responsible for acquiring content from different content providers (with different format or service provision mechanisms) and making it available to the IM in a uniform way.

3.2 Intelligent Module (IM) System's Analysis and Design Issues

The Gaia methodology [21] was employed for system analysis and design. The Gaia methodology is an attempt to define a complete and general methodology that it is specifically tailored to the analysis and design of multi-agent systems (MASs). Gaia is a general methodology that supports both the levels of the individual agent structure and the agent society in the MAS development process. MASs, according to Gaia, are viewed as being composed of a number of autonomous interactive agents that live in an organized society in which each agent plays one or more specific roles. Gaia defines the structure of a MAS in terms of a role model. The model identifies the roles that agents have to play within the MAS and the interaction protocols between the different roles.

Other competent agent oriented software engineering (AOSE) methodologies like MaSE [20] or ZEUS [2] were evaluated along with Gaia so as to select the best one. The major arguments for selecting Gaia were its simplicity and the fact that in order to take full advantage of the benefits of the other methodologies their respective development tools (AgentTool [5] and ZEUS [1]) should be selected for implementation, whereas for several reasons we preferred JADE. The Image project required an open environment, compliant with the standardizing efforts of the Foundation for Intelligent Physical Agents (FIPA). The multi agent platform that would be used should be able to communicate with other FIPA [7] compliant applications. Furthermore, issues that had to be taken into account were maintenance and availability. Under these aspects, the platforms that were selected and examined are JADE and FIPA-OS, that are also used widely by other IST projects (e.g. [14], [3]). They are both open source projects with constant maintenance and support and they are both FIPA compliant. They were analysed in terms of ease of installation and application development, architecture, agent management, communication features and interoperability. Also, a test application was created for each platform in order to verify the platform robustness, resource optimisation and execution time.

In the context of this work a kind of roadmap, based on our experience within this project, of how one can combine the Gaia methodology for agent-oriented analysis and design and JADE for implementation purpose, was proposed [12].

3.3 The IM System's Architecture

During the Gaia design phase the following roles were identified. Briefly the main characteristics of these roles are:

- *Interface*: This role is responsible for interfacing the multi-agent system (MAS) with the user interface (UI) or any other network operator and for providing white and yellow page information to other agents fulfilling also an interface role. Summarizing the interface agent can be considered as a middle agent [19].

- *Travel Guide*: This role provides routing, mapping, proximity search, user location acquisition services to the MAS by invoking relevant web services provided by GS, DM or any external provider.

- *Educator*: This role provides information about points of interest (POIs) to the MAS by invoking relevant web services provided by DM or any external provider.

- *Events Handler*: This role forwards to the user information about current events that may be of interest to him/her by invoking relevant web services provided by DM. These events can be traffic or leisure events such as traffic jams or exhibitions' openings and are sent to the user without his/her prior request.

- *Services*: This role serves as a supervisor of the multi agent system, initializing the system parameters, launching new agents when necessary and monitoring the agents' operation. This role is responsible for system maintenance and disaster recovery.

- *Social*: This role is responsible for dynamically locating new agents that are added to the system and for maintaining an acquaintances structure that contains white and yellow page information about other agent-contacts.

- *Assistant*: This role serves unregistered users (guests) in the two core IMAGE functionalities: display the user position in a map along with the POIs that the user has requested and calculate a route according to the user provided origin and destination. This role interacts with the Travel Guide and Educator roles and combines their input to produce the final result.

- *Personalized Assistant*: This is the most complex role and it serves a registered user, stores and manages his/her profile and personal data and uses the requests' history in order to adapt the services to his/her habitual patterns. Service adaptation is achieved by hour of the day dependent profile management and continuous refinement of user selected POI types whenever the user requests to view specific POI types around him.

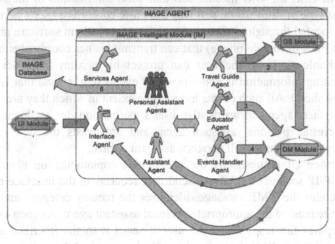

Figure 2 Intelligent Module's agents types and possible interactions

The Gaia model creates agent types by aggregating roles. In the IMAGE system all roles are implemented as agent types with the exception of the Social role, which is realized by all agents that need to be acquainted with their collaborative partners (see the resulting agent types in Figure 2). Thus, the IMAGE Intelligent Module is composed of several types of agents through a layered approach. These agent types and their interaction with one another and with the rest of the IMAGE modules are presented in Figure 2. The interaction among agents is accomplished through ACL messages with standard FIPA performatives [7]

The numbered interaction paths presented in Figure 2 between the agents of IM module and the other modules are:

1. Request geo-reference, request maps generation, request routes generation messages: all these requests are invocations of web services and are set up individually (a URL for each web service), so that any service provider can be used.

2. Request nearby points of interest (POIs), request user location messages: these are invocations of web services currently provided by the DM

module, but any service provider can be used instead since they are set up individually. These web services are for requesting a type of a location point that is within a center range from an origin (e.g. find all restaurants within 100 meters from the user's location). The user's location in co-ordinates format is also requested in a similar fashion.

3. Request POIs service: this is an invocation of a web service for obtaining information about a specific POI from the DM module or an external provider.

4. Request push events: this is an invocation of a web service that requests DM to push information about an event to a specific user.

5. Inform about a user login or logout action: these are web services invocation messages that inform the DM about user login status.

6. Receive user's permission to be located, new recreation and traffic events from DM: the DM module can thus push information to the MAS. The first type of information that DM can push, concerns a user's permission to be located through his/her tracking client (i.e. a client software installed on his PDA or mobile phone) that can transmit his/her coordinates using GPS technology. Thus, the user can protect his privacy. The next type of pushing information is about new city events (e.g. a road that is closed, a new show). All such events have a time extent in which they are valid. The interface agent forwards the user's permission to be located to the interested personal assistant agent and broadcasts the new traffic and recreation events to all personal assistant agents.

7. Service UI requests: by the use of this communication channel (plain TCP/IP sockets) the UI can send user requests to the interface agent who decodes the XML message, identifies the request category and forwards the request to the appropriate personal assistant agent. As soon as the latter prepares the response to the user it sends it to the interface agent who encodes it in XML format and sends it back to the UI.

8. Get profile, update profile, register new user, etc: the IMAGE database is currently part of the DM module and is used for information storage.

3.4 Achievements

The major IM achievements for the provision of advanced infomobility services were, the complex "Where am I" and "Plan a trip" services, the transfer profile feature and finally, the learning about the user. Here we will present for space reasons, only the service "Where am I" and the transfer profile feature.

The complex service *"Where am I" (or WAI)* is one of the most important ones. It is realised as behaviours of the personalised assistant agent. The way the WAI is implemented is as follows. It is JADE *FSMBehaviour*s with many states/sub-behaviours.

The finite state machine implemented behaviours are presented graphically in Figures 3. Thus, for example the *REQUEST_REMOTE_AGENTS_INFO_STATE* corresponds to the *RequestRemoteAgentsBehaviour* that sends a relevant request message to the interface agent. Depending on its reply, the next behaviour (i.e. *RespondRemoteAgentsBehaviour*) that actually listens for a reply from the interface agent in order to undertake some action when that arrives or another behaviour will be added to the agent scheduler. For example if the request is local the *CheckOriginAndRequestGeocodingBehaviour* will be the next scheduled behaviour for the WAI service.

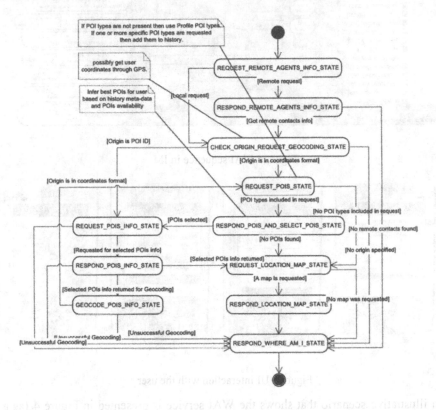

Figure 3 WAI behaviour

Regarding the WAI service the user request has a number of technical device-dependent parameters like screen size in pixels, but the important ones are the visibility around the user (range), the location of the user (origin) and the types of points of interest that he wants to see around him. A guest user will have to submit all this information (origin, though, can be either in coordinates format or the id of a POI that was previously displayed in the user's screen). In the registered user's case all this information can be either supplied (and this time the user can select one of his bookmarks as an origin) or inferred by the personalised assistant agent. Range and POI types can be extracted from his profile while his location can be obtained with the use of GPS. When the available POIs around the user are retrieved by the travel agent, the ones that are closer to the user's interests at that time of the day are selected. This selection is based on a procedure that monitors user requests for specific POI types around him and stores the time that the request was made. For example, if a user has frequently asked for restaurants around him during noon, then if he uses the WAI service with no POI type parameter (at noon) he will see more restaurants than other POI types that might be included in his profile.

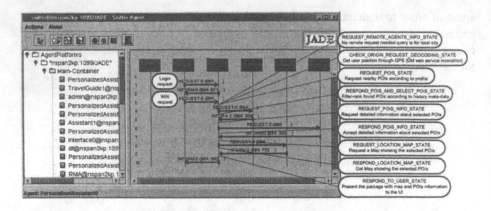

Figure 4 WAI sequence in IM

Figure 5 UI interaction with the user

An illustrative scenario that shows the WAI service is presented in Figure 4 (as a sequence of messages exchange by agents in the IM) and in user actions in Figure 5 (PDA usage). Notice that the user logs in and then selects the "guide" button. As soon as the WAI service is concluded he gets a link to the map and the links to the POIs visible on the map. He clicks the link to the map and sees the map screen. Notice that the only sent information is the size of the screen and the city at which the user is.

For the *transfer profile* use case there are two personalised assistants that participate in the process along with the two interface agents of the different Image platforms. The sequence for this service is presented in Figure 6 (the two participating personalised agents are referred to as the *initiator* and the *responder*).

This service sequence commences as soon as a user requests that one of his profiles (i.e. commuter, tourist, business traveller) "accompanies" him during a trip to a remote city. The user would do so in order to use the remote city's Image services and be informed about local events, there, corresponding to the migrating profile. It is a complex protocol that requires that a personal assistant in the remote city is not servicing, as usually, a registered user but he is dedicated to a user who will be arriving to the remote city. The *request_remote_agents_info* protocol (which can also be used by the WAI service) is also revealed by this sequence.

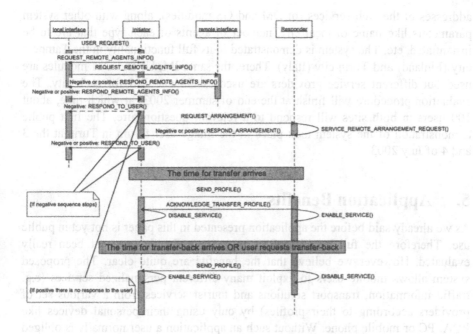

Figure 6 Transfer profile sequence

Each interface agent retains in his acquaintances only remote interface agents, who every time inform him about agents that perform specific services. After obtaining a remote personalised assistant contact, the *initiator* continues with the *transfer_profile* protocol, a three more steps process. At each step the process can be disrupted and in that case the *initiator* resumes servicing the user, informing him that the profile transfer request wasn't completed. At the first step the *initiator* sends to the *responder* a request message for an arrangement (when the user wishes to transfer his profile and for how long). If the response is affirmative the *initiator* continues serving the user normally until the date for the transfer arrives. At that time he sends the user profile to the *responder*. If the *responder* acknowledges the profile receipt the *initiator* stops servicing the user while the *responder* assumes responsibility of the service. From that time forward, the user has to login to the remote Image platform and be serviced from there. If the time frame of the arrangement expires or the user chooses to terminate his trip the profile is returned to the *initiator* and the service continues normally at the user's home.

4. Application Building

The application was developed in a year. JADE is a framework implemented in the Java language so the IM application is a Java application that can be executed in every operating system that has installed the Java 1.4 version and later. The procedure is very simple; the application is packaged in a *jar* file and is accompanied by an IM administrator's manual that describes the parameters that can be changed at installation time by editing an *ini* file. These parameters are the addresses of the web services (of DM and GS modules), along with other system parameters like name of local city, number of agents of each type that are to be instantiated, etc. The system is demonstrated in its full functionality in the Tampere city (Finland) and Turin city (Italy). There, the same IM, UI and DM modules are used but different service providers are used as GS and PM for each city. The evaluation procedure will finish at the end of summer 2003, at which time, about 100 users in both sites will respond to a relevant questionnaire. The first public demonstration of the system took place in the Image user forum in Turin at the 3 and 4 of July 2003.

5.   Application Benefits

As we already said before the application presented in this paper is not yet in public use. Therefore the full benefits of its use cannot for the moment been really evaluated. However we believe that the benefits are quite clear. The proposed system allows mobile users to exploit many different personalized services (e.g. traffic information, transport solutions and tourist services from a various set of providers according to their profiles) by only using their personal devices like PDA, PC or mobile phone. Without such an application a user normally is obliged to search each of the above services to different providers separately. For example, he has to use a touristic content web site in order to find a hotel located nearby him, memorise or somehow record its address and then use another web site that calculates routes in order to get there. Note that the user should know such useful web sites for each city that he travels to otherwise he has to visit a traditional travel agency.

6.   Related Work and Conclusions

In this paper, a real world application, the IMAGE system, and more particularly a multi-agent system implementing the functionalities of the Intelligent Module within the IMAGE system as proposed in the context of the IMAGE IST project, is presented. This system integrates a set of intelligent agents having different functionalities (e.g. personalized assistance, travel information, cultural events information), which are necessary in order to cover the needs presented by this specific application field called "mobile, personalized location-based services". In this paper, through the detailed description of the implemented system, we have shown that agent technology responds perfectly to the basic requirements of such applications and thus is well suited for developing information systems for a modern and important domain of application, the one providing integrated services for mobile users.

To our knowledge, relevant work in this area is sparse and mainly in the research field. A relevant European Union research project is CRUMPET [14]. The overall aim of CRUMPET is to implement, validate, and trial tourism-related value-added services for nomadic users (across mobile and fixed networks). The services provided by CRUMPET take advantage of integrating four key emerging technology domains and applying them to the tourist domain: location-aware services, personalized user interaction, seamlessly accessible multi-media mobile communication and smart component-based middleware that uses multi-agent technology. Comparing to this work, the system we propose presents some advantages. Firstly is the ability to access the IMAGE services through various devices (PDAs, mobile phones, PCs) due to the fact that user profiles are stored at the IMAGE server and not at the user's device. Secondly, IMAGE services can be offered by any network provider who can opt to use an entirely new user interface. PTA [8] used agents on the devices, like CRUMPET, and agents on the service providers. This is a difference with IMAGE, because our agents exploit existing web services of different service providers. Another difference is that in our architecture agents have knowledge of the other agents with whom they need to cooperate. Thus, the system is more robust because we avoid the use of a unique broker agent whose failure can lead to system malfunction. Lastly, the IMAGE system adapts the service to user habits. There also exist works that don't use agent technology like Maporama [13] and Kivera [10]. The advantages of our work compared to these works (besides the previously mentioned) are the ability to exploit external to IMAGE electronic service and middleware providers as well as the ability to seamlessly interoperate with other servers (i.e. IMAGE servers). Other advantages, directly linked to agent technology use, are the expandability, which means that new agents may appear offering new or evolved services with no modifications to the existent ones.

Our future work aims on one hand to expanding the IMAGE service in order to offer inter-regional and international trip planning and management, and on the other hand to offer the IMAGE services to other, possibly heterogeneous agents built using different frameworks. The latter will be achieved by exploiting developments in the semantic web [11].

References

1. Collis, J. and Ndumu, D. Zeus Technical Manual. Intelligent Systems Research Group, BT Labs. British Telecommunications, 1999

2. Collis, J. and Ndumu, D. Zeus Methodology Documentation Part I: The Role Modelling Guide. Intelligent Systems Research Group, BT labs, 1999

3. Bergenti, F, Poggi, A. LEAP - A FIPA platform for handheld and mobile devices. In ATAL01, 2001

4. DAML Services Coalition (Ankolekar, A., Burstein, M., Hobbs, J., Lassila, O., Martin, D., McIlraith, S., Narayanan, S., Paolucci, M., Payne, T., Sycara, K., Zeng, H.): DAML-S: Semantic Markup for Web Services. In Proceedings of the International Semantic Web Working Symposium (SWWS), 2001

5. DeLoach S. and Wood, M.: Developing Multiagent Systems with agentTool. In: Castelfranchi, C., Lesperance Y. (Eds.): in ATAL00, LNCS1986, 2001

6. Eloranta, P., et al. Agent Concept Definition, Functionality and Dependencies & System Integrated Architecture. Intelligent Mobility Agent for Complex Geographic Environments (IMAGE, IST-2000-30047) Project D1.1 Deliverable. (http://www.image-project.com), 2002

48

7. FIPA specification document: SC00061G: FIPA ACL Message Structure Specification (http://www.fipa.org), 2002

8. Gerber, C., Bauer, B. and Steiner, D.: Resource Adaptation for a Scalable Agent Society in the MoTiV-PTA Domain. Hayzelden/Bigham (Eds): Software Agents for Future Communication Systems, Springer, 183-206, 1999

9. IST: A programme of Research, Technology Development and Demonstration under the 5th Framework Programme. 2000 Workprogramme, Information Society Technologies (IST, http://www.cordis.lu/ist), EC, 2000

10. Kivera Location Based Services (http://www.kivera.com/), 2002

11. McGuiness, D., Fikes, R., Hendler, J., Stein, L.: DAML+OIL: An Ontology Language for the Semantic Web. IEEE Intelligent Systems Journal, Vol. 17, No. 5, 72-80, 2002

12. Moraitis, P., Petraki, E. and Spanoudakis, N.. Engineering JADE Agents with the Gaia Methodology. In Kowalczyk R., Muller J., Tianfield H. and Unland R. (Eds), Agent Technologies, Infrastructures, Tools and Applications for E-Services, LNAI 2592, pp. 77-91, Springer Verlag, 2003

13. Pétrissans, A. Geocentric Information. IDC (http://www.maporama.com/), 2000

14. Poslad, S., Laamanen, H., Malaka, R., Nick, A., Buckle, P. and Zipf, A. CRUMPET: Creation of User-friendly Mobile Services Personalised for Tourism. Proceedings of: 3G 2001 - Second International Conference on 3G Mobile Communication Technologies. London, UK, 2001

15. Sonnen, D. What Does the Future Hold for Mobile Location Services, BusinessGeographics (http://www.geoplace.com/bg/2001/0101/0101mrk.asp), 2001

16. W3C: Extensible Markup Language (XML): http://www.w3.org/XML/

17. W3C: Web Services Activity. http://www.w3.org/2002/ws/

18. Weiss, G. Multi-Agent Systems: A Modern Approach to Distributed Artificial Intelligence, MIT Press, 1999

19. Wong, H.C. and Sycara, K. A taxonomy of middle-agents for the Internet. Proceedings of the Fourth International Conference on MultiAgent Systems, pp. 465 - 466, 2000

20. Wood, M.F. and DeLoach, S.A.: An Overview of the Multiagent Systems Engineering Methodology. AOSE-2000, The First International Workshop on Agent-Oriented Software Engineering. Limerick, Ireland, 2000

21. Wooldridge, M., Jennings, N.R., Kinny, D.: The Gaia Methodology for Agent-Oriented Analysis and Design. Journal of Autonomous Agents and Multi-Agent Systems, 3(3) 285-312, 2000

Context Boosting Collaborative Recommendations

Conor Hayes, Pádraig Cunningham
Computer Science Department,
Trinity College Dublin

Abstract

This paper describes the operation of and research behind a networked application for the delivery of personalised streams of music at Trinity College Dublin. Smart Radio is a web based client-server application that uses streaming audio technology and recommendation techniques to allow users build, manage and share music programmes. Since good content descriptors are difficult to obtain in the audio domain, we originally used automated collaborative filtering, a 'content less' approach as our recommendation strategy. We describe how we improve the ACF technique by leveraging a light content-based technique that attempts to capture the user's current listening 'context'. This involves a two stage retrieval process where ACF recommendations are ranked according to the user's current interests. Finally, we demonstrate a novel on-line evaluation strategy that pits the ACF strategy against the context-boosted strategy in a real time competition.

1. Introduction

This paper describes a personalised web-based music service called Smart Radio, which has been in operation in the computer science department at Trinity College Dublin for the past three years. The service was set up to examine how a personalised service of radio programming could be achieved over the web. The advent of on-line music services poses similar problems of information overload often described for textual material. However, the filtering/recommendation of audio resources has its own difficulties. Chief amongst these is the absence of good content description required by content-based or knowledge-based systems. This drawback is conventionally overcome using collaborative filtering, a technique that leverages similarity between users to make recommendations. As such it is often termed a 'contentless' approach to recommendation because description of the items being recommended is not required. Apart from the obvious advantage of a 'knowledge–light' approach to recommendation, ACF is often credited with being able find recommendations that would otherwise escape content-based recommender strategies. This is because it relies upon user preferences that may capture subtle qualities such as aesthetic merit that may escape current content-based systems. However, ACF does have well documented drawbacks such as the problem of bootstrapping new users and new content into the system. In this paper we examine a less documented weakness, that of *context insensitivity*, and provide a solution using a lightweight, case-based approach. Since our technique imposes a ranking based on what the user is currently listening to in the system we do not consider off-line approaches to evaluation such as cross validation or measures of recall/precision appropriate for this situation. Instead we measure whether a user was inclined to make use of the recommendations presented to them. We evaluate our approach using a novel on-line methodology in which a pure ACF strategy and a context boosted ACF strategy are concurrently deployed. We measure how well both techniques perform and find that context-boosted ACF significantly outperforms ACF. Section 2 briefly describes the system operation, and introduces the idea of a playlist, a user-compiled collection of music tracks that we use as the basic unit of recommendation. In section 3 we introduce some of the principles of Automated Collaborative filtering (ACF). We point out some of the deficiencies of using ACF as the sole recommendation strategy, and in section 4 we introduce the idea of a *context* and the strategy we use to further refine recommendations made by the ACF engine. Section 5 describes the integration of our hybrid approach. Finally, in section 6 we discuss our choice of evaluation methodology and present our results.

2. Smart Radio

Smart Radio is a web-based client-server application that allows users to build compilations of music that can be streamed to the desktop. The idea behind Smart Radio is to encourage the sharing of music programmes using automated recommendation techniques. The unit of recommendation in Smart Radio is the *playlist*, a compilation of music tracks built by one listener and recommended to other like-minded listeners. In terms of music delivery it is a better-understood format than a single song recommendation system. It has the advantage of allowing a full programme of music to be delivered to the user. In this way, the *work* involved in compiling a playlist of music is distributed to other listeners. The playlist format is also attractive in that it allows individual users to personalise their own selections of music, with the understanding that these will be passed on to like-minded listeners. This is often reflected in the titles Smart Radio listeners give to their playlists. Our original hypothesis was that the playlist format also would also capture the implicit 'rules of thumb' that people may use when putting together selections of music, such as "don't mix techno and country". However, this hypothesis has yet to be fully tested.

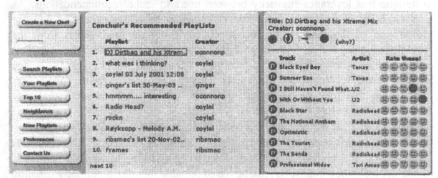

Figure 1. The Smart Radio recommendation panel. Recommended playlists are presented as an ordered list. By default the first playlist is automatically displayed.

3.   ACF and its Drawbacks

Automated Collaborative Filtering (ACF) is a recommendation technique which operates by making recommendations from users that are correlated based on items they have rated in common. Its great strength is that it operates without using any representations of the items being filtered, relying instead on the pooled preference data from positively correlated users to recommend or reject from the resources available. Therefore it can be considered to *implicitly* capture the subtle distinctions people make when selecting or rejecting from any set of items. A distinction can be drawn between ACF and a strategy like Case-Based Reasoning in which content description is used to make recommendations. ACF user profiles are represented simply by rating data as shown in Table 1. As such it has been referred to as a 'contentless' approach to filtering or recommendation [2, 13]; Accordingly, ACF is a particularly suitable recommendation strategy where content description is hard to come by, such as in the music domain.

Table 1.   The table illustrates user-preference data the type of data used in ACF systems. Although this type of data is ordered, this ordering is not used in the ACF algorithm.

	item A	item B	item C	item D	item E	item F	item G
User 1	0.6	0.6	0.8	?	?	0.8	0.5
User 2	?	0.8	0.8	0.3	0.7	?	?
User 3	0.6	0.6	0.3	0.5	?	0.7	0.5
User 4	?	?	?	?	0.7	0.8	0.7

The first version of Smart Radio used ACF as its recommendation strategy [8]. One serious drawback with ACF is that it is not sensitive to a user's interests at a particular moment. Even though a user's preference data is an ordered set of ratings collected over time, the data is treated in an *accumulative* fashion by the ACF algorithm (see Table 1). The sparsity of the data necessitates taking all ratings into account in order to make sound correlations with other users. However, the resulting recommendation set will contain a mix of items reflecting each user's accrued interests. This may not be a real drawback if we are using ACF as a passive filter. However, where ACF is required to produce recommendations on demand, its lack of sensitivity to the users current interests may cause frustration and distrust. For instance, if a user is engaged in specialised activity, such as reading documents on a particular subject, or listening to music of a particular genre many of the recommendations will be inappropriate and untimely. The problem is complicated by the fact that many ACF recommender systems operate in domains where there is very little content description, making it difficult to ascertain the transitions between interests of a particular type. As we illustrate in figure 2, our goal is to enhance the usefulness of an ACF based system by using a lightweight content-based strategy like CBR to rank ACF recommendations according to the user's current interests. The darker shaded cases in the diagram indicate ACF recommendations that are most similar to the user's current *context*. In the next section we explain the concept of *context*, a representation of the user's interests at a particular moment and we present our case-based representation of playlist context. In section 5 we present our hybrid ACF system which uses a novel MAC/FAC retrieval strategy.

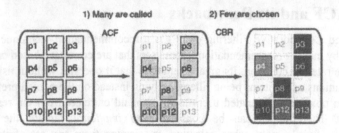

Figure 2. The ACF module selects a subset of the case base. A second stage retrieval process then ranks these primed cases according to their similarity to the user's listening context. This is indicated by the darker shaded cases on the right.

4. Context boosted ACF

This concept of isolating localised interest has been referred to in user-modelling research as *context*. It is a slippery term that has a wider variety of meanings as it is also used to describe sets of environmental parameters in the area of ubiquitous computing [15]. Our use of the term is similar to what would be termed 'task context' within the same community. This is a description of the explicit goals, tasks, actions, background and activities of the user at a particular time and place. The objective in isolating context in user-modelling is that tasks being undertaken by the user may be anticipated and a portion of the work carried out automatically in advance. An example of such a technique is *Watson* [4] an application which monitors the user's current writing or reading behaviour on desktop applications such as Microsoft Word or Windows Explorer, and using information retrieval techniques for content analyses, automatically issues requests to search engines in order to retrieve related material. Another such is Letizia [11,12], an application that tries to predict the most relevant links the user should explore based on the pages he or she has viewed in the previous session. Letizia operates concurrently while the user is browsing, building a keyword based user profile of the current browsing session. It downloads linked pages and generates a score for each link based on the user-profile. Letizia presents a recommendation set of links that indicate a preference ranking according to the current state of the profile. The objective is to recommend a certain *percentage* of the currently available links. Both Watson and Leitizia have been termed 'Reconnaisance' applications [12]. In both cases the user-profile is a *short-term* representation of the user's current interests designed to capture the context of the current task undertaken by the user. The context is a content-based representation of items currently being used. This can be viewed as an approximation of a task-based representation where the user's explicit task goals are known. Obviously the approximation is noisy because it is based upon an implicit concept of the user's interests. If the user digresses or switches subject while researching a topic, both reconnaissance aides will require time to respond. However, the advantage of an implicitly generated profile is that the user does not need explicitly to describe his/her goals, prior to working. Measuring the success of the short-term user profile is a difficult issue. The problem boils down to analysing the correctness of the ranking produced according to their relevance to the user profile. Whereas analyses of recommender systems have been reliant on off-line evaluation (as is standard in machine learning and information retrieval), ranking problems such as these are not as easily studied in on off-line manner. In section 6 we present an evaluation technique suited to measuring the success of contextually motivated recommendations.

4.1   Contextualising by instance

The objective to context-guided ACF is to recommend items based on neighbour endorsement as before, but to promote those items that may be of interest to the user based on his/her current context. Unlike the examples of the *reconnaissance* aides described earlier, which used information retrieval analyses to build a short-term user profile, the Smart Radio domain suffers from a deficit of content descriptions. Our goal is to enhance the ACF technique where very little content is freely available, and where the knowledge engineering overhead is kept to a minimum. The content descriptors we use are found in a few bytes of information at the end of the mp3 file. The type of information available is *TrackName, artistName, albumName, genre* and *date.* However, since this information is often voluntarily uploaded to sites such as the CD database (www.cddb.com), track information has to be scanned for inaccuracies in spelling and genre assignation. Furthermore, we do not use the potentially useful *date* feature since it is often missing or inaccurate.

4.1.1 Context Event

Smart Radio is a closed domain with a finite number of playlist resources. By playing a playlist the user triggers a context event. The contents of the playlist are assumed to indicate the user's current listening preference. We term this *contextualising by instance*. In the taxonomy suggested by Lieberman, this is a "zero input" strategy in which the system uses a short term, *implicit* representation of the user's interests [12]. Rather than extracting features from the playlist in a manner similar to Watson or Letiza, we transform the playlist representation into a *case-based* representation where the case features indicate the *genre/artist* mixture within the playlist. Since the playlist is a compilation, the goal is to capture the type of music mix, using the available features that would best indicate this property.

4.1.2 Case Representation

We have two feature types associated with each track, `genre_` and `artist_`. The semantics we are trying to capture by our case representation is the composition of a playlist in terms of *genre* and *artist*, where we consider *genre* to be the primary feature type. The most obvious way to represent each case is to have two features, `artist` and `genre` that contain an enumeration of the genres or artists in each feature. However, this case representation does not adequately capture the idea of a compilation of music tracks, in that it ignores the quantities of each genre/artist present in the playlist. Our case description must contain the quantities of individual genre and artists within each playlist. Furthermore, our case representation should not ignore retrieval issues. Even though we only have two features, the enumerated set of values for each feature means that similarity matching will require an exhaustive search through the case base. Since many cases will have no genres or artists in common, this is highly inefficient. Our goal is to produce a case representation that allows us to index closely matching cases, so that retrieval takes place only over the relevant portion of the case base. Finally, since one of the advantages of an instance-based representation is the ease with which explanations can be derived from retrieved cases, our case representation should be an intuitive depiction of what constitutes a compilation of music tracks.

The case representation we used in Smart Radio is illustrated in table 2. The case captures the composition of the playlist in terms of the quantity of genres and artist present. This representation allows each case to be indexed in a retrieval-efficient memory structure such as a case retrieval net which we discuss in section 5. The case mark-up demonstrated in table 2 is an example of CBML v1.0, Case Mark-up Language, which we developed to represent case data in distributed web applications [4].

Table 2. A CBML representation of the playlist.

```
<case>
<casedef casename="playlist_930">
<attributes>
  <attribute name="genre_1">1</attribute>
  <attribute name="genre_11">2</attribute>
  <attribute name="genre_17">3</attribute>
  <attribute name="genre_7">4</attribute>
  <attribute name="artist_1201">1</attribute>
  ...
</attributes>
</casedef>
</case>
```

4.2 Feature Weights

The transformed playlist has two types of feature, genre_ features and artist_ features. The maximum number of features in a playlist is 20 where it is composed of 10 separate genres and 10 artists. The minimum number of features a playlist can have is two, in which case the playlist contains tracks by the same artist, and with the same genre. The currently playing playlist is used as the target for which we try and find the most similar cases available in the recommendation set. Playlist similarity is determined by matching the proportions of genre and artist contained in a playlist. When calculating playlist similarity we apply two sets of weights to theses features.

4.2.1 Feature Type Weight

The first, the *feature type weight*, is general across each query and represents the relative importance of each *type* of feature. We consider the genre_ type more important in determining the property of playlist mix and allocate it a weight of 0.7. The artist_ type features receive a 0.3 weighting. The reason for this is that artist features are essentially used to refine the retrieval process, boosting those playlists that match well on the genre_ type features. This is particularly pertinent where a target playlist contains a lot of tracks by one artist. Playlists that match well on the genre_ features are then boosted by the contribution of the artist_ features, pushing those lists with the artist to the top of the retrieval result set. The `artist_` features also implicitly designate the degree of mix of the target playlist. A playlist with one or two artists and one or two genres will match playlists with a similar mix while a playlist with a larger selection of genres and artists will tend to match similarly eclectic playlists. However, we recognise that the weights allocated to each feature type are based only on our view of playlist similarity. This is an inexact science based on a subjective analysis, and different weightings for different listeners could be allocated were we able to capture each listener's outlook on playlist similarity. Stahl [17] and Branting [3] have proposed some techniques for determining local similarity measures, but in the context of Smart Radio it is difficult to see how these could be applied implicitly i.e. without explicitly asking the user to rate how well playlists are matched.

4.2.2 Feature Query Weight

The second weight, the *feature query weight*, is query specific and is determined by the composition of the target playlist. The *feature query weight* represents the degree of importance of each feature in determining similarity. The *feature query weight* is given by calculating the proportion of the feature type that is represented by each feature. For instance, if we consider the `genre_` feature type, the *feature query weight* of the `genre_17` feature is 4/10, where the denominator is the total value for the `genre_` feature types in the target case.

Thus, the *feature query weight* for feature i of type t, can be given as

$$wf_{t,i} = \frac{|f_{t,i}|}{\sum_{j \in t} f_j} \qquad [1]$$

where $|f_{t,i}|$ is the value for feature i of the target case. The denominator is the summation of values for features of type t.

4.2.3 Overall weight

The overall weight, `ow`, for each feature is the product of the *feature type weight* and the *feature query weight*.

```
ow = feature_type_weight × feature_query_weight          [2]
```

Thus, the overall weights for the features in table 2 are given in table 3.

Table 3. The table illustrates how weights are calculated on a per query basis.

Feature	feature_type_weight * feature_query_weight	Overall weight
genre_1	0.7 x (1/10)	0.07
genre_11	0.7 x (2/10)	0.14
genre_17	0.7 x (3/10)	0.21
genre_7	0.7 x (4/10)	0.28
artist_1201	0.3 x (1/10)	0.03

4.3 Similarity Metric

The similarity measure we use is given by equation 3. This measure, which is a modified form of a similarity measure known as the *weighted city block* measure (Equation 4), was chosen because it works well in matching cases where missing values occur. As we see from table 2 and table 3 the target case defines the feature (and feature weights) required in each query. Hence, on a query basis many playlist cases can be considered to have missing attribute values *with respect to the target case*. However, since each case is fully specified in its own right, many matching cases may contain genre_ features that are not relevant to the query. Even though the candidate case may closely match the target in terms of the features they have in common, the presence of irrelevant (or unsuitable) features may mean that the case is less useful than another case that only contains the target features. For this reason we apply a *similarity adjustment*, c, to each retrieved case that depends on the proportion of the *playlist* containing the genre features specified by the target (see Equation 5). This weight diminishes similarity scores that are based on a partial match with the genre_ features of the target, and preserves similarity scores that are based on full matches.

$$sim(A, B) = c \sum_{i=1}^{p} w_i \frac{|a_i - b_i|}{range} \qquad [3]$$

$$sim(A, B) = \sum_{i=1}^{p} w_i \frac{|a_i - b_i|}{range} \qquad [4]$$

$$c = \frac{|num\_tracks\_with\_t \arg et\_genre|}{|total\_number\_of\_tracks|} \qquad [5]$$

5. Integrating Context Ranking and ACF

Integrating the ACF procedure and similarity-based context ranking requires weighing up a number of factors. Burke suggests that a hybrid strategy must be a function of the characteristics of the recommender systems being combined [5]. For content and collaborative recommender systems this is largely dependent on the quantity and quality of data available. Another factor is the history of the application: is it new, in which case both techniques are untested, or is the proposed hybrid an enhancement of an already running system. For historical and logistical reasons the quantity and quality of the ACF data in the Smart Radio system is greater than the content data. Smart Radio has a greater amount of ACF data because it was originally designed and run as an ACF–based playlist recommender system [8]. Content-based recommendation systems at least require a content extraction process and, in the case of knowledge-based system, they may also require a knowledge engineering process [5]. The content extraction process in Smart Radio involved mining the ID3 tags in each mp3 file which contained the genre_ and artist_ information. As such it was a lightweight, inexpensive process. Although, the information it yielded was not particularly rich the alternatives in the music domain are costly. The automatic extraction of audio features suitable for content based retrieval is a difficult task and still the subject of much research [7]. While annotated music databases are available, license fees are prohibitively expensive reflecting the man-hours and knowledge required to keep up to date with the shifting music scene [1].

5.1 ACF/Content-Based Cascade architecture

The content-based strategy in Smart Radio was never designed as a stand-alone recommendation strategy. Rather it evolved through our identification of the problem of insensitivity to user-context in version 1.0 of the system. For this reason, the content-based strategy was always designed as an augmentation of the primary ACF strategy. Since one of the benefits of ACF is its 'knowledge light' approach to recommendation, our goal in designing a hybrid, content-based approach was to augment the ACF process with a similarly lightweight content-based strategy. Within the taxonomy of hybrid strategies suggested by Burke, the Smart Radio hybrid is best described as a *Cascading* system. This involves a staged process where one technique produces a candidate set which is then refined by a secondary process. Burke identifies the EntréeC system as the only other hybrid system using a *Cascading* strategy. In the EntréeC system, a content rich, knowledge-based system is the primary means of recommendation. A light ACF system is employed to decide between tied recommendations produced by the first stage by promoting those recommendations that have been 'endorsed' by EntréeC users. The Smart Radio system, on the other hand, uses ACF as its primary recommendation strategy that is then refined by a content-based process. As a result of this, SmartRadio is an *automated* recommendation system whereas EntreeC requires the user to explicitly enter the terms of their restaurant requirements. The SmartRadio approach is to use the full user profile for ACF recommendations but to then refine these recommendations based on similarity to the current context. The implementation of this strategy is a type of MAC/FAC retrieval well known amongst CBR researchers [6]. In a novel slant on this we integrate the ACF process into this retrieval strategy.

5.2 MAC/FAC

Gentner and Forbus's MAC/FAC (Many Are Called but Few Are Chosen) retrieval technique has its origins in cognitive science where it was suggested as a model of the memory access exhibited by human beings. The technique involves a two-stage retrieval in which the MAC component provided a relatively inexpensive wide search of memory based on a surface representation of the problem. The FAC stage pruned the results from the MAC stage using a much more rigorous, examination of the structural representation of each case. In applied case based reasoning the technique has become understood as a two-stage retrieval in which a wide net search is followed by a refinement stage. Our use of the term is in this context. Our implementation of the two-stage retrieval is novel in that the first stage (MAC) is carried out by the ACF module, which returns a set of results, of which we need to decide which is the most pertinent to our user context. The second stage (FAC) involves finding matches to the context probe in the result set.

5.3   Case Memory

The Smart Radio case memory consists of the total number of playlists in the system organised as a case retrieval net with each case represented in terms of its constituent genre_ and artist_ features. Each playlist case can be considered to have missing features since it is impossible for a single playlist to contain all possible genre_ and artist_ features. As illustrated in figure 3, the case retrieval net structure will only link those cases with features in common. This ensures optimal retrieval while only traversing the relevant portions of case memory [10].

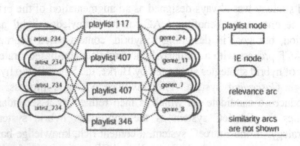

Figure 3.   A schema of the playlists indexed using a case retrieval net.

The output for the ACF module is a set of candidate playlists. These are the playlists the system has found using the resources of the ACF neighbourhood. The key idea at this point is that only a portion of these may be particularly relevant to the user at this time. Each retrieved playlist has a caseIndex which refers to its position in the case retrieval net. Using these indexes a subset of the case retrieval net is automatically primed. The most recently played playlist, the *context* playlist, is then presented as a target case. The CRN retrieval mechanism is activated only through the primed subset of the case retrieval net. Those programmes that have the highest activation after this process are those that are most similar to the target playlist. The overall activation metric is the similarity score calculated using equation 3. The top 5 playlists are then ranked according to their activation score.

5.4   Presenting Recommendations

The presentation strategy employed by Smart Radio is to give the user a list of ten recommended playlists per page. By default the top recommended playlist is displayed automatically (see Figure 1). The further a list is from the top the less likely the user will view it [18]. For this reason, the 5 most similar playlists to the context playlist are displayed at the top of the Smart Radio home page. Users quickly understand that the top 5 recommendations are particularly relevant to their listening interests at the time. After the first 5 playlists the recommended lists are displayed according to the predicted vote of the ACF module. As we shall see in the next section we amend this presentation strategy when we are evaluating the efficacy of our context-based recommendations.

6. Evaluation

Increasingly, there has been a demand for objective evaluation criteria for on-line Recommender systems. This stems from a difficulty in evaluating which recommender is better than another, and in judging which criteria to use when making this evaluation. Normally, evaluations are performed *off-line* using techniques from machine learning and information retrieval such as cross validation, Leave-One-Out evaluation and measures of recall/precision. However, these techniques are not suitable for measuring the success of a recommender strategy like the content-boosted ACF that produces a ranking based on user actions at a particular time. To be sure that our new hypothesis is working we need to perform a comparative analysis of how it performs against a pure ACF strategy. We draw attention to the fact that evaluation has to measure whether real people are willing to act based on the advice of the system. Unlike the off-line analysis, this methodology plays one recommendation strategy against the other in an on-line setting and measures relative degree of success of each strategy according to how the user utilises the recommendations of either system. This framework doesn't measure absolute user satisfaction but only relative user satisfaction with one system over another. Our evaluation methodology draws upon an on-line evaluative framework for recommender systems which we have earlier defined [9]. In the interests of space we only discuss issues related to our current evaluation and refer the reader to the earlier paper for a fuller discussion.

6.1.1 Evaluation Environment

Our evaluation environment consists of a live on-line application used by a community of users, with a well-defined recommendation task using a specific user interface. The application is serviced by two competing recommendation strategies: ACF and context-boosted ACF. In order to be able to gauge a relative measure of user satisfaction with the two strategies, it is necessary to log the user interactions with respect to the recommendation engines. In order to isolate the recommendation strategies we keep other aspects that might influence user satisfaction (interface, interaction model) the same. The proposed methodology can be seen as a competition between two different approaches to solving the same problem (in this case, winning user satisfaction) in which the winner is defined by how the user makes use of recommendations. We define three evaluation policies.

Presentation policy: The recommendations in Smart Radio are presented as an ordered list (see figure 1). For evaluative purposes we interleave items from each strategy. Since the item presented first in a recommendation set is considered to have priority, access to this position is alternated between each recommender strategy after each playlist 'play' event.

Evaluation policy: defines how user actions will be considered evidence of preference of one algorithm over the other. In this case a preference is registered for one strategy over the other when a user plays a playlist from its recommendation set.

Comparison metric: defines how to analyse the evaluative feedback in order to determine a winner. The simplest way is to count the number of rounds won by the competing systems. However, certain algorithms, such as collaborative filtering, may only start to perform well after sufficient data has been collected. Therefore, we also need to analyse the performance of each system over time.

7. Results

The results refer to the listening data of 58 users who played a total of 1012 playlists during the 101 day period from 08/04/2003 until 17/07/2003. The graph in figure 4 shows the source of playlists played in the system for this period. The recommendation category was by far the most popular means of finding playlists. We should also note that building playlists from scratch or explicitly searching for playlists should not be considered 'rival' categories to the recommendation category since an ACF based system requires users to find a proportion of new items from outside the system itself.

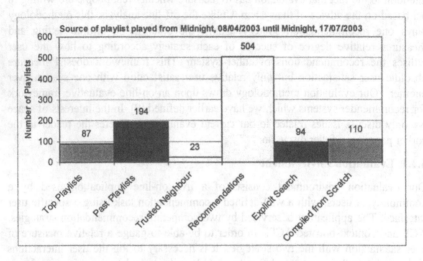

Figure 4. The source of playlists played in Smart Radio during the evaluation period.

Figure 5 illustrates the cumulative breakdown of recommendations between pure ACF recommendations and context boosted ACF for the period. From a total of 504 recommended playlists which were played, 311 were sourced from content boosted recommendations, while 177 came from normal ACF recommendations. 16 came from bootstrap recommendations which we haven't discussed here.

In order to check that these results were consistent throughout the evaluation period we divided the period into 15 intervals of one week. The graph in figure 6 shows the proportions of ACF to context boosted recommendations analysed on a weekly basis for the period. We can see that the context boosted ACF continually outperformed the pure ACF recommendation strategy. We have tested these results using a paired t-test and found them to be statistically significant.

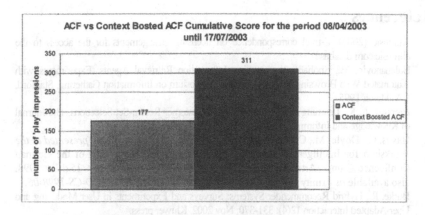

Figure 5. The cumulative scores for the ACF vs. context boosted ACF analysis

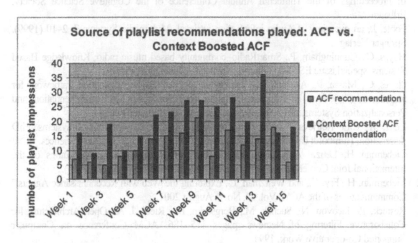

Figure 6. ACF vs. context-boosted ACF over 15 weekly intervals

8.   Conclusion

In this paper we introduced the Smart Radio system, a community-based recommendation service where users compile and share music playlists with the aide of an automated collaborative filtering system. However, since ACF techniques are insensitive to the user's current listening preferences we have used a lightweight content-based retrieval mechanism to rank playlist recommendations according to their current relevance to the user. The principle idea is that the user's most recent interests are represented as a target case. The ACF module retrieves a set of recommended playlists and primes a subset of the playlist Case Retrieval Net. Using the spreading activation mechanism of the Case Retrieval Net, the ACF recommendations are then ranked according to their similarity to the target case. We evaluated our strategy with an on-line methodology in which ACF and context-boosted ACF simultaneously competed. Our results would suggest that the context boosted ACF significantly out performs standard ACF.

References

1. Allmusic (2002). E-mail correspondence on licensing arrangements for the access to the allmusic.com database
2. Balabanovic, M., Shoham, Y., Learning Information Retrieval Agents: Experiments with Automated Web Browsing, in AAAI Spring Symposium on Information Gathering, Stanford, CA, March 1995
3. Branting, L. K., Learning Feature Weights from Customer Return-Set Selections. The Journal of Knowledge and Information Systems (KAIS). To appear, 2003.
4. Hayes, C., Doyle, M., Cunningham, P., Distributed CBR Using XML, *presented at the* Workshop for Intelligent Systems and Electronic Commerce as part of the German Conference on Artificial Intelligence (KI-98) September 15-17 1998. also available *as* Trinity College Dublin Computer Science Report *TCD-CS-1998-06*.
5. Burke, R., Hybrid Recommender Systems: Surveys and Experiments in User Modelling and User-Adapted Interaction 12(4): 331-370; Nov 2002. Kluwer press.
6. Gentner, D., and Forbus, K. D., MAC/FAC: A model of similarity based access and mapping. In Proceedings of the Thirteenth Annual Conference of the Cognitive Science Society. Erlbaum
7. Foote, J., an overview of Audio information retrieval. Multimedia Systems 7: 2–10 (1999). Springer Verlag
8. Hayes, C., Cunningham, P., SmartRadio–community based music radio; Knowledge Based Systems, special issue ES2000, Volume 14, Issue3-4, June 2001, Elsevier
9. Hayes, C., Massa, P., Avesani, P., Cunningham, P., An on-line evaluation framework for recommender systems in the proceedings of the IWorkshop on Recommendation and Personalization Systems, AH 2002, Malaga, Spain, 2002. Springer Verlag.
10. Lenz, M., Case Retrieval Nets as a model for building flexible information systems. PhD dissertation, Humboldt University, Berlin. Faculty of Mathematics and Natural Sciences.
11. Lieberman H, Letiza: An Agent That Assists Web Browsing" in Proceedings of the International Joint Conference on Artificial Intelligence IJCAI-95.(Montreal 1995).
12. Lieberman, H., Fry, C., and Weitzman, L., Exploring the Web with Reconnaissance Agents," Communications of the ACM, Vol. 44, No. 8, August 2001.
13. Resnick, P., Iacovou, N., Suchak, M., Bergstrom, P., Riedl, J. An Open Architecture for Collaborative Filtering of Netnews. pages 175--186. ACM Conference on Computer Supported Co-operative Work, 1994.
14. Schafer, J.B., Konstan, J.A., and Riedl, J., Recommender Systems in E-Commerce. In ACM Conference on Electronic Commerce (EC-99), pages 158-166, 1999.
15. Schlit B. et al, Context-Aware Computing Applications, IEEE Workshop on Mobile Computing Systems and Applications 1994
16. Shardanand, U., and Mayes, P., Social Information Filtering: Algorithms for Automating 'Word of Mouth', in Proceedings of CHI95, 210-217, 1995.
17. Stahl, A., Learning Feature Weights from Case Order Feedback. Proceedings of the 4th International Conference on Case-Based Reasoning, ICCBR 2001
18. Swearingen, K., Sinha, R., Beyond Algorithms: An HCI Perspective on Recommender Systems, ACM SIGIR Workshop on Recommender Systems, 2001.

CBR for SMARTHOUSE Technology

Nirmalie Wiratunga*   Susan Craw*   Bruce Taylor†

Genevieve Davis*

* School of Computing   † Scott Sutherland School

The Robert Gordon University

Aberdeen, AB10 1FR, Scotland, UK

{nw|craw}@comp.rgu.ac.uk   b.taylor@rgu.ac.uk

Abstract

SMARTHOUSE technology offers devices that help the elderly and people with disabilities to live independently in their homes. This paper presents our experiences from a pilot project applying case-based reasoning techniques to match the needs of the elderly and those with disabilities to SMARTHOUSE technology. The SMARTHOUSE problem is decomposed into sub-tasks, and generalised concepts added for each sub-task. This decomposition and generalisation enables multiple case reuse employing a standard decision tree index based iterative retrieval strategy. Documented real situations were used to create a small case base. A prototype implemented using RECALL [1] with TCL script is evaluated empirically using leave-one-out testing, and separately with the domain expert on newly created test cases. Results show the generated solutions to be comparable to those of a domain expert. Importantly, the iterative retrieval strategy employing multiple indices generated solutions that were significantly better compared to a best match retrieval without indices.

1 Introduction

Smart House Technology has been around for about twenty years and aims to encourage independent living for the elderly and disabled. This technology may consist of something as simple as a telephone amplifying unit for those with hearing impairments, to a field bus system, where large numbers of sensors and actuators each with their own microprocessors are connected together, for people with severe mobility problems.

Occupational Therapists usually match assistive technology to people's needs by observing people engaged in daily tasks. If patients have difficulty doing these tasks then a technological solution may be suggested, often based on similar past patients. In recent years the range of technology has increased considerably. This additionally makes it harder for occupational therapists

---

[1]RECALL is a CBR development tool supplied by Isoft (www.isoft.fr).

to keep abreast with SMARTHOUSE devices, thereby creating a real need for automated tools to help match SMARTHOUSE technology to people's needs [6].

A case-based reasoning (CBR) system solves new problems by reusing solutions from previously correctly solved similar problems [7]. These past experiences consisting of problem descriptions and associated solutions are called cases and are stored in a case base. For the SMARTHOUSE domain a case consists of a person's disability needs together with the SMARTHOUSE devices that can enable this person to live independently. Case retrieval is the first stage of the CBR cycle in Figure 1. Here given a description of the new problem (a person's disability needs) a similar case or a subset of similar cases most useful for solving the new problem are retrieved from the case-base. Depending on the differences between the current problem and the retrieved cases some adaptation of the retrieved cases might be necessary before the retrieved solution can be reused. Subsequent stages include verification of the proposed solution and if necessary retention of the new problem and the modified solution with the aim of reusing it in the future.

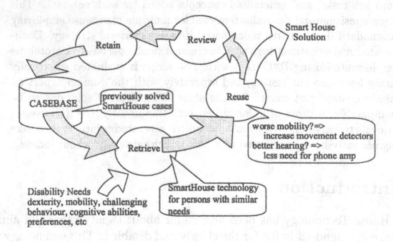

Figure 1: CBR cycle applied to the SMARTHOUSE task (Kolodner 1993)

Retrieval of relevant cases is crucial for the successful operation of any CBR system. This is particularly true when adaptation knowledge is difficult to acquire [4]. This paper tackles two important issues for a retrieval only system in the context of the SMARTHOUSE domain:

- Case representation enabling storage of cases in the case base according to a predefined structure; and

- An iterative retrieval strategy primarily comprising an indexing scheme to restrict the similarity matching to just a selection of cases, but also facilitating multiple case reuse.

Typically case representation has a flat structure consisting of feature-value pairs. Additionally the SMARTHOUSE case representation captures the inherent task decomposition within this domain. The similarity measure used for case retrieval can be a straightforward distance function, but it may also involve some knowledge intensive matching of cases [5]. Retrieval knowledge typically comprises weights reflecting importance of features and relevance of features for index creation. Given the relatively small size of the SMARTHOUSE case base here we were able to acquire this knowledge from the domain expert.

In the rest of this paper we will describe how a prototype was built to match people's needs to SMARTHOUSE technology. Section 2 discusses case representation issues, and an iterative retrieval strategy is presented in Section 3. Evaluation results are presented in Section 4 followed by related work in Section 5, and conclusions in Section 6.

2 Case Representation

The EU funded Custodian project created a SMARTHOUSE technology simulation tool to illustrate how different SMARTHOUSE devices function in the house [3]. More importantly for the work presented in this paper eleven real scenarios consisting of people needs and matching technology solutions were acquired during this project.

The first task for developing our prototype CBR system was to *manually* translate the documented textual cases into a more structured representation of feature-value pairs. This involved identifying relevant features that belonged to the problem space and the solution space; and establishing the data labels with which to instantiate these features. For example given;

... Ms M is an indoor wheelchair user with cerebral palsy. She is a tenant in her own ground-floor flat, and whilst living moderately independently, did have support from care workers to assist her in getting dressed and bathed... She required an intercom that was both hands free and with video so that she could operate it from her wheel chair ... also electrically operated locks were fitted on her external door ...

We can extract the following to describe the problem: wheel-chair-indoor Yes, wheel-chair-outdoor unknown, house-type ground-floor-flat, care-staff Yes, able-into-bath with-help; and the solution described by: electrically-operated-locks-external-door Yes, intercom-front-door video-hands-free. Converting the textual descriptions into problem and solution features required establishing quantifiable values with which to instantiate these nominal features, Some features are binary valued (e.g. Yes/No) but many are multi-valued (e.g. the feature able-into-bath can have values Yes, No or with-help). Missing values was another common problem because the cases were documented for an entirely different purpose from that of developing a CBR tool. Although the domain expert could have made informed guesses in some situations, often it was left as unknown.

A total of 108 features were identified of which 64 describe the problem in terms of the person, their home, abilities and needs; and a further 44 features

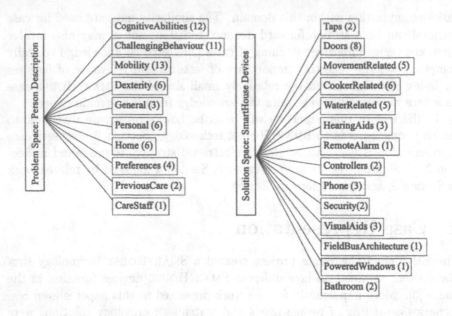

Figure 2: SMARTHOUSE case representation

describe the solution; i.e. SMARTHOUSE devices. With increased numbers of features and values it made sense to group these features particularly the solution features, according to their context, forming 10 problem space groups and 14 solution space groups consisting of SMARTHOUSE devices (see Figure 2). The number within brackets denotes the number of devices in each group e.g. 5 MovementRelated devices. We will refer to solution space groups as device groups and for consistency use the same terminology for the 3 singleton groups (RemoteAlarm, FieldBusArchitecture and PoweredWindows). Grouping devices is generally a straightforward task for the domain expert and in difficult instances a pragmatic decision was made, e.g. would it make a difference if the devices associated with Doors is split into exterior and interior doors. Importantly this grouping decomposes the task thereby enabling retrieval to concentrate on each sub-task separately.

3 Retrieval Strategy

Several commercial CBR tools (e.g. RECALL, REMIND and KATE) use decision trees (DTs) to index the case base in order to improve retrieval efficiency [1]. Although efficiency is a primary reason for using an index, a DT index formed using C4.5's information gain ratio heuristic [12] additionally provides a useful means to explain the underlying reasoning behind the retrieval; a desirable

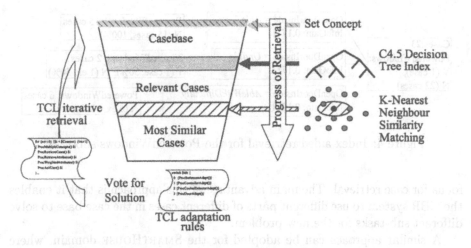

Figure 3: Multiple case retrieval

feature for CBR applied to the SMARTHOUSE domain. Essentially the index is created for a selected concept (or class) and acts as a filter enabling the CBR system to locate the relevant subset of cases for a given problem (see Figure 3). The most similar k cases to the current problem are then identified from this subset by applying the k Nearest Neighbour algorithm (k-NN).

Let us consider a retrieval sub-task within the SMARTHOUSE domain. Figure 4 illustrates a case base index created by inducing a C4.5 DT for the sub-task PoweredWindows (i.e. powered windows required or not). Given a new problem the tree is traversed and depending on the person's ability to open internal doors the relevant leaf node and its cases are retrieved. These cases form the neighbourhood and the majority solution obtained using k-NN instantiates the PoweredWindows part of the solution for the new problem. Notice that the DT is built with the aim of partitioning cases according to a specified concept; here it is PoweredWindows with possible instantiations values: Yes or No. Generally the partitioning tends to result in leaf-nodes containing cases with similar instantiations for PoweredWindows. However, with the second leaf node in Figure 4 we have 2 cases that relate to persons who are unable to open doors, yet one has powered windows, while the other does not, because existing sash windows cannot be powered. Therefore if cases were retrieved from this leaf node and the new problem also consisted of a house with sash windows then applying k-NN would result in the PoweredWindows part of the solution to be instantiated with No.

3.1 Using Multiple Indices for Iterative Retrieval

In previous work [2], we have shown how multiple DTs can be employed to solve design problems, where each tree concentrates on retrieving cases pertinent to solve a different part of a design task. Essentially this involves an iterative retrieval strategy whereby at a given iteration a different sub-task becomes the

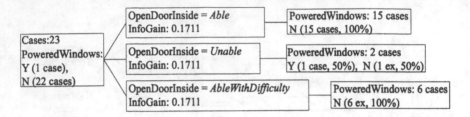

Figure 4: Index aided retrieval for the PoweredWindows sub-task

focus for case retrieval. The main advantage of this approach is that it enables the CBR system to use different parts of different cases in the case base to solve different sub-tasks for the new problem.

A similar approach can be adopted for the SMARTHOUSE domain, where identifying a suitable SMARTHOUSE device is a sub-task and is solved in conjunction with a separate DT index given the new person's description. Traversal of each tree identifies a different subset of cases to solve each sub-task. This is the approach we use for RemoteAlarms, PoweredWindows and FieldBus Architecture requiring 3 DT indices. However if we were to insist on separate indices for the remaining devices we would need a further 41 DTs, which from an efficiency point of view does not make sense. Instead we exploit the fact that these 41 devices are already grouped in 11 device groups. We create a generalised concept feature, for each group. This means we induce 11 DTs (instead of 41), in addition to the 3 DTs for RemoteAlarm, PoweredWindows and FieldBusArchitecture.

3.2   Creating Generalised Concepts

The new generalised concept feature that we wish to create for a given group should be an abstraction or summarisation of the devices that are members of that device group. We will now look at how a value can be assigned to such a feature created for a device group with the aid of an example. Consider two cases from the case base and their solution instantiations for just the CookerRelated device group (see Table 1). With CaseX we have a solution involving a timer-based automatic cooker shut-off, together with a detector that can detect gas, heat or smoke, and three alarms; while CaseY does not require detectors or alarms. So how do we establish a value for the new generalised concept feature, F_{cooker}? The simplest approach is to instantiate it with value Needed, if at least one of the cooker devices are needed, otherwise Not-Needed. Accordingly, in our example, F_{cooker}, is instantiated with Needed for CaseX and Not-Needed for CaseY.

In this manner all cases in the case base are modified by adding a generalised concept feature, per device group[2]. We can then induce a DT for each device group with the new feature selected as the concept. For example, to establish suitable devices related with cookers for a given new problem,

---

[2]Note this generalisation is not required for the 3 singleton device groups.

Table 1: Case values for the CookerRelated device group

CookerRelated Group	Instantiations For	
	CaseX	CaseY
auto-cooker-shut-off	{gas, heat, timer}	No
detectors-over-cooker	{gas, heat, smoke}	unknown
alarm-for-carers	No	No
cooker-isolation-alarm	No	No
fire-alarm	Yes	No
gas-alarm	Yes	No
F_{cooker}	Needed	Not-Needed

the CookerRelated DT (induced with F_{cooker} as the concept) is traversed to identify the leaf node cases, and then k-NN is applied to access the k nearest neighbours. The majority solutions for cooker detectors and alarms from these k cases are reused and instantiate the cooker related solution part of the new problem.

4 Evaluation

In our experiments we implemented the SMARTHOUSE prototype using the RECALL CBR shell together with a TCL script to drive the retrieval. MULTIPLE is the iterative retrieval strategy described in Section 3, where multiple indices enable reuse of multiple cases to solve different sub-tasks. Traversal of each index identifies the relevant subset of cases to which 1-NN is applied, and the solution part from the nearest neighbour corresponding to the sub-task is reused. MULTIPLE is compared with SINGLE, where the entire solution of the best match case is reused. Unlike MULTIPLE, SINGLE does not use indices, instead applies 1-NN to the entire case base, once.

Eleven real-cases were supplemented with another twelve cases invented by our domain expert, forming a case base of 23 cases. Evaluation was carried out in two ways:

Leave-One-Out Testing: 10 cases from the real cases were each used in turn as the probe to the CBR system containing a case base of the remaining 22 cases. This provides results from 10 different leave-one-out test runs; and

User Testing: Comparison of the system's and expert's solutions for 3 new problem scenarios supplied by the expert.

Ascertaining the quality of a generated system solution involves establishing its similarity to the expert's solution. When the solution contains nominal values it is typical to employ the standard overlap similarity metric for this purpose [11]. However this metric can be misleading when the distribution of nominal values is highly skewed. Although there are 44 devices, a SMARTHOUSE solution would very rarely require an instantiation consisting of all devices. Instead it is more likely for a solution to require fewer than half of these devices.

Table 2: Comparing system and expert solutions

Doors Group	Solution		Categories			
	System	Expert	TP	TN	FP	FN
alarm-when-open	No	No	0	1	0	0
contacts-on-external-doors	Yes	No	0	0	1	0
contacts-on-bedroom-door	No	No	0	1	0	0
contacts-on-bathroom-door	No	No	0	1	0	0
contacts-on-kitchen-door	No	No	0	1	0	0
intercom-to-front-door	Audio	Video-HF	0	0	1	0
powered-external-doors	Yes	Yes	1	0	0	0
electric-locks-external-doors	No	Yes	0	0	0	1

Consider the example in Table 2 listing the system's and expert's solution for the Doors device group. Of the 8 listed devices we have an exact match in 5, of which 4 are True Negatives (TN) and only one is a True Positive (TP). A False Negative (FN) is a system fault caused when it fails to propose a device, as with electric-locks-external-doors. In contrast with contacts-on-external-doors we have the system incorrectly proposing a device, referred to as a False Positive (FP). A similar situation arises with intercom-to-front-door, but here the difference is that, although the system has proposed a device, it is not the right one (Audio instead of Video-HF). We will consider such a system failure also as a FP although it is actually referred to as a failing positive [10].

The overlap similarity metric (Sim), is the number of matching devices divided by all the devices; $(TP+TN)/(TP+TN+FP+FN)$. In the Table 2 example, this overlap is 0.625. Here the influence of the lesser important TNs can suggest an overly optimistic similarity between solutions. Therefore, we also employ traditional Information Retrieval measures [9] in the context of SMARTHOUSE devices:

- Precision (P) is the proportion of proposed devices that are actually correct $P = TP/(TP + FP)$; and

- Recall (R) is the proportion of required devices that are correctly proposed $R = TP/(TP + FN)$.

Generally high recall is desirable because lower FN and higher TP is important for the SMARTHOUSE domain. The combined effect of these two measures is commonly measured by the F-measure (F) calculated as their harmonic mean; $2PR/(P + R)$. By applying this to the Doors example in Table 2 we have a far more realistic similarity based comparison of system and expert solutions;

P is 0.33, R is 0.5 and F is 0.4. Significance is reported from a one-sided paired Wilcoxon signed rank test.

4.1 Leave-One-Out Testing

The average results from 10 leave-one-out test runs appear in Table 3. The first column lists the 14 device groups and the adjacent column indicates the number of devices in each group. For comparison purposes both the Sim and F values are provided for SINGLE and MULTIPLE.

Table 3: Averaged results from 10 leave-one-out test runs

Device group	No Of Devices	Single Sim	F	Multiple Sim	F
Bathroom	2	0.85	0	0.85	0
Controllers	2	1	1	0.9	0.67
Cooker Detectors	6	0.83	0	0.83	0
Doors	8	0.85	0.57	0.89	**0.71**
Hearing Aids	3	0.93	0.8	1	1
Movement Detectors	5	0.86	0.46	0.86	0.46
Phone Related	3	0.73	0.42	0.8	**0.7**
Remote Alarms	1	0.9	0.8	0.9	0.67
Security	2	0.85	0	1	1
Taps	2	0.9	0	1	1
Technology Architecture	1	0.9	0	1	1
Visual Aids	3	0.9	0	0.9	0
Water Detectors	5	0.98	0	1	1
Windows	1	0.6	0.33	0.8	**0.67**
Overall Average		*0.86*	*0.31*	*0.91*	*0.63*

MULTIPLE shows a significant improvement in 8 of the 14 groups over SINGLE; with both F (p=0.016) and Sim (p=0.029) measures. The domain expert indicated that some interesting valid alternative solutions were proposed by MULTIPLE. For instance in connection with Water Detectors for a person with cognitive impairments, learning problems and challenging behaviour, MULTIPLE suggested the need for flood detectors in the bathroom while the expert solution contained a special push to operate Taps. With another problem, MULTIPLE suggested the use of a pendant activated community alarm plinth as one of the 3 devices grouped under Phone. Although the expert solution also had the community alarm plinth the need for a pendant was documented as a future need.

With Controllers, MULTIPLE incorrectly suggests the use of environment and lighting controllers for a person that only has some mobility problems requiring the use of a wheelchair indoors, but otherwise having good manual dexterity and therefore able to operate switches. However MULTIPLE's suggestion of an environmental controller is not a totally wrong suggestion. Yet if this overly expensive solution had been implemented it would have gradually reduced the person's range of movements which would be both physically and psychologically detrimental to the person. This highlights the fact that system generated solutions should not be taken on board as the all encompassing definitive solution, and instead should be treated as a guide that localises search to potential solution areas. The over estimation of similarity with the overlap measure (Sim) is clearly seen with 7 of the device groups; SINGLE has a Sim measure > 0.85 (because there are many TNs) but the F measure is 0 (because TP is 0).

4.2 User Testing

Three new problem scenarios authored by the expert were used as probes to the CBR system. Test cases A and B were created by making minor variations based on existing cases while test case C was created from scratch, hence a more challenging problem. Importantly these test cases were generated to portray realistic problem scenarios with different levels of similarity to existing cases in the case base, and also with different levels of problem difficulty.

A comparison of the expert's and MULTIPLE's solutions for test cases A and B, appear in table 4. It is clear that these 2 test cases have a relatively low level of difficulty; they each require only 3 and 5 devices in the solution. Therefore it is not surprising that MULTIPLE's solution can be obtained by SINGLE's one-shot retrieval. We further investigated solution quality by increasing the nearest neighbours of MULTIPLE from 1 to 3. However due to the small case base size this increase actually had a detrimental affect on the solution.

Generally the domain expert felt that there was sufficient overlap between the actual and system solutions for test cases A and B. With Controllers for case A the expert solution suggests a lighting-controller while the system solution fails to suggest this device. The reason for this is that the DT for Controllers selected ambulant-mobility as a discriminatory feature to partition the case base. Since the only case with a lighting-controller device in the case base differed from test case A in ambulant-mobility, it did not fall under the same leaf node as test case A. This is an obvious problem with the limited number of cases in the case base. Similar explanations hold for test case B with for instance the Doors device group.

The use of DTs was well received by the expert because the decision nodes provides a useful explanation mechanism of the system's retrieval stage. For instance the selection of ambulant-mobility as the decision node for the Controllers device group, enabled the expert to conclude that although test case A related to a person with good ambulant mobility, a lighting-controller device was necessary because of the inability to operate light switches.

Test case C was a harder case to solve because the expert's solution consisted of 11 devices compared to 3 and 5 devices for A and B. Therefore it was encouraging to see that the iterative retrieval strategy reflects this problem

Table 4: Comparison of MULTIPLE and expert solutions

Device	Test Case A				Test Case B			
group	TP	TN	FP	FN	TP	TN	FP	FN
Bathroom	0	2	0	0	0	2	0	0
Controllers	0	1	0	1	0	2	0	0
Cooker Detectors	0	6	0	0	0	6	0	0
Doors	0	8	0	0	1	5	2	0
Hearing Aids	0	3	0	0	0	3	0	0
Movement Detectors	0	5	0	0	0	5	0	0
Phone Related	1	2	0	0	1	2	0	0
Remote Alarms	0	1	0	0	0	1	0	0
Security	1	1	0	0	0	2	0	0
Taps	0	2	0	0	0	2	0	0
Technology Architecture	0	1	0	0	0	1	0	0
Visual Aids	0	3	0	0	0	3	0	0
Water Detectors	0	5	0	0	3	2	0	0
Windows	0	1	0	0	0	1	0	0
Total	2	41	0	1	5	37	2	0

solving difficulty in that it reused 9 different cases to solve different sub-tasks of C. In Table 5, although MULTIPLE and SINGLE have equal Sim values, the Recall measure drops from 0.64 to 0.18 with SINGLE. Since the quality of the proposed solution is best ascertained by the system's ability to predict (true) devices here the increase in recall with MULTIPLE is most encouraging.

Overall the poor performance with device groups containing a greater number of devices; such as Doors, CookerRelated and MovementRelated, may suggest that the binary valued approach adopted with generalised concept creation (F_i), needs to be extended to a multi-valued concept.

5 Related Work

Task decomposition is commonly employed for complex problem solving, and is particularly successful when sub-tasks have few interactions [14]. One of the main advantages of task decomposition is multiple case reuse, and a good demonstration of this is seen with a hierarchical CBR system developed for automating plant-control software design [13]. The design case base is organised as a hierarchy and interestingly uses abstract and concrete cases; top level nodes are abstract cases decomposing the problem at subsequent levels in the hierarchy, while leaf nodes contain concrete sub-solutions. Since concrete cases can be attached to more than one parent the same case can be retrieved for different sub-tasks, thereby facilitating multiple case reuse. With the SMART-HOUSE prototype, task decomposition was achieved by tackling device groups

Table 5: Comparison of SINGLE and MULTIPLE solutions for test case C

Device group	SINGLE				MULTIPLE			
	TP	TN	FP	FN	TP	TN	FP	FN
Bathroom	0	2	0	0	0	2	0	0
Controllers	0	2	0	0	0	2	0	0
Cooker Detectors	0	4	0	2	0	4	0	2
Doors	0	5	0	3	1	5	0	2
Hearing Aids	0	2	0	1	1	0	2	0
Movement Detectors	0	3	0	2	2	0	3	0
Phone Related	1	1	1	0	1	1	1	0
Remote Alarms	1	0	0	0	1	0	0	0
Security	0	1	0	1	1	1	0	0
Taps	0	2	0	0	0	2	0	0
Technology Architecture	0	1	0	0	0	1	0	0
Visual Aids	0	3	0	0	0	3	0	0
Water Detectors	0	5	0	0	0	5	0	0
Windows	0	1	0	0	0	1	0	0
Total	2	32	1	9	7	27	6	4
Recall	0.18				0.64			
Precision	0.67				0.54			
Sim	0.77				0.77			

separately. Retrieval employed an automatically created DT structure as the index for each of these groups. Although abstract cases can be viewed as an index structure in a hierarchical case base, the knowledge engineering effort involved with identifying abstract cases and manually discovering connections between these would have been far more demanding for our domain expert. Instead DT based indexing greatly relieves this burden by automatically inducing a tree like structure which can then be examined by the expert.

The use of DTs as indices for sub-task retrieval has been applied with the tablet formulation domain [2], where instantiation of each component of a tablet is treated as a sub-task and a DT-based retrieval is triggered for each sub-task. The main difference with the SMARTHOUSE domain is that the sub-tasks are too numerous to be dealt with separately and hence a grouping of sub-tasks into device groups and the addition of generalised concepts is required before iterative retrieval is manageable.

Iterative retrieval applied to decomposable tasks stands to gain much from a well designed case structure. In fact it is the discovery of device groups that enabled multiple case reuse with the SMARTHOUSE prototype. The Auguste Project, operating in a similar application domain, aids decision making with regards to prescribing a neuroleptic drug for Alzheimer's patients [8]. The case representation consists of a grouping of features where the top level view contains personal information, physical health, behavioural aspects, etc. We have also adopted this general approach of grouping areas of the problem and solution space, although with SMARTHOUSE devices the solution space being more complex benefitted from concept generalisation. An example of a hierarchical case representation can be seen with the NIRMANI system [15]. This hierarchic structure is employed as a means to enforce context guided retrieval, where parts of cases are retrieved in stages. Presently the SMARTHOUSE case representation involves a single level hierarchy however it is possible that a multi-level hierarchy might be appropriate particularly to cope with the increasing range of devices in this domain.

6 Conclusion

We have presented our experiences with developing a prototype CBR system for the SMARTHOUSE problem domain, where the task involved matching SMARTHOUSE technology to the needs of the elderly and people with disabilities. The main users of a SMARTHOUSE CBR system will be suppliers of assistive technology, enabling them to match appropriate devices from supplier catalogues. The number of companies supplying SMARTHOUSE devices to support independent living at home is growing as they recognise the market opportunities in the increasing aging populations of developed countries.

Organising the solution space into device groups decomposed the SMARTHOUSE task into manageable sub-tasks. Task decomposition with concept generalisation enabled the use of a standard DT-based iterative retrieval strategy. Importantly the use of multiple indices enabled re-use of different cases to solve different parts of a given test case, thereby encouraging best use of the relatively small case base. An empirical evaluation has clearly shown significant improvement in solution quality with MULTIPLE's retrieval strategy over SINGLE's best match retrieval without indexing. Subjective evaluation with the expert has been promising, but we are conscious of the fact that these results are partly based on cases invented by the domain expert. Therefore a more realistic evaluation is needed before operational feasibility of this approach can be fully justified.

The ability to explain the reasoning behind the proposed system's solution is a desirable facility and with the SMARTHOUSE prototype the domain expert found that the display of both index trees and similarity of cases at leaf nodes to be a useful step in this direction. Finally it is worth mentioning that it was the prototype's ability to use multiple cases to solve different parts of a given SMARTHOUSE problem that most impressed our domain expert.

References

[1] David W. Aha and Leonard A. Breslow. Comparing simplification procedures for DTs on an economics classification task. Tec. Report AIC-98-009, Navy Center for Applied Research in AI, Washington DC, 1998.

[2] Susan Craw, Nirmalie Wiratunga, and Ray Rowe. Case-based design for tablet formulation. In *Proc. of the 4th European Workshop on CBR, EWCBR-98*, pages 358–369, Dublin, Eire, 1998. Springer.

[3] G. Dewsbury, S. Bonner, B. Taylor, and M. Edge. Final evaluation of tools developed. Tec. Report custodian/rgu/wp7.3/re/004, CUSTODIAN Project, EU Telematics Initiative for Disabled and Elderly People, 2001.

[4] Kathleen Hanney and Mark T. Keane. The adaptation knowledge bottleneck: How to ease it by learning from cases. In *Proc. of the 2nd International Conference on CBR, ICCBR-97*, pages 359–370, Providence, RI, USA, 1997. Springer-Verlag.

[5] Jacek Jarmulak, Susan Craw, and Ray Rowe. Genetic algorithms to optimise CBR retrieval. In *Proc. of the 5th European Workshop on CBR, EWCBR-2K*, pages 137–149, Trento, Italy, 2000. Springer-Verlag, Berlin.

[6] Janet Kolodner. Improving human decision making through case-based decision aiding. *AI Magazine*, 12(2):52–68, 1991.

[7] Janet Kolodner. *Case-Based Reasoning*. Morgan Kauffman Publishers, Inc., San Mateo, CA., 1993.

[8] Cindy Marling and Peter Whitehouse. CBR in the care of alzheimer's disease patients. In *Proc. of the 4th International Conference on CBR, ICCBR-01*, pages 702–715, Vancouver, BC, Canada, 2001. Springer Verlag.

[9] David McSherry. Precision and recall in interactive case-based reasoning. In *Proc. of the 4th International Conference on CBR, ICCBR-01*, pages 392–406, Vancouver, BC, Canada, 2001. Springer Verlag.

[10] D. Ourston and R. Mooney. Theory refinement combining analytical and empirical methods. *Artificial Intelligence*, 66:273–309, 1994.

[11] Terry Payne and Pete Edwards. Implicit feature selection with the value difference metric. In *Proc. of the ECAI98 Conference*, pages 450–454, Brighton, UK, 1998. John Wiley and Sons Ltd.

[12] J. R. Quinlan. *C4.5: Programs for Machine Learning*. Morgan Kaufmann, San Mateo, 1993.

[13] Barry Smyth and Padraig Cunningham. Hierarchical case-based reasoning - integrating case-based and decompositional problem-solving Techniques for Plant-Control Software Design. *IEEE Transactions on Knowledge and Data Engineering*, 13:793-812, 2001.

[14] Armin Stahl and Ralph Bergmann. Applying recursive CBR for the custumization of structured products in an electronic shop. In *Proc. of the 5th European Workshop on CBR, EWCBR-2K*, pages 297–308, 2000.

[15] Ian Watson and Sunil Perera. A hierarchical case representation using context guided retrieval. *Knowledge-Based Systems*, 11:285–292, 1998.

SESSION 2:

E-COMMERCE AND RESOURCE MANAGEMENT

An eNegotiation Framework

John Debenham

University of Technology, Sydney,
Faculty of Information Technology,
PO Box 123, NSW 2007, Australia
debenham@it.uts.edu.au

Abstract. Negotiation between two trading agents is a two-stage process. First, the agents exchange offers whilst acquiring and exchanging information. Second, they attempt to reach a mutually satisfactory agreement in the light of that information. This process aims to reach informed decisions in eMarket bargaining by integrating the exchange of offers and the acquisition and exchange of information drawn from the environment. Negotiation proceeds by a loose alternating offers protocol that is intended to converge when the agents believe that they are fully informed. The eNegotiation framework is a prototype for developing agents that exploit an information-rich environment in one-to-one negotiation. This work is part of a program that is investigating deeper issues of market evolution and business network development in an immersive, virtual worlds eMarket environment.

1. Introduction

The economic (game theoretic) and multiagent interest in negotiation became fused in "Agent Mediated Electronic Commerce" which has attracted increasing attention since the mid-1990s. Much of this work has studied economically rational strategies and mechanisms in an eMarket context; for example, the use of auction mechanisms for multi-unit and multi-attribute trade [1]. From an artificial intelligence perspective humans do not always strive to be utility optimisers. Sometimes they do so, for example, traders taking short-term positions in exchanges act to make short-term profits. And sometimes they do not, for example when buying a house or an automobile an intelligent human may have intelligent, justifiable but completely irrational motives. The study of negotiation between artificially intelligent agents should not be bound by economic rationality; see also [2].

Here, two agents reach a mutually beneficial agreement on a set of issues because they have chosen to become well informed. The aim is to reach *well-informed* decisions rather than *economically rational* decisions. "Good negotiators, therefore, undertake integrated processes of knowledge acquisition combining sources of knowledge obtained at and away from the negotiation table. They learn in order to plan and plan in order to learn" [3]. The work described here attempts to encapsulate this intimate link between the negotiation itself and the knowledge generated both by and because of it. During a negotiation, an agent may actively acquire information that it may, or may not, choose to place on the negotiation table. Information is a strategic weapon in competitive interaction [4].

The eNegotiation framework is a prototype for developing negotiation agents that exploit an information-rich environment in one-to-one negotiation. The *negotiation agents* are responsible for conducting the negotiation on behalf of another. They are purely self-interested agents. Eventually, the negotiation architecture will consist of two further generic agent types: mediation agents and observer agents. *Mediation agents* are impartial observers of negotiations and develop expertise in how to lead multi-attribute negotiations to a successful conclusion [5]. *Observer agents* analyse unsuccessful negotiations. A failed negotiation is a missed business opportunity and so may be a clue to the discovery of an innovative, evolutionary way of doing business.

The eNegotiation framework is being built by members of the eMarkets research group in the Faculty of IT at UTS in Sydney: http://research.it.uts.edu.au/emarkets/ where the project is named the "Curious Negotiator" [6]. Minghui Li, a PhD student in the group is building the eNegotiation framework. To date a version has been roughed up in Java. Woralak Kongdenfha, another PhD student is developing negotiation strategies for the framework. Bots that access the World Wide Web have been designed and built by Dr Debbie Zhang, a Senior Researcher in the group. A fully integrated demonstrable version of the framework will be operational in July when it will be trialed on an exemplar application described below and made publicly available. Plans are to then re-engineer the framework using the Australian Jack agent building-environment and to apply it to a variety of richer negotiation situations.

The following *exemplar application* will be used in initial trials of the framework. An agent has owned a digital camera for three years and wants to upgrade to a better model. This agent has set some money aside, and has a pretty good idea of the features that she wants in her next digital camera. She is in no hurry to buy. She has let it be known that she will consider buying a second-hand camera as long as it is in as-new condition. On receiving an opening offer from a seller to buy a camera she then negotiates with that seller—hopefully leading to a mutually satisfactory deal. This problem is simple in that the actual negotiation is single-attribute—namely the price of the camera. It involves an assessment of the extent to which the camera offered is suited to her requirements—this involves multi-attribute reasoning. It also involves an assessment of the market value of the camera. Both of these two issues are resolved by reference to information on the World-Wide-Web that is accessed by information gathering bots. The negotiation uses a "loose" alternating offers protocol in which each agent may make an offer at any time but is under no contractual obligation until a deal is made [7]. During a negotiation the agent is expected to be able to feed information to its opponent such as "that model does not have the features that I am looking for" and "your price is higher than I could buy it for on the Web". This exemplar application has been chosen to enable us to make the whole negotiation apparatus work in a satisfactory way on a moderately simple problem. Future plans are to use the augmented negotiation framework in the group's two long-term projects that are in eMarket evolution and in the development of business networks in an eMarket environment.

Game theoretic analyses of *bargaining* are founded on the notion of agents as utility optimisers in the presence of complete and incomplete information about their opponents [8]. To deal with incomplete information, agents are typically assumed to know the probability distribution of that which is not known completely [9]. Likewise, game theoretic analyses of auction mechanisms in *markets* are typically base on assumptions concerning the probability distributions of the utilities of the agents in both the private and public value cases [10]. Further, game theoretic analyses of *exchanges* focus on price formation, strategies and mechanisms for agents with complete and incomplete information. Game theory tells us what to do, and what outcome to expect, in many well-known negotiation situations, but these strategies and expectations are derived from assumptions. For example, in auction theory, the most restrictive of these are that the players are utility opimisers with SIPV (symmetric, independent, private valuations) [10].

Impressive though the achievements in game theory are, the significance of that work in describing how humans negotiate—and so too how artificially intelligent systems should negotiate—is questionable. When confronted with the SIPV formula for an optimal bid in a first-price sealed-bid auction a colleague once remarked: "Look, I may simply want to buy it". The sense in this remark is that utility optimisation is not always the motivation for a negotiation.

The work here is based on the notion that when an intelligent agent buys a hat, a car, a house or a company she does so because she *feels comfortable* with the general terms of the deal. This "feeling of comfort" is achieved as a result of information acquisition and validation. This information includes both that which the agent is given and information that which the agent chooses to acquire. Here negotiation is as much of an information exchange process as it is an offer exchange process. The exchange of information is equally as important as the exchange of offers—one feeds off the other. In so far as game theory aims to reach a *rational* solution, the aim here is to reach an *informed* solution.

2. Managing an Information-Rich Environment

The form of negotiation considered is between two agents in an information-rich environment. That is, the agents have access to general information that may be of use to them. They also exchange information as part of the negotiation process. The two agents are called "me" and my opponent ω. The environment here is the Internet, in particular the World Wide Web, from which information is extracted on demand using special purpose 'bots'. So my agent, "me", may receive information either from ω or from one of these bots. In a 'real life' negotiation, the sort of information that is tabled during a negotiation includes statements such as "this is the last bottle available", "you won't get a better price than this", and so on. To avoid the issue of natural language understanding, and other more general semantic issues, the interface between each of the negotiating agents and these information sources is represented using the language of first-order, typed predicate logic, and a set of pre-agreed, pre-specified predicates. All information passed to "me" is expressed in this way.

As well as being unambiguous, the use of first-order typed predicate logic has the advantage of admitting metrics that describe, for example, how "close" two statements are. These metrics are useful in enabling the agent to manage the information extracted from the environment in a strategic way. The terms predicate, term, function, variable and constant are used in their well-accepted sense. In typed logic a term, constant or variable appearing as part of a proposition belongs to a certain domain determined by the argument in which it occurs in the predicate of that proposition. If functions can be avoided then these metrics are simpler. Functions are not used in this discussion, although their inclusion does not introduce any technical problems beyond making the Herbrand universe unbounded. The notation: <variable>/<term> denotes the substitution in which the named variable, the *subject*, is replaced by the term wherever that variable occurs in an expression.

Using the usual notation and terminology for Horn clauses, given a set of facts—ie: unit clauses with just one positive predicate—the following defines a partial ordering of those facts:

$P(\underline{x}) \geq_s P(\underline{y})$ if there exists set of substitutions J whose subjects are variables in $\underline{x}$ such that: $\underline{y} = \underline{x} / J$

where $\underline{x}$ and $\underline{y}$ are complete sets of arguments of P. If this holds then $P(\underline{x})$ *subsumes* $P(\underline{y})$. This ordering between two literals captures the notion of one being *more general* than the other.

Given two positive propositions, p_1 and p_2, both of which have the same predicate symbol, then the *unification* of those two propositions is denoted by $p_1 \cap p_2$, and the *anti-unification*—using the terminology of Reynolds—by $p_1 \cup p_2$. [The anti-unification of two positive literals is the unique literal that subsumes both of them and of all such literals is minimal with respect to the partial order $\geq_s$.]

Suppose that G is a finite set of ground literals that is closed with respect to unification and anti-unification. G is a non-modular lattice where unification and anti-unification are the meet and join respectively. Given a literal c, the function λ_G : {the set of all literals} $\rightarrow$ {the positive integers} is defined as $\lambda_G(c) =$ the number of literals in G with which c is resolvable. $\lambda_G(c)$ is a measure of the "generality" of c with respect to unification over G. It is a measure of how "general" c is over G. Given an isotone valuation v on the vertices of G, the function:

$\delta_1(c_1, c_2) = v[c_1] - v[c_2]$

is a measure of how much "more general" c_1 is compared with c_2. Further

$\delta_2(c_1, c_2) = v[c_1 \cup c_2] - v[c_1 \cap c_2]$

is a measure of the "distance" between c_1 and c_2. There is a problem with δ_2 when the meaning of the partial ordering is such that: if $c_1 \leq c_2$ then knowing c_2 means that knowing c_1 brings no new information—this is the case with the partial ordering $\geq_s$. In this case the function:

$\delta_3(c_1, c_2) = v[c_1 \cup c_2] - v[c_2]$

is a measure of how much more "novel" c_1 is compared with c_2. [Another possibility is $v[c_1] - v[c_1 \cap c_2]$ but that is not so useful when the intersection is likely to be empty—ie: at the "bottom" of the lattice—if $c_1 \leq c_2$ then $\delta_3(c_1, c_2) = 0$.

Suppose that J is any subset of G, given a literal c, then:

$\delta_i(c, J) = \min_{s \in J} \delta_i(c, s)$ \qquad for i = 1, 2, 3.

are generalisations of the measures between two vertices to measures between a vertex and a set of vertices. Suppose that S is the set of literals that agent "me" knows, let H be set of all possible literals obtained by instantiating the predicates in $\{c\} \cup S$ over the Herbrand universe for $\{c\} \cup S$, then the above two measures are:

$\delta_1(c, S) = \min_{s \in S} [\lambda_H[c] - \lambda_H[s]]$

$\delta_2(c, S) = \min_{s \in S} [\lambda_H[c \cup s] - \lambda_H[c \cap s]]$

$\delta_3(c, S) = \min_{s \in S} [\lambda_H[c \cup s] - \lambda_H[s]]$

If there are functions present then the Herbrand universe will be non-finite. In this case H may be defined as the set of such instantiations up to a certain chosen function nesting depth. As long as that chosen nesting depth is greater than that occurring in the literals in $\{c\} \cup S$ the resulting measures are generally useful.

This leads to a general approach to managing information in negotiation:

- develop a predicate logic representation
- introduce a partial ordering on that representation that captures the meaning of "generalisation" in a way that is relevant to the application
- define lattice meet and join operations
- define an isotone valuation on the lattice that is consistent with the ordering—this valuation need not necessarily treat each argument (domain) in the same way (as in the example above)—it may be useful to introduce weights that give some arguments more significance than others.

and then apply the ideas above. The introduction of two additional measures, of "cost" of acquiring the information and of "belief" in its validity, complete the machinery required to manage the acquisition and maintenance of an information base in a strategic way.

To illustrate this, in the exemplar system one job that the information bots do is to find the cheapest camera that has a certain set of features. This is achieved by scraping the sites of various information providers $\{P_i\}$. My agent knows what sites are available to it. To my agent, the bot that scrapes site P_j is represented as:

Cheapest(P_j:$\{P_i\}$, f_1:F_1,..., f_n:F_n; c:C, p:\$) [1]

where f_i is the i'th feature (such as, whether the camera has an on-board, electronic flash), F_i is the domain (ie: all possible values) for each of these features, c is the cheapest camera with those features (according to source P_j), and p is its price (according to source P_j). The ";" separates the "inputs" from the "outputs". It is assumed that each domain F_i contains the features dc_i meaning "I don't care what f_i is". So to my agent the bots appear as a set of as yet uninstantiated literals. If my agent chooses to activate the j'th bot then it does so by setting the P_j and all of the f_i to particular values and the result of the scraping exercise is then, for example:

Cheapest(P_2, "no flash",..., dc_n; Kodak123, \$54)

meaning that "according to site P_2 the Kodak123 camera is the cheapest camera available with the set of features specified and it costs \$54". In so far as that information is valid, it can only be assumed to be valid at the time that bot is activated. Here it is assumed that information is valid for the period of the negotiation. There is also the matter of how reliable the information is—with what degree of belief should the agent believe it to be true? This is achieved by attaching a certainty factor to each retrieved tuple that is based solely on an assessment of the general reliability of the information provider P_j.

The "don't care" value, dc, may be a value for any or all of the $\{f_i\}$. [Sites vary in their accuracy and completeness—some do not contain information for every such combination.] At some time after activation a bot, information will be received by my agent also in form [1] but with the "output" values (ie: values for c_x and p_x) specified. This completes the first step—the predicate logic representation. Introduce the partial order defined by the values of the first $(n+1)$ arguments only. If the first $(n+1)$ arguments of expressions e_1 and e_2 are the same except that e_1 contains dc values where e_2 does not then $e_1 \geq_D e_2$. $\geq_D$ is the partial ordering. If e_1 and e_2 can be "unified" by setting dc input values in one expression to the corresponding value in the other then define $e_1 \cap e_2$ to be the expression with that "unified" set of input values, [output values remaining undefined as they play no part in this ordering], otherwise $e_1 \cap e_2$ is the empty expression. In defining this ordering the constant dc is treated rather like a logic variable in conventional unification, but *it is a logical constant.* The expression $e_1 \cup e_2$ is defined similarly—ie: to reflect the sense of "generality" in the "Cheapest" predicate. Let S be the set of ground literals that the agent believes to be true, then define H as above by treating dc as a "variable", and λ_H as above.

After all of this the measures of "how general" statements are [11], and how "close" statements are, may be used to strategically gather information. In the exemplar system this amounts to managing the "information lattice" in a fairly common sense manner. It enables the agent to explore "nearby" alternatives, and to obtain a "more general feeling" for price. More importantly, it has been shown that this approach may be used for first-order resolution logic—it is proposed that this approach may be applied to any application that can be expressed in first-order logic, including those of greater complexity, to strategically manage the acquisition of information. This approach relies on the hand crafting of the lattice structure and the lattice ordering for each predicate involved.

3.   Accepting an Offer

A mechanism decides whether to accept an offer or to cease the negotiation—neither of these may occur in which case either one of these two agents has to "think again". This mechanism is the first step towards automatic negotiation in which agents aim to reach comfortable agreements through managing both the exchange of offers and requests for information in an integrated way. The goal here is to design something that works. The solution described does work, but is not claimed to be the best, or even a particularly good, way representing "comfort". The following section embeds this mechanism into a negotiation framework.

Suppose that a negotiation between two agents, my opponent ω and me, stands alone—that it is not part of a related sequence of negotiations. Each agent aims to reach an agreement on a deal. A *deal* Δ is a commitment for me to do something, τ (my "terms"), subject to the other agent agreeing to do something, υ, $\Delta = (\tau, \upsilon)$. Suppose my negotiation with ω is conducted in the light of information, ι, (ie: ι is the information available to me, but not necessarily to ω) then:

Acc($\omega, \tau, \upsilon, \iota$)

is a proposition in which the predicate "Acc" means "taking account of information ι, if I agree to do τ, subject to ω agreeing to do υ, then I will feel comfortable with the deal". This raises the two questions of defining what it means to say that I feel comfortable with a deal, and determining the point in time at which that determination should be made. It makes acceptable sense to the author to state "looking back on it, I made the right decision at the time"—those two questions are not addressed further here. The information, ι, consists of any information tabled by either party as part of the negotiation process, and any information extracted by me from the environment as described in the previous section. The commitments, τ and υ, may be quite complex and may include staggered payments or related "sweeteners"—in general they will contain multiple attributes [12]. A deal is normally associated with a time, or time frame, when the respective commitments of the two agents are to be performed. In addition, the "Acc" predicate could contain an assessment of the guarantees, assurances, escrow services and "after sales service", γ—but this has been omitted for simplicity. In addition to the Acc predicate, a "Cea" predicate aims to detect when a negotiation should cease—possibly because it appears to be a "waste of time". The Cea predicate is not described here.

A probability is attached to the "Acc" proposition so that it may be used as the basis for making a decision on whether or not to accept the terms τ. This probability aims to represent the likelihood that the proposition will turn out to be true in due course—see the comment above concerning the point in time at which "I may feel comfortable". A fuzzy set is introduced to define "Accept" to some level of confidence χ. Its membership function $\mu_A : [0, 1] \rightarrow [0, 1]$ is monotonic increasing. μ_A is applied to

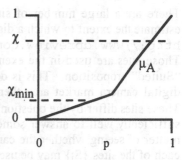

Figure 1. Fuzzy Accept

P(Acc($\omega, \tau, \upsilon, \iota$)). This function is a matter for each agent to specify, and in general may be a function of the terms, τ, and maybe υ, and so there is no claim that this work is leading to context-independent super-negotiator. See Fig. 1 for an example of a piece-wise linear fuzzy membership function μ_A. The μ_A function just scales the values—it accepts offers when P(Acc) $\geq \mu_A^{-1}(\chi)$. It is included so that the framework will support experiments with cooperative agents seeking to reach a compromise deal with equivalent certainty—the μ_A function enables agents to have different "types" analogous to Kasbah's "anxious", "cool-headed", and "frugal" [13]. The value χ_{min} is the greatest value of confidence χ for which both:

P(Acc($\omega, \tau, \upsilon, \iota$)) $\in$ Accept, and
P(Cea($\omega, \tau, \upsilon, \iota$)) $\in$ Cease

are true. χ_{min} is the confidence value at which the agent will be equally disposed to accept the offer *and* to cease negotiation—values of χ at or below χ_{min} are of no interest here. The level of confidence χ is vaguely related to the notion of "risk averseness" in game theory. If, to confidence χ,

P(Acc($\omega, \tau, \upsilon, \iota$)) $\notin$ Accept, and
P(Cea($\omega, \tau, \upsilon, \iota$)) $\notin$ Cease

then the agent continues to negotiate as described in the following section.

The probability attached to the "Acc" proposition—and similarly for the "Cea" proposition—is derived from probabilities attached to four other propositions:
Suited(ι, υ), Good(ι, ω), Fair(ι, τ, υ), and Me(ι, τ, υ)
meaning respectively: "taking account of information ι, terms υ are perfectly *suited* to my needs", "taking account of information ι, ω will be a *good* agent for me to be doing business with", "taking account of information ι, τ are generally considered to be *fair* terms in exchange for ω agreeing to do υ given that ω is impeccable", and "independent of what everybody else believes, on strictly subjective grounds, taking account of information ι, τ are fair terms in exchange for ω agreeing to do υ given that ω is impeccable". The last two of these four explicitly ignore the suitability of υ and factors out the appropriateness of the opponent ω. If ω's reputation is doubtful then the mechanism will compensate for these doubts by looking for better terms than would be comfortable for me if I had dealt with an impeccable opponent. The difference in meaning between the third and fourth proposition is that the third captures the concept of "a fair market deal" and the fourth a strictly subjective "what υ is worth to me". The "Me" proposition is closely related to the concept of private valuations in game theory.

To deal with "Suited" depends on what the terms υ are. In the exemplar system the terms will be a second-hand camera if I am buying, and money if I am selling.

There are a large number of sites on the World Wide Web that may be used to estimate the extent to which a digital camera will suit me. For example: http://www.dpreview.com/reviews/compare.asp
Those sites are used in the exemplar system to attach a level of confidence in the "Suited" proposition. This is described in detail in the following section. In the digital camera market area there are a variety of such advisory sites $\{S_1,..,S_n\}$. These sites differ by the questions that they ask. If the agent's preferences are known sufficiently well to answer some of the questions on one of these sites then it is a matter of seeing whether the camera, υ, is amongst the recommended choices. So each of the sites $\{S_i\}$ may be used to generate evidence for "Suited". These sites are designed to help a buyer choose a camera—they are used here for a rather different task: to check that a given camera is suitable for me. A Bayesian revises the *a priori* probability attached to "Suited" in the light of evidence obtained from the $\{S_i\}$. For any seller it is assumed here that ω is a commitment to deliver money, and that the probability of money being "suitable" is 1.0. That is, P(Suited("money")) = 1.0. Another approach to dealing with the suitability of a deal is used in some B2B e-procurement reverse auctions [14]. There the buyer specifies various packages and attaches a factor to them as a real number ≥ 1.0. The sellers bid on the various packages. The bids are then multiplied by the factor associated with the relevant package to determine the winner—ie: the lowest bid.

Attaching a probability to "Good" involves an assessment of the reliability of the opposing agent. For some retailers (sellers), information—of possibly questionable reliability—may be extracted from sites that rate them. For individuals, this may be done either through assessing their reputation established during prior trades in a multi-agent environment [15], or through the use of some intermediate escrow service that in turn is deemed to be "reliable" in which case the assessment is of the individual *and* the escrow service. In the exemplar system this factor has been ignored as the camera is assumed to be offered for sale by an individual. That is, P(Good(ω)) = 1.0.

Attaching a probability to "Fair" is achieved by reference to an appropriate market. When a deal is to purchase retail goods for money this may be achieved by using bots to scrape a set of sites. In the exemplar system the second-hand camera, υ, is assumed to be in "as new" condition, and so its fair market value, α_υ, is obtained by discounting the best price, β_υ, that is found for that item in new condition, say by 30%. The sites

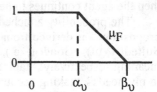

Figure 2. Fuzzy Fair

scraped are those merchant sites that are linked from the sites used for "Suited" above. These are shown as $\{\overline{S}_1,..,\overline{S}_n\}$. There is no causal link between the $\{S_i\}$ and the $\{\overline{S}_i\}$. If the terms τ specify that money is to be exchanged for the camera then the set $\{ \tau : \text{Fair}(\tau , \omega) \}$ is defined by a fuzzy membership function such as that shown in Figure 2.

Attaching a probability to "Me" is a purely subjective matter. For a single-attribute, real-valued τ it is dealt with in a similar way to "Fair" above using a fuzzy membership function that is zero at my upper limit, $\overline{\sigma}_\upsilon$, and 1.0 at the greatest price that "I would be delighted to pay", σ_υ. Figure 3 shows a possible fuzzy membership function for "Me" for such a τ. That function aims to encapsulate the notion of "τ

are personally fair terms to me in exchange for ω doing υ". My upper limit, $\bar{\sigma}_\upsilon$, is my "valuation" in game theoretic terms—it is a link between this informed-decision approach and economically rational approaches.

The whole "accept an offer" apparatus is shown in Figure 4. There is no causal relationship between the four propositions, with the possible exception of the third and fourth. So to link the probabilities associated with the five propositions, the probabilities are treated as epistemic probabilities and form the nodes of a simple Bayesian net. The weights on the three arcs of the resulting Bayesian net are meaningful in practical

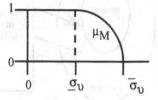

Figure 3. Fuzzy Me

terms. They are a subjective, high-level representation of what "comfortable" means to an agent. More important, the resulting net divides the problem of assessing "Accept" into four more convenient sub-problems.

Figure 4 shows the structure of the hybrid net for the general case—ie: including the machinery for "Good". The top half of the hybrid net combines data obtained from the Internet through the "fuzzy filters" represented by •'s on that figure. There "Good" is derived as a result of scraping a set of sites $\{M_1,..,M_m\}$ as would most likely be the case in a 'real'

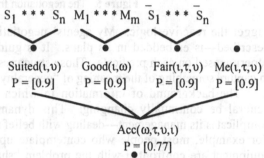

Figure 4. Hybrid net to accept an offer

electronic business application. The product of these "fuzzy filters" are treated as probabilities and attached to the bottom half of the hybrid net that is a conventional Bayesian belief network. The probability attached to "Acc" is then passed through the fuzzy filter μ_A also denoted by a • on that figure. The conditionals on the Bayesian network are subjective—they are easy to specify because 12 of them are zero—for the cases in which I believe that either Fair or Me is "false". With fairly optimistic priors of 0.9 on each of the four evidence nodes, and the conditionals set to:

P(Acc | Suited, Good, Fair, Me) = 1.0, P(Acc | ~Suited, Good, Fair, Me) = 0.7, P(Acc | Suited, ~Good, Fair, Me) = 0.8, P(Acc | ~Suited, ~Good, Fair, Me) = 0.6

the probability P(Acc) = 0.77, and so the membership function, μ_A, for the fuzzy set "Accept" and the confidence value χ should be defined so that $\mu_A(0.77) << \chi$. It then remains to access the information from the available sources to, hopefully, increase P(Acc) so that the deal is acceptable.

4.   The Negotiation Process

The ideas in the previous two sections are summarised in Figure 5. My agent is a hybrid agent. Its beliefs are derived first from incoming messages in the "Information received" box, expressed in pre-determined predicates, from ω (and from "John")—these beliefs activate the deliberative machinery. They are time-stamped on arrival as they include offers from ω. Second, beliefs are also derived from information that arrives because a plan has activated a macro tool—these beliefs

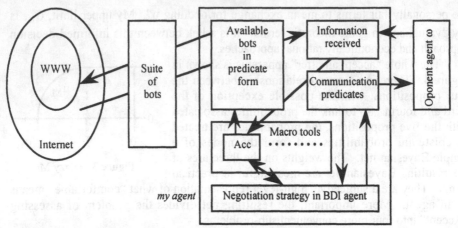

Figure 5. The negotiation framework

trigger the reactive logic. My agents' negotiation strategy—which has yet to be described—is embedded in its plans. It is guided by the lattice structure that is superimposed on each predicate. Those structures are built by hand and are intended to capture something of the meaning of "generality" for each predicate.

The background of information in which a negotiation takes place will in general be continually changing. This dynamic nature of information greatly complicates its management—dealing with belief revision is one consequence of this. For example, most people who contemplate upgrading their personal computing equipment are confronted with the problem "shall I buy now or wait to see what becomes available next month". In the markets for stocks and bonds the background information is continually changing, and only experienced traders are able to detect deep patterns in the information shift on which to build their trading strategies. To simplify the discussion here we assume that the background information remains constant during the period of each negotiation. Specifically we assume that any information derived from information sources during a negotiation remains valid for the period of the negotiation.

A negotiation here is a sequence of offers tabled together with attendant information. The offers in this sequence may originate from the two agents in turn—the alternating offers model—or the agents may table offers at random. As time progresses during a negotiation my agent will have access to an increasing amount of information—shown in the lower half of Figure 6. The source of that information will be the information bots, information tabled by my opponent ω, and the deals themselves. Of this information, only the terms offered by my agent, τ, are certain. The

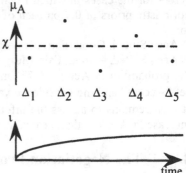

Figure 6. The negotiation process

validity of the information extracted by the bots will be uncertain, as will the information tabled by ω, and even ω's terms, υ, may be uncertain in that if I accept an offer, (τ, υ), ω may not meet her commitments—she may "renege" on the deal.

The μ_A value of acceptable offers will be above my confidence level χ—five offers are shown in the top half of Figure 6.

The negotiation process is in two stages—first, the exchange of offers and information, and, second, the end-game. As the information is assumed to be static, there will come a time during the exchange of offers and information when the agents believe that have all the information that they require. They are then "fully informed", and should be in a position to take a final position. The development of the offer sequence, the construction of counter-offers [16], and the tabling of information are all part of the negotiation game. This can be a game of bluff and counter-bluff in which an agent may not even intend to close the deal if one should be reached. Strategies for playing the "negotiation game" in an information rich environment are the subject of on-going research. The aim here is to present the machinery that those strategies will have at their disposal.

4.1 Stage 1: Offer, counter-offer, re-offer and information exchange

The current version of the exemplar application has two pre-defined bot predicates in addition to the "Cheapest" predicate (described above):

Features(c:C, P_j:{P_i}; f_1:F_1,..., f_n:F_n, r:*s, p:$)

Cameras(P_j:{P_i}, f_1:F_1,..., f_n:F_n, r:*s, p:$; {c_k:C})

where the meaning of Features and Cameras is self-evident—in Features "r:*s" is a rating in *s (typically one to five). The lattice structure for Cameras is defined similarly to that for Cheapest. The structure for Features is null—it could be given a trivial structure by including "dc" in C but this serves no useful purpose.

There are four pre-defined interaction predicate templates:

Message("John", "me", IWant(f_1:F_1,..., f_n:F_n; c:C))

Message(a_1:A, a_2:A, Offer(τ:{ $, C }, υ:{ $, C }))

Message(a_1:A, a_2:A, Accept τ:{ $, C }, υ:{ $, C }))

Message(a_1:A, a_2:A, Unacceptable((τ:{ $, C }, υ:{ $, C }) , <reason>)

where the meaning of IWant is self-evident, "A" is the domain of agent names (eg: me or ω), and <reason> is derived here by identifying the evidence node with lowest probability in the Accept Bayesian net. A "Message" is from agent a_1 to agent a_2 and here contains either an "Offer", an "Accept", or a reason for an offer being "Unacceptable". At present my agent does not understand received "Unacceptable" messages but it sends them if wishes to do so. It should not do so as a matter of course as that would then give ω a sure way to discover my threshold. My agent is presently unable to receive tabled information from ω.

If an agent's confidence in accepting an offer is close to her threshold then she may decide to seek further information—either from the bots or from ω—in the hope that she will be able to accept it. An issue here is what information to request, particularly when costs are involved.

In 'real' negotiation it is common for an agent to table information in an attempt to encourage the opposition to see her point of view: "I really wanted a blue one". Advising an agent that its terms are not quite what I wanted is not difficult, but we can do more subtle things than that. In the exemplar system, when assessing an offer my agent may ask its information bots "to find if there is a camera whose features nearly match those of the one on offer but which sells new for less than the offer price". If such a camera exists then it is used as fodder for the Unacceptable predicate.

In the exemplar application my agent's offer strategy is to make a, possibly empty, sequence of counter offers. The price in the initial counter offer, if any, is the greatest such that both P(Fair) = P(Me) = 1.0 and the confidence in Accept > χ. Then the subsequent prices are chosen so that the confidence in Accept tends asymptotically to χ so as to more or less reach χ is 5 steps. This sequence will be empty if P(Suited) and P(Good) are such that confidence in Accept does not exceed χ for any positive price. If ω were to discover this simple strategy then it should take advantage of it. This is not seen as a weakness in these experiments that aim primarily at trialing the information management machinery.

More important, it is proposed that more complex applications may be supported in the same way as long as the information in the application is expressed in first-order predicates with lattice orderings for each predicate that capture "generalisation". For example, the same machinery could in principle handle a negotiation to purchase a house where features could include the number of bedrooms, the size of the house, the "aspect" (sunny or otherwise), the extent to which there are views from the property, the prime construction method, number of car spaces and so on.

4.2   Stage 2: Fully informed agents and the end-game

If my agent believes that it has all the information it requires to make an informed decision—with the exception of the position of the opposing agent—and no matter what the opposing agents position is it will make no difference to my agents position then my agent is *fully informed*. An agent may believe that it is fully informed prior to any negotiation taking place, or it may come to believe that it is fully informed during the exchange of offers and information.

If both agents in a negotiation believe that they are fully informed then they should be prepared to enter a final, single round of the negotiation process that determines a final, definitive outcome of either "no deal" or "a deal will be conducted under these terms..." [17].

If:

$\{ (\tau, \upsilon) \mid P(Acc_{me}(\omega, \tau, \upsilon, \iota_{me})) \in Accept_{me} \} \cap$
$\{ (\tau, \upsilon) \mid P(Acc_{\omega}(me, \upsilon, \tau, \iota_{\omega})) \in Accept_{\omega} \} = PosDeals$

is non-empty then a deal is possible. There will typically be a large or unbounded number of such possible deals. The structure of the admissible deals in this intersection may be quite complex if the negotiation involves multiple attributes. The comfort level of any acceptable deal will be no less than my level of confidence χ_{me}, and clearly no greater than 1.0. It will be less than 1.0 as the deal must also be acceptable to my opponent ω. The best confidence level that I may hope for, β_{me}, for will be determined by ω's confidence threshold χ_{ω}, and *vice versa*. This is illustrated in Figure 7. The [χ, β] intervals are vaguely related to the idea of players having different "types" in the game-theoretic analysis of bargaining [9].

There are no ready answers to the following questions. Could some analogue of the Nash Bargaining Solution of 1950 [9] be used here? In so far as the Nash solution yields a fair distribution of the surplus utility, perhaps the basis for a final definitive outcome could be based on a fair distribution of "comfort"? Perhaps some mechanism that split each agent's range of feasible confidence in fair proportions would satisfy an analogue of the Myerson-Satterthwaite [1983] result [19] for the linear equilibrium in "split the difference" bargaining? The linear equilibrium in the raw form of "split the difference" bargaining yields the highest expected payoff of any mechanism *ex ante*, but it is not truth-revealing—there are associated truth-revealing mechanisms—this mechanism is not optimal *ex post*. These questions require some serious analysis, and have yet to be addressed. Two possible ways in which a final, single round of negotiation could be managed are now described.

First, two fully informed agents table their final, proposed deals simultaneously. If either the terms that I propose are unsatisfactory to ω, or *vice versa*, then there is no deal. Otherwise a trusted intermediary sets about constructing a compromise deal based on the agents' two proposals. If the difference between the deals concerns one continuous attribute—such as an amount of money—then the intermediary may simply "split the difference"—although this will not lead to truth-revealing behaviour by the agents. If there are multi-attributes, or attributes with discrete values then this intermediation will be more complex, although the second method following may be employed.

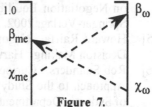

Figure 7.
Expected confidence range

Second, two fully informed agents make their whole reasoning apparatus available to a trusted intermediary who determines whether the set PosDeals is empty. If it is not then the intermediary attempts to find a deal that divides the two agent's $[\beta, \chi]$ intervals into equal proportions $\pi:1$. If this proves impossible, as may be the case if one of the deal attributes is non-continuous, then a deal is selected at random from the pair of deals that most closely match with one deal's μ_A value above and one below the $\pi:1$ division.

5.   Conclusion

The eNegotiation framework is the first step in the design of agents that can exploit information-rich environments in one-to-one negotiation. Such agents should be adept at handling both the exchange of information and the exchange of offers. The negotiation protocol used is a loose exchange of offers and information in an initial stage, followed by an end-game mechanism when the agents believe that they have become fully informed. This protocol assumes that sufficient information is available and that the currency of the information is sustained throughout the negotiation process. Semantic issues [18] are avoided by introducing pre-defined, pre-agreed predicates. The information is managed by representing it in these predicates and then by overlaying a lattice structure with isotone valuations on each predicate. It is proposed that this method may be applied to a wide range of negotiation situations, and if so then general negotiation strategies may be developed to manage both the offers and the information. To date this work has raised more problems than it has solved. Initial indications are that it appears to work and so it is expected to lead to the design of sound negotiation agents that strive to make informed decisions rather than economically rational decisions.

References

[1] Martin Bichler.   The Future of E-Markets: Multi Dimensional Market Mechanisms. Cambridge University Press, 2001.

[2] Felix Brandt and Gerhard Weiß. Antisocial Agents and Vickrey Auctions. in Intelligent Agents VIII proceedings ATAL 2001. Springer Verlag, 2002.

[3] Watkins, M. Breakthrough Business Negotiation—A Toolbox for Managers. Jossey-Bass, 2002.

[4] S.S. Fatima, M. Wooldridge and N. R. Jennings. The Influence of Information on Negotiation Equilibrium. In: Agent Mediated Electronic Commerce IV, Springer-Verlag, 2002.

[5] Howard Raiffa. Negotiation Analysis: The Science and Art of Collaborative Decision Making. Harvard, 2002.

[6] Rob Saunders. Curious Design Agents and Artificial Creativity: A Synthetic Approach to the Study of Creative Behaviour. Ph.D. Dissertation. University of Sydney, Department of Architectural and Design Science, 2001.

[7] Sarit Kraus. Strategic Negotiation in Multiagent Environments. MIT Press, 2001.

[8] Muthoo, A. Bargaining Theory with Applications. Cambridge UP, 1999.

[9] Martin J. Osborne and Ariel Rubinstein. Bargaining and Markets. Academic Press, 1990.

[10] Elmer Wolfstetter. Topics in Microeconomics. Cambridge UP, 1999.

[11] Hilderman, R.J. and Hamilton, H.J. "Evaluation of Interestingness Measures for Ranking Discovered Knowledge." In Cheung, D., Williams, G.J., and Li, Q. (eds.), Proceedings of the 5th Pacific-Asia Conference on Knowledge Discovery and Data Mining (PAKDD'01), Hong Kong, April, 2001, pp. 247-259.

[12] Gerding, E.H., van Bragt, D.D.B. and La Poutre, J.A. Multi-issue negotiation processes by evolutionary simulation: validation and social extensions. In proceedings Workshop on Complex Behavior in Economics. Aix-en-Provence, France, May 4-6, 2000.

[13] Anthony Chavez, Daniel Dreilinger, Robert Guttman and Pattie Maes. A Real-Life Experiment in Creating an Agent Marketplace. in proceedings of the Second International Conference on the Practical Application of Intelligent Agents and Multi-Agent Technology (PAAM97). London, UK, April 1997.

[14] Birgit Burmeister, Tobias Ihde, Thomas Kittisteiner, Benny Moldavanu and Jörg Nikutta.. A Practical Approach to Multi-Attribute Auctions. in proceedings Third International Workshop on Negotiations in Electronic Markets, Aix-en-Provence, France, 2002.

[15] S. Ramchurn, N. Jennings, C. Sierra and L. Godo. "A Computational Trust Model for Multi-Agent Interactions based on Confidence and Reputation". in proceedings workshop on "Proc. 5th Int. Workshop on Deception, Fraud and Trust in Agent Societies" AAMAS-2003, Melbourne, Australia, July 2003.

[16] Peyman Faratin, Carles Sierra and Nick Jennings. Using Similarity Criteria to Make Issue Trade-Offs in Automated Negotiation. Journal of Artificial Intelligence. 142 (2) 205-237, 2003.

[17] Jeffrey S. Rosenschein and Gilad Zlotkin. Rules of Encounter. MIT Press, 1998.

[18] Steven Wilmott, Monique Calisti and Emma Rollon. Challenges in Large-Scale Open Agent Mediated Economies. In: Agent Mediated Electronic Commerce IV, Springer-Verlag, 2002.

[19] R. Myerson and M. Satterthwaite. Efficient Mechanisms for Bilateral Trading. Journal of Economic Theory, 29, 1–21, April 1983.

A Mixed Approach towards Formulating Global Marketing Strategies and Related E-Commerce Strategies: Group Judgment + a Fuzzy Expert System

Shuliang Li and Gill Sugden

Westminster Business School, University of Westminster, UK

lish@wmin.ac.uk

Abstract

This paper presents a three-stage mixed approach towards formulating global marketing strategies and related e-commerce strategies. Aiming at supporting the key stages of the strategy development process, the mixed approach combines the advantages of a fuzzy expert system with the strengths of judgment and intuition from a group of decision-makers. The overall value of the mixed approach is evaluated with 46 MSc students in Business IT and Information Management at a British business school. The evaluation findings suggest that the mixed approach is effective in terms of the 11 measurements used.

1. Introduction

In the 21st century, the world economy will be increasingly globalized. The competition for customers and market share will continue to escalate [7]. Decision-makers in global marketing are faced by more challenges as a result of the increasingly complex environments in which they operate. Managerial needs for appropriate techniques and tools in support of formulating timely and sound global marketing strategies have never been greater.

In the past decades, attempts have been made by researchers to develop computer-based systems to support the process of global marketing planning. Some related typical work in this field may be found in [4], [8], [18], [20], [21], [25] and [31].

In most of the previous reported work in this field, however, efforts have been focused on applying relevant technologies, such as expert systems, fuzzy logic, decision support systems, hybrid systems, etc., to the problems of global marketing decision-making. The critical importance of combining groups of managers' judgment and intuition with fuzzy expert systems in support of global marketing planning has not been highlighted adequately.

It is also argued that the Internet can complement traditional ways of competing [37]. Appropriate Internet applications can improve communications with actual and potential customers, suppliers and collaborators abroad; and can be a powerful

93

international promotion and sales tool [16]. Internet technologies and e-commerce applications can be used strategically for creating competitive advantage in global markets. Devising e-commerce strategies as an organic part of business strategies is something that business today should not neglect.

The intent of this research is to establish a mixed approach that integrates the advantages of a fuzzy expert system with the benefits of judgment and intuition from a group of decision-makers and combines global strategy development with e-commerce strategy formulation. In this paper, a mixed approach towards formulating global strategies and related e-commerce strategies is developed and tested by the first-named author. The paper is structured as follows. The opening section outlines the logical process, the functional components and judgmental ingredients of the mixed approach. The next section presents the evaluation of the overall value of the mixed approach. The final section offers some general conclusions with further work discussed.

2. An Outline of the Mixed Approach

Global marketing strategy development is concerned with designing means to match unique company resources with overseas market opportunities to accomplish competitive advantage [17]. A right and clear strategy is always the key to success. However, strategy formulation presents a challenge to the experience, knowledge, judgment and intuition of individual managers. A group of managers from different functional departments may bring a variety of knowledge, experience and judgment to the strategy formulation process [3, 26]. Porter [36] points out that strategic planning should employ multifunctional planning teams. People who have the power to act should be involved in the process of strategy development [12]. Despite groupwork can often be plagued with process losses such as social pressures of conformity and inappropriate influences of individuals, decision-making in groups may have the following benefits: groups are better than individuals at catching errors; groups are better than individuals at understanding problems; a group has more information or knowledge than any one member; and synergy may be produced [40].

Webler et al. [43] proposed a technique, called group Delphi, in which a group of participants can input, debate and discuss their judgment concerning existing information and knowledge. With group Delphi, views are discussed openly and any ambiguities are clarified immediately. Furthermore, debate and discussions among participants provides an internal check for consistency in accepted points of view [43]. Group Delphi can be used as a technique for reducing uncertainty surrounding the group inputs to the strategy development process. It can also be applied to resolve disagreement and build consensus on creating and choosing final global strategies.

It is also argued that the appropriate uses of computer-based support systems can improve the process of marketing strategy development [21, 44]. Keen and Scott Morton [19] point out that computer-based decision support implies the use of computers to: assist decision-makers in their decision processes; support, rather than replace, managerial judgment. Therefore, both computerised support and managerial judgment are important.

Computerised models are consistent and unbiased, but rigid, while managers are inconsistent and often lack analytical skills but are flexible in adapting to changing environments [6, 22] and have knowledge about their products and markets [28, 29 & 30]. The key idea is, hence, the combination of the decision makers into the computerized models. It is also found that marketing strategy development is typically the shared collective responsibility of managers in many large companies [22]. Thus, combining computerised models with a group of decision-makers' judgment and intuition would lead to better strategic decisions.

In this paper, a mixed approach is proposed to integrate group judgment with computer-based fuzzy expert systems and to combine the development of global marketing strategies with the formulation of related e-commerce strategies. The mixed approach aims at supporting some key stages of global strategy and e-commerce strategy making, namely:

- Global marketing environments assessment and strategic analysis;
- Global marketing and e-commerce portfolio summary;
- Setting global marketing strategies and related e-commerce strategies.

The framework of the mixed approach is illustrated in Figure 1.

The framework of the mixed approach shown in Figure 1 is based on the intercommunicating hybrid method [15] that enables independent and self-contained components to exchange information and perform distinct functions to produce solutions. Within this framework, a group Delphi process supports groups of managers in conducting environments assessment and strategic analysis. A fuzzy expert system developed by the first-named author is then utilized to perform fuzzy rule-based reasoning for generating strategic advice and recommendations. Finally, a group of decision-makers review the system's output and various alternatives and judge their overall viability. The group Delphi technique is again applied to resolve disagreement and build consensus on selecting global strategies.

The mixed approach can be described in more detail as a three-stage procedure with a fuzzy expert system and group judgment hybridised:

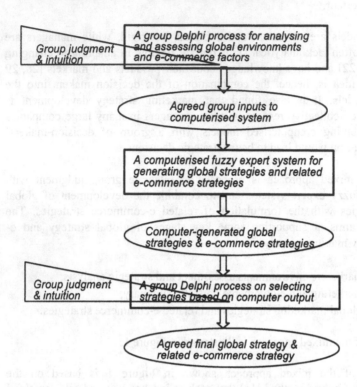

Figure 1. A mixed approach towards formulating global strategies
and related e-commerce strategies

Stage 1

Applying the group Delphi technique [43], combined with group judgment and
intuition, to assess global marketing environments and perform strategic analysis. In
order to build group consensus and obtain agreed group judgment, a structured
seven-step group Delphi process is specified on the basis of Webler et al. [43] and
Gear and Read [14]'s work:

Step 1. In a meeting room, a moderator raises the issue and establishes the task –
global marketing and e-commerce environment assessment and strategic
analysis;

Step 2. Get judgmental inputs to relevant strategic factors from group members
using data forms;

Step 3. Record, analyse the inputs and provide a display of the responses back to
the group members using a computer-connected multi-media projector;

Step 4. Encourage discussions and debate of points of agreement and
disagreement;

Step 5. Ask the group members to re-input judgmental data to relevant strategic factors after the display feedback and debate;

Step 6. Repeat *Steps 2, 3, 4* and *5* until there is some form of group consensus or agreement;

Step 7. Conduct voting if disagreement still exists.

Stage 2

Employing a fuzzy expert system developed by the author to produce global marketing and e-commerce portfolio summary and generate strategic recommendations based on the group inputs obtained from Stage 1.

Within this mixed approach, the computerised global strategy models and strategic advice are based on Harrell and Kiefer [17]' work and McDonald [23, 24]'s four-box directional policy matrix and relevant guidelines. Within the software system, the criteria considered for assessing country attractiveness and the company's competitive strengths or compatibility with the target overseas markets are derived from Harrell and Kiefer [17], Albaum et al. [2], Chee and Harris [9], and Levy and Yoon [20]. An illustrated example of computerised Harrell and Kiefer [17]'s model with fuzzification and group judgment is shown in Figure 2. Other strategic analysis models, such as McDonald [23, 24]'s four-cell portfolio model can be computerised in the same way.

The computerised e-commerce strategy model is based upon Watson and Zinkhan [42]'s four-cell matrix. The factors considered for strategic choices and the relevant strategic alternatives and guidelines used in the software system are derived from Watson and Zinkhan [42], O'Brien [32], Hamill [16], and Peattie and Peters [35]. The computerised e-commerce strategy model with fuzzification and group judgment is illustrated in Figure 3. Other e-commerce portfolio models such as O'Brien's grid [32, p.52] can be converted in a similar way.

Based upon group inputs and computerised strategy models, the computer-based fuzzy expert system then performs intelligent reasoning and derives advice or recommendations. The fuzzy inference process of the fuzzy expert system includes fuzzification of user inputs, evaluation of fuzzy rules, and output of strategic recommendations.

(1) Fuzzification of the strategic factors

First of all, the system receives agreed numeric scores (ranging from 1 to 10) and relative importance or weights (ranging from 0 to 1) for each strategic factor. The system then calculates an overall score for each dimension of the matrix or grid illustrated in Figures 2 and 3. The calculated scores are then converted into fuzzy memberships as shown in the Figures where trapezoidal membership functions are used.

98

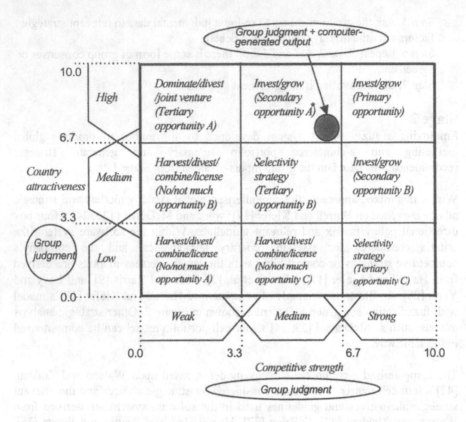

* **Invest/grow (secondary opportunity A):** *Opportunities are identified but political or economic risks and company weaknesses are perceived. The market would be handled in a pragmatic way due to potential risks and company weaknesses identified. This strategy calls for company commitment to a good market position. A rapid share in a growing market will require substantial financial investments. Equally important are the investments in people to sustain a good competitive position. Product development and modification will be important to match products closely with specific market requirements. Foreign direct investment in sales and service facilities is often required for the sake of rapid market response, delivery and service, because major competitors will also operate in such growing markets. Marketing support of all kinds should be expansive and should be related to personnel, advertising, quality of services, etc. [17]*

Figure 2. Computerised global strategy model with fuzzification and group judgment (Extended and adapted from Harrell and Kiefer [17])

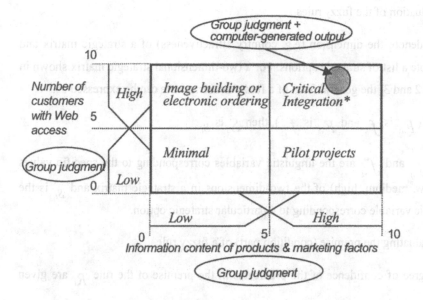

* **Critical Integration:** *Organisations falling in this quadrant have many existing and potential customers with Internet access and have products with a high information content. There are needs for on-line marketing. Therefore, it is critical for these companies to link their business plans and global strategies to their Internet marketing strategies. Customers expect to interact with these companies via their Web sites [42].*

Figure 3. Computerised Internet marketing strategy model with fuzzification and group judgment (Extended and adapted from Watson and Zinkhan [42])

For real numbers $a <= b <= c <= d$, the trapezoid $T = (a, b, c, d)$ with amplitude one is defined as:

$T(u) = 0$ if $u <= a$;
$T(u) = (u - a)/(b - a)$ if $a < u <= b$;
$T(u) = 1$ if $b < u <= c$;
$T(u) = (d - u)/(d - c)$ if $c < u <= d$;
$T(u) = 0$ if $d < u$;
$T(a) = 1$ if $a = b$;
$T(d) = 1$ if $c = d$.

(2) Evaluation of the fuzzy rules

Let F_i denote the dimension (e.g. country attractiveness) of a strategic matrix and S_i denote a list of strategic options. For a two-dimensional strategic matrix shown in Figures 2 and 3, the general form of a fuzzy inference rule can be expressed as:

$$R_i: \text{If}\,(F_{i1} \text{ is } f_{i1} \text{ and } F_{i2} \text{ is } f_{i2}), \text{ then } S_i \text{ is } s_i$$

where f_{i1} and f_{i2} are the linguistic variables corresponding to the specific values (e.g. low, medium, high) of the two-dimensions in a strategic matrix and s_i is the linguistic variable corresponding to a particular strategic option.

(a) Evaluating the premise (condition part) of a fuzzy rule

The degree of confidence of the predicates in the premise of the rule R_i are given by:

The degree of confidence of ' F_{i1} is f_{i1} ' is c_{i1}
The degree of confidence of ' F_{i2} is f_{i2} ' is c_{i2}

The overall degree of confidence in the premise of R_i can be denoted as a joint probability:

$$c_i = (c_{i1}) \times (c_{i2})$$

(b) Determining the degree of confidence for the consequent (conclusion part) of the rule

For rule R_i, the degree of confidence of its consequent will be the same as the overall degree of confidence of its premise. Therefore, the degree of confidence of the consequent ' S_i is s_i ' is also equal to c_i.

(3) Strategic recommendations

After execution of the fuzzy rules, the system produces one or more strategic options or recommendations in the form of:

$$S_j \text{ is } s_{j1}: c_{j1}$$
$$S_j \text{ is } s_{j2}: c_{j2}$$

... ...

S_j is $S_{jk} : C_{jk}$ where $k \leq 4$ for a four-cell or nine-cell strategic matrix

The outputs are not aggregated because we want to provide a list of strategic options with corresponding degrees of confidence. The decision-makers then review the system's outputs and judge which option is sound and select a particular strategy.

An example of the inference results is given below:

The calculated score for country attractiveness = 7.2
The calculated score for competitive strength = 6.5
The score for the population of customers with Web access = 6.5
The score for information content of the product = 6.0

Fuzzy country attractiveness is medium (Conf=0.247) and high (Conf=0.753)
Fuzzy competitive strength is medium (Conf=1)
*Fuzzy global strategy is **Invest/grow** (secondary opportunity A) (Conf=0.753) and **Selectivity** (tertiary opportunity B) (Conf=0.247)*

Fuzzy number of customers with Web access is large (Conf=1)
Fuzzy information content of the product is low (Conf=0.02) and high (Conf=0.98)
*Fuzzy Internet strategy is **Critical integration** (Conf=0.98)*
... ...

Stage 3

Using the group Delphi process [43] coupled with group judgment and creativity, to select the final global strategies and related e-commerce strategies based upon the system output generated at Stage 2. At this stage, the decision-making group may follow the similar group Delphi process as described in Stage 1, but with a focus on selecting and creating final strategies.

At this stage, group creativity should always be stimulated to produce new ideas and strategic choices when choosing and making final strategies. For example, while considering the strategies generated by the computerised models, the decision-making team may also create novel alternatives or take into account other relevant competitive strategies such as differentiation, innovation, etc.

It is worthy of note that the computer-based support system, embodying domain expertise and providing some general strategic analysis models, can deliver consistent support. On the other hand, "judgment seems to be the favored mode of selection, perhaps because it is the fastest, most convenient and least stressful ..." [27]. Experienced managers have good knowledge about their company, products, customers and their competitors [28, 29 & 30]. Thus, a combined use of the support system's general knowledge and the managers' specific knowledge about their products and markets should always be encouraged. The rationale is that the fuzzy expert system must be coupled with a group of decision-makers' judgment, intuition and insight.

It is also essential to point out that the group Delphi process specified in this mixed approach is not a replacement for group decision support systems (GDSSs) or groupware. GDSSs and groupware have been used for a variety of planning tasks such as idea generation, electronic brainstorming, evaluation of alternatives, and voting [1, 13, 18 & 40]. If the strengths of GDSSs and groupware can be combined with the advantages of computer-based fuzzy expert system to support the strategy formulation process, there is likely to be more benefits. Thus, one interesting part of future work is to integrate an on-line group support system with the mixed approach proposed in this paper.

The mixed approach established in the paper has some weaknesses. The first disadvantage of the mixed approach is that it could be slow and time-consuming when trying to integrate agreed group judgment with a fuzzy expert system. The second limitation lies in the limited provision of strategic analysis models although managerial creativity and imagination are encouraged and stimulated. Another problem may arguably be the surrender of anonymity during discussions and debate in the group Delphi process within the mixed approach. However, face-to-face debate can be one useful form of communication to ensure that participants exchange knowledge and information [3, 26]. Differing points of view on inputs to the model and disagreement on selecting final strategies may be best resolved through face-to-face verbal communication.

3. The Overall Value of the Mixed Approach

The overall value of the mixed approach is measured in terms of decision confidence [10, 34 & 41], level of consensus [11, 39], performance of the decision activity [19], helping understand relevant strategic factors [25], helping strategic thinking, and helping couple strategic analysis with managerial judgement [28, 29].

The mixed approach has been evaluated with 46 MSc students in Business IT and Information Management at a British business school. The evaluation work focused on the use of the fuzzy expert system developed by the first-named author and its integration with group judgment and intuition as illustrated in Figures 1-3. The MSc students in a British Business School were selected as subjects because they were receiving formal business and information management training and are the potential users of relevant decision support techniques and technologies. While the subjects were not real decision-makers in actual companies, they were being prepared for potential decision-making roles. The evaluation was based upon a case study of marketing COMPAQ Presario Desktops in the UK home computers markets.

Prior to the evaluation session, the author covered the rationale, relevant techniques and technologies, and the components of the mixed approach in a lecture. The students were then asked to visit the website: **http://thenew.hp.com** to look at the case study details including product information and the company's background.

During the evaluation seminar, the participants were first invited to use their individual judgment as input to drive the fuzzy expert system to formulate global strategies and e-commerce strategies for marketing COMPAQ Presario Desktops in the UK home computers market. They were then requested to fill in questionnaires to assess the effectiveness of their individual judgment coupled with the fuzzy expert system.

The case-based evaluation procedure for the mixed approach was conducted as follows. The 46 participants were divided into two decision-making groups with a moderator appointed for each group in the seminar. They were asked to combine their group judgment with the fuzzy expert system to develop strategies for marketing COMPAQ Presario Desktops in the UK home computers market, following the mixed approach illustrated in Figure 1. The outcomes from the two groups were surprisingly similar. The participants were then asked to answer a questionnaire to assess the overall value of the mixed approach for formulating global strategies and related e-commerce strategies. The collected evaluation findings are summarised in Table 1.

Table 1. The evaluation findings with t-test results

Measurement	Individual judgment + a fuzzy expert system (averaged score)	Group judgment + a fuzzy expert system) (averaged score)	Ccalculated t-value	Two-tailed p-value
Confidence in the output produced	2.91	3.72	-4.46291	0.00005
Helping build group consensus	2.89	3.85	-12.6086	0.00000
Improving the performance of the decision activity	3.37	4.02	-5.21006	0.00000
Helping strategic analysis	3.35	4.02	-5.58782	0.00000
Helping understand the factors affecting strategy development	3.39	4.00	-4.97748	0.00001
Helping the coupling of strategic analysis with judgment	3.32	3.82	-3.30072	0.00189
Helping supplement judgment	3.39	3.96	-4.32799	0.00008
Helping strategic thinking	3.48	3.91	-3.42773	0.00131
Helping deal with uncertainty	2.96	3.70	-4.31029	0.00009
The quality of the results produced by the system	3.26	3.91	-4.05650	0.00001
Helping improve the quality of strategic decision-making	3.15	3.96	-6.54756	0.00000

Note: Significance level, alpha, is 0.05. The degrees of freedom, df, are 45. Two-tailed t-critical value is 2.01410. The sample size is 46 MSc Business IT and Information Management students. All the measurements use a scale of 1 to 5 where higher scores indicate more favourable replies.

The participants' responses before and after using the mixed approach were compared using matched pair t-test. All the null hypotheses were rejected. The t-test results given in Table 1 show that the mean scores of "group judgment + a fuzzy expert system" are significantly higher than those of "individual judgment + a fuzzy expert system". The findings suggest that the mixed approach, group judgment plus a fuzzy expert system, is more effective than individual judgment combined with a fuzzy expert system in terms of the 11 measurements listed in the Table:

1) Confidence in the output produced
2) Helping build group consensus
3) Improving the performance of the decision activity
4) Helping strategic analysis
5) Helping understand the factors affecting strategy development
6) Helping the coupling of strategic analysis with judgment and intuition
7) Helping supplement managerial judgment and intuition
8) Helping strategic thinking
9) Helping deal with uncertainty
10) The quality of the results produced by the fuzzy expert system
11) Helping improve the quality of strategic decisions

The findings reported here, however, may be preliminary due to the type of the subjects used and sample size of the participants involved, although the nature of the evaluation is case-based assessment.

4. Conclusions and further work

In this paper, a three-stage mixed approach towards formulating global marketing strategies and related e-commerce strategies has been established and evaluated by the first-named author. The mixed approach provides a systematic way to combine a fuzzy expert system with group judgment and intuition to support the key stages of global marketing strategy and e-commerce strategy formulation. Within this approach, the group Delphi technique is utilized to reduce the uncertainty surrounding the group inputs to the strategy development process; to resolve disagreement group inputs to the computerized models; and to build group consensus on selecting final strategies. A fuzzy expert system is developed to provide strategic analysis models and domain expert knowledge to supplement managers' weaknesses in analytical skills. Group judgment and intuition are incorporated to work with computerised models to ensure flexibility and creativity for the global strategy development process.

The mixed approach has been evaluated with 46 MSc Business IT and Information Management students at a British business school. The evaluation findings and related t-test results indicate that the mixed approach, group judgment plus a fuzzy expert system, is more effective than individual judgment coupled with a fuzzy expert system, in terms of confidence in the output, group consensus, quality of strategic decisions, usability, etc.

It is important to note that groups perform at a level rarely as well as their most proficient members [38]. Thus, with the mixed approach proposed in this paper, sound judgment and intuition of the most proficient members of the decision-making group should always be considered and incorporated into the whole strategy development process.

It should also be mentioned that the evaluation findings reported in the paper may be limited to the type of the subjects used and the small number of participants involved, although the nature of the evaluation is case-based assessment. Hence, evaluating the mixed approach with different type of subjects (e.g. industrial users) or larger number of participants would be an option for future work.

As an important part of further work in this field, a Web-based intelligent advisory system, called *WebStra*, has been developed by the first-named author to support the formulation of global marketing strategies and related Internet marketing strategies. The *WebStra* system contains more strategic analysis models. The following propositions are to be tested in the next stage of research:

Proposition 1. Use of the Web-based approach will improve the effectiveness of the process of global marketing planning and related e-commerce planning

Proposition 2. Use of the Web-based approach will improve the efficiency of the process of global marketing planning and related e-commerce planning

Proposition 3. Use of the Web-based approach that combines Web-based intelligent support with group judgment will improve the quality of the strategic decisions

Proposition 4. Use of the Web-based approach that integrates Web-based intelligent support with group judgment will improve users' confidence in the strategic decisions

Proposition 5. The Web-based approach will be able to help reduce some barriers to the use of computerised support for global marketing planning

References

1. Aiken, M., Hawley, D. and Zhang, W. Increasing meeting efficiency with a GDSS. Industrial Management and Data Systems 1994; 94(8): 13-16
2. Albaum, G., Strandskov, J. and Duerr, E. International Marketing and Export Management. Addison Wesley Longman Limited, Harlow, Essex, 1998
3. Bass, B. M. Organisational Decision Making. Richard D. Irwin, Illinois, IL, 1983
4. Belardo, S., Duchessi, P. and Coleman, J. R. A strategic decision support system at Orell Fussli. Journal of Management Information Systems 1994; 10(4): 135-157
5. Beveridge, M., Gear, A. E. and Minkes, A. L. Organisational learning and strategic decision support. The Learning Organization 1997; 4(5): 217-227
6. Blattberg, R. C. and Hoch, S. J. Database models and managerial intuition: 50% model + 50% manager. Management Science 1990; 36(8): 887-899
7. Carlsson, C. and Turban, E. DSS: directions for the next decade. Decision Support Systems 2002; 33(2): 105-110

8. Cavusgil, S. T. and Evirgen, C. Use of expert systems in international marketing: an application for co-operative venture partner selection. European Journal of Marketing 1997; 31(1): 73-86

9. Chee, H. and Harris, R. Global Marketing Strategy. Pitman Publishing, London, 1998

10. Davey, A. and Olson, D. Multiple criteria decision making models in group decision support. Group Decision and Negotiation 1998; 7(1): 55-75

11. DeSanctis, G. and Gallupe, B. Group decision support systems: a new frontier. DATA BASE 1985; Winter: 3-10

12. Eden, C. Strategic thinking with computers. Long Range Planning 1990; 23(6): 35-43

13. Finlay, P. N. and Marples, C. Strategic group decision support systems. Long Range Planning 1992; 25(3): 98-108

14. Gear, A. E. and Read, M. J. On-line group process support. OMEGA: International Journal of Management Science 1993; 21(3): 261-274

15. Goonatilake, S. and Khebbal, S. Intelligent hybrid systems: issues, classifications and future directions. In: Goonatilake, S. and Khebbal, S. (Eds), Intelligent Hybrid Systems. John Wiley & Sons, Chichester, 1995

16. Hamill, J. The Internet and Internet marketing. International Marketing Review 1997; 14(5): 300-323

17. Harrell, G. D. and Kiefer, R. O. Multinational market portfolios in global strategy development. International Marketing Review 1993; 10(1): 60-72

18. Jessup, L. M. and Kukalis, S. Better planning using group support systems. Long Range Planning 1990; 23(3): 100-105

19. Keen, P. G. W. and Scott Morton, M. S. Decision support systems: An organisational perspective. Addison-Wesley, Reading, Massachusetts, 1978

20. Levy, J. and Yoon, E. Modelling global market entry decision by fuzzy logic with an application to country risk assessment. European Journal of Operational Research 1995; 82(1): 53-78

21. Li, S. The development of a hybrid intelligent system for developing marketing strategy. Decision Support Systems 2000; 27(4): 395-409

22. Li, S., Kinman, R. Duan, Y. and Edwards, J. Computer-based support for marketing strategy development. European Journal of Marketing 2000; 34(5/6): 551-575.

23. McDonald, M. H. B. Marketing Plans: How to Prepare Them, How to Use Them. Butterworth-Heinemann, Oxford, 1989

24. McDonald, M. H. B. Strategic marketing planning. Kogan Page Ltd, London, 1996

25. McDonald, M. H. B. and Wilson, H. N. State-of-the-art developments in expert systems and strategic marketing planning. British Journal of Management 1990; 1: 159-170

26. Minkes, A. L. The Entrepreneurial Manager, Decisions Goals and Business Ideas. Penguin Books, Harmondsworth, 1987

27. Mintzberg, H., Raisinghani, D. and Theoret, A. The structure of unstructured decision processes. Administrative Science Quarterly 1976; 21: 246-275

28. Mintzberg, H. Rethinking strategic planning Part 1: Pitfalls and fallacies. Long Range Planning 1994; 27(3): 12-21

29. Mintzberg, H. Rethinking strategic planning Part 2: New roles for planners. Long Range Planning 1994; 27(3): 22-30.

30. Mintzberg, H. The Rise and Fall of Strategic Planning. Prentice Hall International (UK), 1994

31. Mitri, M., Karimalis, G., Cannon, H. and Yaprak, A. Targeting foreign markets: a structured approach for determining a market entry strategy. Journal of Targeting, Measurement and Analysis for Marketing 1999; 8(1): 71-82

32. O'Brien, J. A. Management Information Systems: Managing Information Technology in the E-Business Enterprise. McGraw Hill, New York, 2002

33. O'Keefe, R. M., Balci, O. and Smith, E. P. Validating expert system performance. IEEE expert 1987; 2(4): 81-90

34. Oz, E., Fedorowicz, J. and Stapleton, T. Improving quality, speed and confidence in decision-making. Information & Management 1993; 24: 71-82

35. Peattie, K. and Peters, L. The marketing mix in the third age of computing. Marketing Intelligence & Planning 1997; 15(3): 142-150

36. Porter, M. E. Corporate strategy: the state of strategic thinking. The Economist 1987; May 23: 21-22, 27-28

37. Porter, M. E. Strategy and the Internet. Harvard Business Review 2001; 79(3): 63-79

38. Rohrbaugh, J. Improving the quality of group judgment: social judgment analysis and the nominal group technique. Organizational Behavior and Human Performance 1981; 28: 272-288

39. Sharda, R., Barr, S. H. and McDonnell, J. C. Decision support system effectiveness: a review and an empirical test. Management Science 1988; 34(2): 139-159

40. Turban, E. and Aronson, J. Decision Support Systems and Intelligent Systems (6th edition). Prentice Hall International, Upper Saddle River, New Jersey, 2001

41. Van Bruggen, G. H., Smidts, A., Wierenga, B. The impact of the quality of a marketing decision support system: An experimental study. International Journal of Research in Marketing 1996; 13(4): 331-344.

42. Watson, R. T. and Zinkhan, G. M. Electronic commerce strategy: addressing the key questions. Journal of Strategic Marketing 1997; 5(4): 189-210

43. Webler, T., Levine, D., Rakel, H. and Renn, O. A novel approach to reducing uncertainty. Technological Forecasting and Social Change 1991; 39: 253-263

44. Wilson, H. and McDonald, H. H. B. Critical problems in marketing planning: the potential of decision support systems. Journal of Strategic Marketing 1994; 2: 249-269

A Two Stage Optimisation System for Resource Management in BT

Botond Virginas, Gilbert Owusu,
Chris Voudouris, George Anim-Ansah
BT Exact Technologies, Adastral Park,
MLB1/pp12, Ipswich, UK

Abstract

Resource management is a three step process of job demand forecasting, resource planning and resource distribution. Job demand forecasting is data intensive and requires sophisticated algorithms. Resource planning and distribution are complex processes, usually involving the analyses of large amounts of information. The complexity increases when more than one objective is being evaluated and the number of variables to consider is huge. Clearly the amount of effort and time required for accurately managing resources warrant an automated approach, especially for large customer service organisations such as BT. This paper describes a two stage optimisation system which is part of the ARMS architecture for automating resource management in BT. The paper focuses on a hybrid resource planning and distribution system that is underpinned by constraint-based and multi-objective optimisation methods. We have developed Collaborator, a resource distribution system which sits on top of Dynamic Planner, a resource planning system. By using this novel integrated approach, BT aims to optimise resource deployment through increased workforce utilisation and mobility and ultimately to substantially reduce its operational costs.

1.   Introduction

BT has one of the largest telecommunications infrastructures in the world. Resource planning is vital to ensure (a) customers' commitments are met, (b) quality of service is improved, and (c) operational costs are reduced. BT's UK operation is divided into Regional Business Areas (RBAs), which in turn are divided into varying numbers of Customer Service Teams (CSTs). BT has around 24,000 field engineers in the Retail and Wholesale divisions alone. Resource managers hold a telephone conference every morning to ascertain how best to distribute resources across an RBA. Resources are multi-skilled, mobile and have different working shifts (i.e. availability patterns). The RBA resource manager is responsible for ensuring that on a given day there are sufficient engineers available to perform work in the given RBA so as to maintain the Quality of Service (QoS) that the company stipulates, reduce operational costs, and meet customer commitments.

The resource manager at a CST level aims to balance the workforce according to the volume of work. Planning resources at the CST level highlights two outcomes. In the case of over-resourced conditions there will be shortage of resources in the CST, whilst in the case of under-resourced conditions there will be surplus. We view the problem as a two-stage process. This kind of conceptualisation arises because of the combinatorial nature of the problem [1] and the need to optimise resource profiles. A resource profile is defined by its skill, location and availability and each resource is multi-skilled, mobile (i.e. can work in different locations) and has different availability patterns. The problem is combinatorial because as the number of resources increases, the number of profiles to be considered increases as well by a factor of *skills* x *location* x *availability*. Moreover, this also increases further as the number of CSTs increases. The need for optimisation arises because the goal of resource managers is to ascertain how best to deploy the resources. The first stage is to optimise at the CST level and then feed the output of the first stage to the second stage which optimises at the RBA level.

We have developed the Dynamic Planner system (aka DP) [2,3] to optimise at the CST level and the Collaborator system to optimise at the RBA level. DP uses heuristic search algorithms [4,5] to solve a combinatorial optimisation problem, and as a result, the solution could be locally optimal and it might still leave unallocated resources and/or uncleared jobs in the workstack. If there are unresolved jobs, then managers must acquire extra resources from elsewhere. On the other hand if there are excess unutilised resources available to managers, then they should consider lending some of their excess personnel to other CSTs in order to maximise the utilisation of resources within the RBA.

Collaborator has been built on top of the single-domain DP system and integrated with it to support multi-domain resource management functionality. While DP is responsible for resource allocation at a given level (e.g. CST level), Collaborator operates at a level above DP (e.g. RBA level), where one RBA consists of many CST domains. While DP is concerned with the utilisation of the local workforce, Collaborator focuses on balancing the workforce across multiple patches. The aim of Collaborator is to facilitate the acquisition of additional resources to clear the workstack and to identify under-utilised resources. This is made possible because there is surplus of resources elsewhere. Collaborator enhances the deployment process by allowing dynamic distribution of engineers among a group of e.g. CSTs so that resource utilisation is improved from a higher level perspective. Dynamic Planner and Collaborator are subsystems of the ARMS platform for automating resource management in BT.

The remainder of the paper is organised as follows. Section 2 presents the two applications forming a common framework. Section 3 describes the engineering of the system. Section 4 presents the steps involved in a typical use of the application. Section 5 concludes the paper highlighting the benefits offered by the system.

2. Application Description

2.1 The Common Framework

Dynamic Planner and Collaborator work in a common framework. The following figure illustrates the main components of the integrated system:

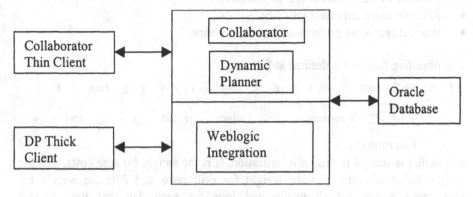

Figure 1: The overall architecture

While Dynamic Planner is launched as an application, Collaborator uses a thin client approach where Web browsers are used to interact with the system. The middle layer is supported by Weblogic Integration incorporated within Weblogic Server 6.1. An Oracle database is providing the backend to the system. The integrated system performs a two stage optimisation first optimising at the local level using DP and then feeding the output of the first stage to the second stage which optimises at a regional level using Collaborator. The two component systems are described in the following sections.

2.2 Dynamic Planner: Resource Planning at the CST Level

DP is a software component built atop iOpt [6] (a Java based toolkit for solving optimisation and combinatorial problems), that optimally assigns area (location), state (availability) and skill (capacity) data to technicians so as to facilitate the optimal scheduling of resources by Work Manager [7], BT's automated job allocation system. The input to Dynamic Planner is planning period, a list of resource profiles and a list of jobs for each day. A profile is a set of attributes for the resource for a particular day. Resource attributes are area, skill and state (availability). For each attribute in the profile there is a domain as well as an actual assignment. There are three types of resources: normal, overtime and required. Normal resources are available to work. Overtime resources are those who are unavailable to work (i.e. their day off) but have registered interest to work should the need arise. Required resources are fictituous resources that are used to identify extra resources in case of over-resource utilisation. Each value in the {area, skill, state} domain has a corresponding preference, 1 being the most preferred. Each skill has a skill productivity. A skill productivity of 1.5 would specify that the resource using this skill on the specified day could clear 1.5 jobs. Job attributes include execution day, the skill required for executing the job, the location of the job, its importance score i.e. either low, medium or high importance.

The overall objective of DP is to find optimal assignments for all the profiles. To achieve this objective we allocate jobs to resources. The overall aims of DP is stated as follows:

- Allocate as many jobs as fast as possible.
- Allocate more important jobs first.
- Respect resources preferences in job allocation.

The objective function is defined as follows:

$$F = \alpha \sum_{1}^{n} \text{cost}(a_i) + \beta \sum_{1}^{n} \text{cost}(t_i) + \chi \sum_{1}^{n} \text{cost}(k_i)$$

$$+ \delta \sum_{jobs} \text{importance score}(job_i) + \sum_{1}^{n} \text{cost}(u_i)$$

Equation (1)

a is skill, t is state, k is skill, u is utilisation. α is the weight for area costs, β is the weight for state costs, χ is the weight for skill costs and δ is the weight for importance scores for all unallocated jobs for each day that they remain unallocated.

In order to speed up the optimisation we do not explicitly allocate jobs to resources. Instead, we employ the notion of buckets to compare a pool of resources to a pool of jobs. A bucket is an aggregation of entities. There are two buckets: resources and jobs. Each resource bucket represents resource capacities. A resource bucket is defined by a normalised execution date, area and skill. Job buckets exist for each possible <day, area, skill, importance, job type> combination. The amount of jobs being cleared is determined with this implicit job assignment, by matching the resource and job buckets. A job bucket and a resource bucket can be described as having a "size", which is essentially the number of jobs and resources respectively that have been assigned to a respective bucket. In the case of the resource buckets, the size thereof is modified by a productivity value and availability. This means that if, for example, resources T1 and T2 both have skill sk2, but T1 is far more productive than T2, T1's contribution to the resource bucket corresponding to sk2 will be larger than T2's contribution (assuming area and state to be the same). The algorithm for optimising profiles is as follows. We generate an initial solution by sweeping over all profiles and set the area-skill-state variables sequentially to their best combination, i.e. all possible area-skill-value-combinations would be assigned for evaluation, and then the most optimal combination would get assigned (for setting the heuristic solution) before going on to the next profile. We then sweep over the profiles to optimise them. We identify surplus resources by making them unavailable and checking their effect on the objective function. If there is no change in the objective function, then they are surplus. For over resource utilisation, we add required resources to the system. Required resources have super-sets of the skill, area and state domains. The output of DP is thus a list of surpluses and required resources.

2.3 Collaborator: Resource Distribution at the RBA Level

Collaborator is a system to facilitate the acquisition of additional resources to clear the workstack (i.e. jobs) for particular CSTs. This is made possible because from the RBA manager's viewpoint there are surplus resources in some of the CSTs he/she oversees. In effect, Collaborator ensures optimal deployment of resources across an RBA.

The starting point for Collaborator is invoking DP for a particular planning period in the future (a period of time set at regional level by the RBA manager). As a result, each CST manager will know about the jobs he has ("shortages") and the unallocated resources ("surpluses") for the planning period. Each manager will decide which "shortages" and "surpluses" to submit to Collaborator. Collaborator therefore will receive as input details of "surpluses" and "shortages" selected by CST managers. These details will contain information like the skill and proficiency of a surplus resource and/or the required skill and the "importance" (level of urgency) of an uncleared job. User preferences like maximum travelling distance and preferred selection criteria can also be specified by a CST manager. At the heart of Collaborator stands the "Central Matchmaker". The "Central Matchmaker" will aim at balancing the load over a geographical area under the same management/cost structure. Since there is no notion of competition, we use a multi-objective algorithm to redistribute resources.

We model the resource distribution problem as a multi-agent co-ordination problem (see Figure 2).

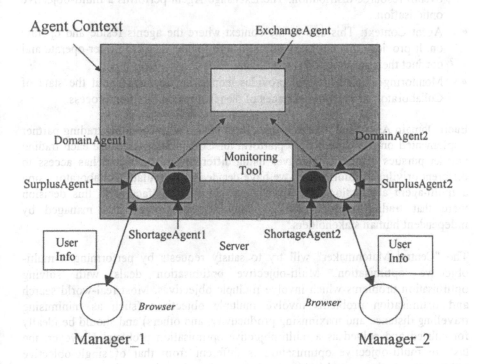

Figure 2: Collaborator Architecture

In this model, the system consists of 2*A+1 agents where there exist two agents representing each CST domain (one agent for "shortages" and another agent for "surpluses"), and an Exchange Agent for the "Central Matchmaker". The Exchange Agent is responsible for collecting all necessary information from each domain agent and performing overall resource distribution.

There are five basic components to Collaborator as shown in Figure 2:

- Domain managers: The Domain managers (e.g. Manager_1 and Manager_2) act as principals of Collaborator. They have resources they wish to exchange. They will interact with the system using a lightweight client approach.
- Domain Agents: The Domain Agents are representatives of managers that reside in the server context. These agents will execute and act according to the desires of their principals. The agents have their own objectives and possess the intelligence to engage in negotiation. The Agents are divided into Surplus Agents and Shortage Agents. Each domain manager will have one Surplus Agent and one Shortage Agent associated with them. The objective of an agent in charge of "surpluses" is to "lend" these excess resources. The objective of an agent in charge of "shortages" is to "acquire" resources to satisfy these "shortages".
- Exchange Agent: At the heart of Collaborator the "Central Matchmaker" role is performed by the Exchange Agent. The Exchange Agent is responsible for collecting all necessary information from each Domain Agent and performing overall resource distribution. The Exchange Agent performs a multi-objective optimisation.
- Agent Context: This acts as the context where the agents reside and operate on. It provides the necessary infrastructure for the agents to inter-operate and conduct their activities on.
- Monitoring Tool: This tool provides monitoring features about the state of Collaborator during various stages of the resource distribution process.

Each Domain Agent and the Exchange Agent have a corresponding trading partner implemented on the chosen B2B platform for Collaborator. Because each trading partner pursues different objectives using different strategies and has access to different privileged information, we have decided to formulate Collaborator using a multi-agent abstraction. Moreover, other contributing factors to this decision were that trading partners are geographically distributed and managed by independent human stakeholders.

The "Central Matchmaker" will try to satisfy requests by performing a multi-objective optimisation. Multi-objective optimisation deals with solving optimisation problems which involve multiple objectives. Most real-world search and optimisation problems involve multiple objectives (such as minimising travelling distance and maximising productivity, and others) and should be ideally formulated and solved as a multi-objective optimisation problem. However, the task of multi-objective optimisation is different from that of single-objective optimisation in that in multi-objective optimisation, there is usually no single solution which is optimum with respect to all objectives. The resulting problem usually has a set of optimal solutions, known as Pareto-optimal solutions, non-inferior solutions, or effective solutions [8].

From a conceptual point of view, the main difference between single and multiple objective optimisation is the definition of optimal solution, that is an extension of the single objective optimum concept. In a multi-objective optimisation problem, there is more than one objective function, each of which may have a different individual optimal solution. If there is sufficient difference in the optimal solutions corresponding to different objectives, the objective functions are known as conflicting to each other. So in the presence of multiple and conflicting objectives, the resulting optimisation problem gives rise to a set of optimal solutions, instead of a single optimal solution.

Multi-objective optimisation can be defined as the problem of finding [9] a vector of decision variables which satisfies constraints and optimises a vector function whose elements represent the objective functions. These functions form a mathematical description of performance criteria which are usually in conflict with each other. Hence, the term "optimise" means finding such a solution that would give the values of all the objective functions acceptable to the user. V. Pareto, a prominent Italian economist, introduced this idea of optimality at the end of the XIX century [10]. A Pareto optimisation almost always gives multiple solutions called non-inferior or non-dominated solutions [11]. A feasible solution to a multi-objective optimisation problem is said to be optimal, or non dominated, if, starting from that point in the design space, the value of any of the objective functions cannot be improved without deteriorating at least one of the others. All feasible solutions can, indeed, be classified into dominated and non-dominated (Pareto optimal) solutions, and the set of non-dominated solutions is called the Pareto front [12]. Solving a multi-objective optimisation problem is, therefore, to find this set of non-dominated solutions. Afterwards the decision-maker's preference may be applied to choose the best compromise solution from the generated set.

In Collaborator the Central Matchmaker will perform a two step Pareto Optimisation using hard and soft constraints. Currently the optimisation algorithm uses two objectives: travelling distance and skill proficiency. Nevertheless, the algorithm can be used with n objectives. The hard and soft constraints will be expressed by Domain managers and maintained by Shortage and Surplus Agents. For each request the Exchange Agent will query the Surplus Agents for matching resources who will respond using their hard constraints. An example of a hard constraint is a maximum travelling distance for a particular resource maintained by the Surplus Agent and specified by the associated Domain manager. Once the Exchange Agent receives all valid responses (the "search space") from all Surplus Agents it will perform a Pareto optimisation. The result will be a subset of non-dominated solutions or the Pareto front. A greedy algorithm is used to construct this Pareto front. In the second step the Exchange Agent will send this subset to the corresponding Shortage Agent for the request to make its selection based on the soft constraints. An example of a soft constraint is the degree of preference for travelling distance or proficiency expressed by the associated Domain manager. The Shortage Agent will then respond with the chosen option.

3. Engineering the Application

The system follows a four-tier architecture: a thin client, servlets, EJB, and Oracle 8.1.5 database running on a SUN E10K. We have two main components in the system: a CST and RBA monitor. The front end comprises of HTML pages and the communication between the principals and their associated agents is provided through Java Servlet Technology and XML using Java Message Service. The CST monitor enables a typical user to invoke DP from Collaborator in order to obtain its input. The input for Collaborator is a list of jobs that a specific CST manager has ("shortages") and a list of unallocated resources ("surpluses") in that CST for the set planning period. DP is implemented as an Enterprise Java Bean (EJB) and DP runs on Weblogic Server 6.1. Collaborator invokes DP to generate a problem model with resource profiles and jobs for the planning period. DP then optimises profiles and highlights "surpluses" and "shortages".

The RBA Monitor on the other hand provides control and monitoring features for the RBA manager. On one hand the RBA Monitor will provide control features for the manager such as set parameters for Collaborator, start Collaborator, stop Collaborator, etc. On the other hand the RBA Monitor will assist the RBA manager in monitoring the distribution of resources between CST(s) in an RBA. It provides monitoring functionality during the three distinctive stages of the resource distribution process: "pre-trading", "trading" and "post-trading".

Pre-trading phase (see Figure 3):
The RBA managers select which CST(s) within the RBA they are interested in monitoring. Once this selection has been made, Collaborator provides the RBA Monitor tool with the number of submitted surplus and required resources for each CST that it is monitoring. The details are then represented visually in different views e.g. graphs, tables and maps.

Trading phase (see Figure 4):
At this stage the tool informs the RBA manager which surplus resources are moving from one CST to another as "provisional deals". This view is represented in the form of a table and a graphical animator.

During this stage CST managers have the option to reject a particular "provisional move" or to withdraw a particular surplus resource/shortage request from Collaborator. The monitoring tool has the capability of visualising these rejections and withdrawals.

Post-trading phase:
Once the resource distribution has been completed, all provisional deals will be declared "final deals". Therefore the RBA Monitor will provide a summary of all activities which have taken place in Collaborator including details of all the moves between CSTs, details of all withdrawals and rejections and summarising views on the state of the market in the post-trading stage.

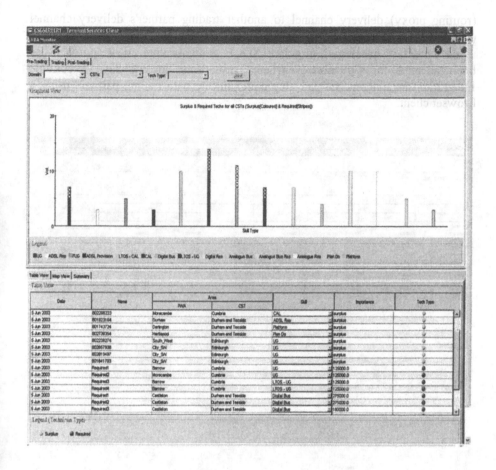

Figure 3: Monitoring the pre-trading phase

Collaborator is using the BEA Weblogic integration B2B platform. This platform supports the building of mission-critical, scalable, real-world e-commerce applications. WebLogic Integration provides an infrastructure platform for integrating business processes that can span over multiple corporate departments, multiple enterprises across the Internet, or both. Enterprises that want to participate in a conversation must first configure their environments. This task includes creating a trading partner, and defining trading partner-specific information and one or more delivery channels. A delivery channel describes a trading partner's message sending and receiving characteristics, including the business protocol to be used in the conversation, a transport protocol, and security parameters. Various trading partners have been implemented on the B2B platform for Collaborator. Each "Surplus Agent" and "Shortage Agent" has an associated trading partner. The "Central Matchmaker" has a trading partner application associated with it as well. The trading partners communicate using their delivery channel through an intermediary delivery channel, in hub-and-spoke mode. In a hub-and-spoke configuration, a trading partner application communicates via an intermediary (routing proxy) delivery channel to another trading partner's delivery channel (spoke delivery channel). In Collaborator various trading partners communicate using the default messaging protocol: XOCP. A lightweight client approach has been adopted for Collaborator where participants do not have WebLogic Integration installations, instead they communicate with trading partners using a browser client.

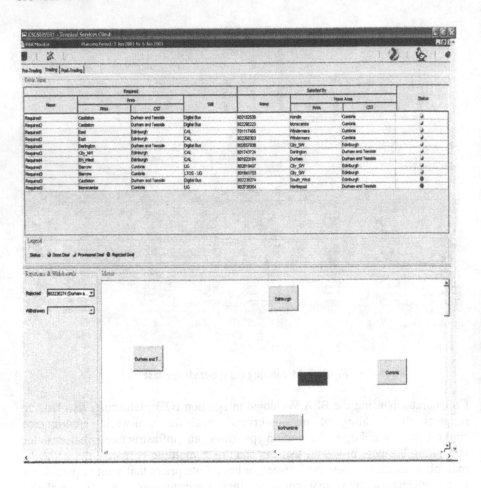

Figure 4: Monitoring the trading phase

The intelligence for each "Surplus Agent" and "Shortage Agent" and the "Exchange Agent" to control their corresponding trading partners is provided in Java classes. In addition, the "Exchange Agent" class incorporates the multi-objective distribution algorithm as well. The monitoring tool has been implemented as a standalone Java application. The various agents communicate with the monitoring tool using Java Message Service.

The development of the current version of Collaborator has involved 10 people over a period of a year.

4.   Using the Application

A typical flow of information in the system follows a three-stage process. The three distinct phases are as follows: "pre-trading", "trading" and "post-trading". Collaborator is launched by the RBA manager using the RBA Monitor tool. This manager will set various parameters for Collaborator, such as the planning period, when to start the "trading phase", when to finish the "trading-phase", etc. Once Collaborator has been launched, the "pre-trading" phase begins.

Pre-trading phase:
The RBA manager has got the option to monitor the state of Collaborator in pre-trading using the RBA Monitor tool as described in Section 3. On the other hand CST managers will login to the CST Monitor tool using a Web browser. They will invoke DP for the particular planning period set by the RBA manager in order to acquire the list of "shortages" and "surpluses". Here DP will optimise resource deployment at the CST level taking as input a pool of resource and work demand profiles. DP outputs profiles of resources that are surplus and highlights resources required to clear the workstack. We would like to emphasise the decision support nature of Collaborator. Once the CST Manager receives the details of all "shortages" and "surpluses" from DP, it is his/her decision which subset of this list to submit to Collaborator. Moreover, CST managers will have the option to set their trading preferences, which in turn will be used for soft and hard constraints during optimisation. They can specify details such as maximum travelling distance for a resource move, preferred selection criteria such as highest proficiency or minimum travelling distance, etc.

Trading-phase:
The RBA manager has got the option to monitor the state of Collaborator in trading using the RBA Monitor tool as described in section 3. On the other hand CST managers will be presented with details of proposed provisional moves. Moreover, because of the decision support nature of Collaborator, they will be able to perform the following actions:
- withdraw a particular surplus resource: in which case the resource becomes unavailable
- reject a provisional move for a surplus resource: in which case the system will try to rearrange a new deal for the resource request
- withdraw a particular resource request: in which case the resource request will be withdrawn
- reject a provisional move for a resource request: in which case the appropriate surplus resource will become available again

Figure 5 presents a screenshot of a typical CST Monitor screen during the trading phase.

Post-trading phase

The RBA manager has got the option to monitor the state of Collaborator in post-trading using the RBA Monitor tool as described in section 3. On the other hand CST managers will be presented with details of all finalised moves and the final state of their CST.

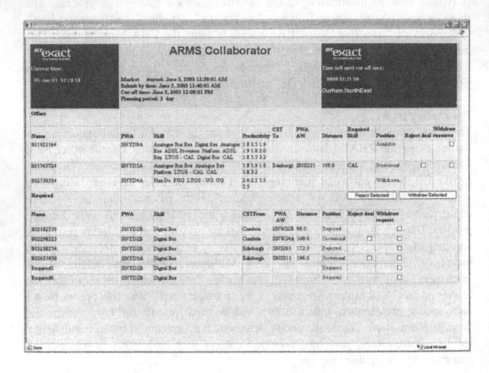

Figure 5: CST monitor during the trading phase

5.   Conclusions

We have presented an integrated resource planning and distribution system for BT. The system is currently on trial in the organisation. This trial involves over 600 engineers located in three different CSTs. Initial feedback is being incorporated in the system. BT aims to reduce its operational cost of employing a workforce of 24,000 engineers by using this application. Substantial customer satisfaction benefits are also expected because of better appointing of work and resource availability where it is required by BT's customers. The tool will also help in identifying training needs, will reduce the number of resources on overtime and will identify optimal deployment opportunities.

The novelty of the system lies in its two stage optimisation approach by first optimising at the local level and then feeding the output of the first stage to the second stage which optimises at a regional level. The first stage is governed by local business policies where the Dynamic Planner will make local decisions based on local calendarised work demand and resource availability profiles. The second stage is governed by global business policies where Collaborator will adopt a centralised view of the system and will perform a load balancing whilst still attempting to maintain the local business objectives as well. This novel way offers a comprehensive human resource exchange solution which ultimately is suitable for both intra-organisational and inter-organisational resource management.

Future plans include the replacement of the centralised approach with a fully distributed multi-agent system, where individual Domain Agents will communicate directly with each other and the Exchange Agent will be replaced by a Directory Agent. In this way Collaborator will become more distributed in nature and the various Domain Agents will become more autonomous and more powerful.

Acknowledgements

We thank Kim Gasson, Graham Connolly, Martyn Gollop, Raphael Dorne, Cedric Ladde, Lyndon Lee, and Nishan Karunatillake for their useful suggestions and input to this project.

References

1. Aarts, E.H.L. and Lenstra, J.K. (eds). Local search in combinatorial optimisation. Kirkpatrick, S., Gelatt, C.D. and Vecchi, M.P. Optimisation by simulated annealing. Science, 1993, 220: 671 – 680.
2. Owusu G., Voudouris C., Dorne R., & Lesaint D. (2002a), Developing a Profiler in the Arms Platform, Proceedings of the Sixth IASTED International Conference on Artificial Intelligence and Soft Computing, pp. 541-546, Banff, Canada, July 2002
3. Owusu G., Dorne R., Voudouris C., & Lesaint D. (2002b), Dynamic Planner: A Decision Support Tool for Resource Planning, ES2002: 22th SGAI International Conference on KBS and Applied AI, Applications and Innovations in Intelligent Systems X, pp.19-31
4. Reeves, C.R. (ed). Modern heuristic techniques for combinatorial problems, Blackwell Scientific Publications, Oxford, 1993.
5. Glover, F.W. and Laguna, M. Tabu search. Kluwer Academic Publishers, 1997.
6. Voudouris, C., Dorne, R., Lesaint, D., & Liret, A. iOpt: A Software Toolkit for Heuristic Search Methods, Principles and Practice of Constraint Programming - CP 2001, ed. Walsh, T., Lecture Notes in Computer Science, vol. 2239, pp 716-729, Springer, 2001
7. Lesaint, D., Azarmi, N. Laithwaite, R. & Walker, P. Engineering dynamic scheduler for Work Manager. BT Technology Journal, 1995, 16, 3: 16-29
8. Steuer R., Multiple criteria optimization: theory, computation and application, John Wiley & Sons, Inc, New York, 1986
9. Osyczka, A. Multicriteria optimization for engineering design. In John S. Gero, editor, Design Optimization, pages 193-227. Academic Press, 1985
10. Pareto, V. Cours D'Economie Politique, volume I and II. F. Rouge, Lausanne, 1896
11. Coello, C.A. An updated survey of evolutionary multiobjective optimization techniques: State of the art and future trends. In: Congress on Evolutionary Computation. (1999) 3-13
12. Srinivas, N & Deb, K Multiobjective optimisation using nondominated Sorting in Genetic Algorithms. Evolutionary Computation, 2(3):221-248, fall 1994

SESSION 3:

HAZARD PREDICTION, FAULT DIAGNOSIS, DESIGN

WMD HAZARD PREDICTION –
Blending three AI techniques to produce a superior defence capability

P. A. Thomas[i], Dr M. Bull[ii] and G. R. Ravenscroft[iii]

[i]Dstl, [ii]RiskAware Ltd, [iii]SciSys Ltd

(Correspondence to P. A. Thomas, Porton Down, Salisbury, SP4 0JQ, UK. pathomas@dstl.gov.uk)

Abstract

This paper describes the development of a hazard prediction system for Weapons of Mass Destruction (WMD) and discusses how three distinct Artificial Intelligence (AI) techniques were found to be necessary to enable operational use of such a system. The three techniques: Bayesian data fusion, Blackboard Architecture and Genetic Algorithm optimisation, are described, along with the novel modifications found necessary for their use in this domain. Furthermore, issues encountered and practical aspects of the development phase are discussed.

Introduction

Weapons of Mass Destruction (WMD) pose perhaps the greatest threat to peace and stability in modern times. Despite the fall of the Iraqi regime, many rogue nations still sponsor offensive WMD programmes and research. Additionally, and of even greater concern, WMD devices remain the ultimate goal for many extreme terrorist groups, providing the ultimate form of asymmetric aggression.

The UK's recently revised defence posture[1] states that "International terrorist groups will continue to explore the potential of innovative and unconventional means of attack in order to achieve global impact. Extreme terrorist groups or possibly rogue states may in future seek to emulate the massive effect of the 11 September attacks."

Hijacked airliners are a special, and hopefully unrepeatable, case of WMD. However, some terrorist groups will be attracted by the use of chemical, biological, radiological or nuclear (CBRN) weapons to achieve major impact. The anthrax attacks in the US illustrate the range of possibilities. CBRN weapons are characterised by creating a hazardous area downwind of the original release point, and, in the case of all but Nuclear, this is where they exert their lethal effect.

125

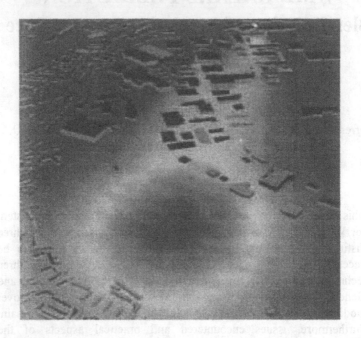

Figure 1: Downwind hazard from a biological release

The downwind hazard area is determined by environmental conditions and physical processes and this gives us a key area of defence against this kind of aggression. Although complex, the physical processes can be modelled and this enables us to predict, evaluate and respond to the hazard to minimise its lethal effect. Atmospheric dispersion modelling is a complex, fascinating science but not the topic of this paper. What are of interest are the techniques needed to enable advanced atmospheric dispersion models to be used in an operational context, reacting to real-time reports and making predictions in time for response action to be taken. This is the area of WMD Hazard Prediction.

WMD Hazard Prediction systems impose three additional requirements in addition to atmospheric dispersion modelling. Since they are being used in a real event they must:

- Have the ability to estimate the parameters of the release from the sparse data received during an event.
- Be able to produce hazard predictions promptly enough for a response to be effective.
- Include the capability of providing support tools for decision makers.

These requirements can be met by the application of advanced techniques from three Artificial Intelligence domains.

Parameter estimation

Covert WMD releases (i.e. Chemical, Radiological and Biological) are a distinctive form of attack in that the actual attack event may go undetected. It is probable that only when effects of such attacks are realised in the form of casualties, remote sensor readings or actual observations will alarms be raised. However, the realisation that some form of attack has occurred is really only the start of the problem. In order to provide warnings to affected personnel we must run an atmospheric dispersion model to predict downwind hazard areas. Before this can be done we need to determine a parameterised causative event (source term) describing the characteristics of the attack(s).

The correlation and association of event reports from WMD attacks presents a number of difficulties for traditional "non-intelligent" systems. Firstly, reports arrive from different sources in differing forms and in non-chronological order. Secondly, association of the incoming report with any reports so far received is an "inverse problem" since terrain-following dispersion models cannot be run in reverse. Thirdly, once a set of associated reports is established, a source term must be generated which best explains all associated reports.

This is a classic Artificial Intelligence problem and can be solved by drawing from "Data Fusion" techniques. Consideration was given to such data fusion techniques as Kalman filters, Endorsement theory, Fuzzy logic, Dempster-Shafer, and Case-based reasoning. Whilst each had a number of benefits in terms of their ability to solve the problems presented within the WMD hazard prediction domain, Bayesian techniques were selected for a number of reasons:

- Bayesian techniques are probability-based and can be based on meta-probabilities which can be readily obtained from either domain experts or experimental data,
- Bayesian methods enable belief to be refined on receipt of further evidence or event reports,
- Bayesian methods are suitable for use in situations where the problem space is non-linear and where the uncertainty is not necessarily Gaussian,
- Bayesian techniques allow greater flexibility in terms of the number of parameters used to describe the system.

Initial research at Dstl focused on developing a Bayesian network solution to the Parameter Estimation problem. However, there was found to be a lack of applicability of static Bayesian networks to derivation of sub-symbolic parameters (such as location or time of release). This led the research program to a technique based on dynamic Bayesian graphical modelling[2,3] extensively used in radar/sonar target tracking[4,5]. Using Bayesian probability reasoning, this technique enabled disparate data to be combined in a mathematically tractable way, allowing update of belief in the system given new information, and conferring a high level of error tolerance.

At its core the dynamic Bayesian graphical modelling algorithm has a sampling / updating cycle summarised by Figure 2. During this cycle, samples are drawn from the prior pdf whenever a new report is received. Each sample represents a hypothesised source term for which a fast dispersion model is run. The degree-of-fit to the new report received is assessed using Bayes' rule and this forms a weighting that is applied to each sample. The resulting collection of weighted samples is re-sampled and reduced, using an adaptive kernel density estimation technique to form a Gaussian mixture model. This model represents the posterior pdf (probability density function), or belief distribution, of source term. This posterior pdf becomes the prior for the next cycle upon receipt of the next report.

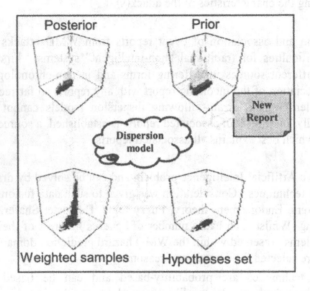

Figure 2: Bayesian sampling / updating cycle.

The prototype algorithm was initially developed using Mathematica™ before being translated into C++ to investigate performance effects. A second generation C++ version focused on integration of this functionality with the WMD Hazard Prediction system presented in this paper. This led to consideration of the effects of such factors as larger spatial domain, greater number of agents and reports from sources other than remote sensors.

While these issues were largely a natural extension of the initial research, the incorporation of different types of event reports, such as observer reports, required some further thought. The solution was found to lie in the treatment of observer reports according to the same underlying methodology (Figure 2) as remote sensors, thus hypotheses sets are created for an observation report (based on bearing or proximality to the observer) and samples are weighted based on a visual model instead of a dispersion model.

Each parameter is represented by a single pdf and each pdf can be updated using Bayes' rule on receipt of event reports. The peak of the posterior pdf gives the most likely estimate of that release parameters. Therefore, the complete set of belief information forms the current source term, which is fed into the most appropriate dispersion model for a full prediction of the resulting hazard profile.

The pdf also provides us with a measure of the uncertainty of our belief, a smaller/larger spread representing less/greater uncertainty. This measure of uncertainty can then be used at the dispersion modelling stage to determine the size of the risk envelope to place around the model output.

The technique allows all information relating to a particular scenario to be maintained within the system so that "less likely" scenarios could ultimately become the "probable" or "most likely" scenario. This applies to the full set of source term parameters, both sub-symbolic (source location, event time, duration, etc.) and symbolic (agent type, weapon system, etc.).

One of the primary benefits of this methodology is that the full probability density function for each parameter is always available allowing the system to refine its belief in the nature of the scenario as further information becomes available. As a result, even situations where initial evidence favours erroneous hypotheses, the system would be able to recover given subsequent 'true' data.

Prompt hazard prediction

There are many important influences upon airborne transport and dispersion. These include meteorology, atmospheric turbulence and features such as land usage, buildings and other obstacles. Dstl Porton Down undertakes a great deal of research investigating these other phenomena and producing methods for modelling each. However, it is important that these models are not used in isolation. Terrain, vegetation, buildings and other structures will be present in almost all modelling scenarios of relevance and so the models need to be used in combination. The next-generation tool for dispersion modelling and hazard assessment is an integrated modelling suite that incorporates near-field effects such as the urban and vegetative environment together with longer range effects. Dstl is working on such a capability called Integrated Modelling Platform with Agent Controlled Tasking (IMPACT) for use as the dispersion modelling and hazard assessment engine for WMD Hazard Prediction systems.

The IMPACT architectural model grew out of a general requirement to integrate diverse collections of existing modelling components together to create modelling and simulation applications, using a generic object-oriented architecture. The internal architecture chosen was based on the Blackboard Architecture. In Blackboard Architectures, several software "Agents" (autonomous modules) collaborate to solve a problem by reading information from a "blackboard" database, and writing their conclusions back to the blackboard database. In the IMPACT system, a set of modelling and connectivity Software Agents collaborate to model dispersion, assess downwind hazard and exchange information with other systems. The Agents function autonomously, recognising their opportunity to make a contribution, performing modelling tasks and returning output data to the Blackboard, and an underlying Object Database. Figure 3 provides a high-level overview of the IMPACT architecture.

IMPACT Architecture

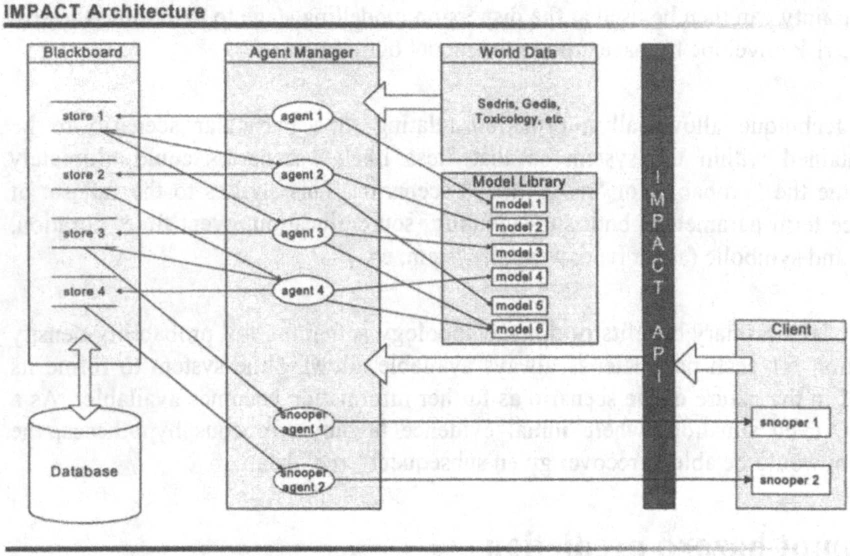

Figure 3: The IMPACT Architecture.

The product framework itself is entirely an in-house development, and has been implemented using ANSI C++ using the Microsoft Visual Studio compiler, although the code base is fully portable to Linux systems utilising the GNU compiler. Extensive use has been made of the C++ Standard Template Library and the Open Source BOOST C++ Class and Template Libraries, in order to streamline development. Initial prototype development began in 1999, but in the last year, the system has been fully re-implemented to create a fully robust product.

The key components of the IMPACT framework are the Agents themselves. Each Agent is derived from a common C++ base class, SoftwareAgent, which implements all necessary housekeeping and thread management functionality, and provides two key public methods, CanContribute, and DoActivity. The Agent Manager, which has no run-time knowledge of the functionality of its Agent complement (the Agents are constructed separately by an Agent Factory) cycles through its list of Agents, and polls the CanContribute method of each. This prompts each agent to check the Blackboard for patterns of new information that the Agent can process. When an Agent recognises an opportunity to contribute, it returns a True value to the Agent Manager, which responds by calling the

DoActivity method on the Agent. This causes the Agent to activate its processing thread, and process the Blackboard information using any relevant modelling routines from the Modelling Library, which includes extensive Third Party and Legacy code, primarily in the form of Dynamic Link Libraries (DLL's).

The IMPACT Blackboard has proved the most challenging component to develop. It forms a layer between the Agents and the Database itself, optimised to the requirements of the Agents, and provides a thread-safe API that allows Agents to: -

- Identify and extract new or updated data in Database Tables,
- Perform queries on Database Tables, including spatial and spatio-temporal queries,
- Write new or updated data back to the Database.

Here, extensive use has been made of the BOOST C++ libraries, for components such as Smart Pointers, Locks, Mutexes and Thread Managers, thus saving development cost and easing cross-platform portability.

Although the IMPACT Database is currently implemented as a configurable memory-resident set of Object Tables, a transactional approach has been taken to the query and update API, which should in future allow a commercial RDBMS, such as Oracle, to be utilised in future generations of the product.

This architecture has proved highly modular, allowing Agents to be developed independently and tested in isolation, before being integrated together with relative ease. The support of multi-threading within the Software Agent base class allows IMPACT to take advantage of the additional power of multi-processor hardware configurations where possible. Since all updates to the Blackboard are recorded to file, the system can restore its previous state easily after a system crash, and resume modelling.

Throughout the product, a very high level of configurability has been provided, by allowing Agents, Blackboard and Database to be selected and reconfigured at run-time. This was necessary in order to allow IMPACT to be deployed for the WMD Hazard Assessment system.

Figure 4 shows a sample of the IMPACT output displayed here in 3D. In this simulation, IMPACT has been supplied with simulated real-time meteorological data. For the sources shown, IMPACT has chosen to model the transport and diffusion using Dstl's Urban Dispersion Model (UDM)[6]. All the modelling is carried out automatically by IMPACT in faster than real-time without any input from the user.

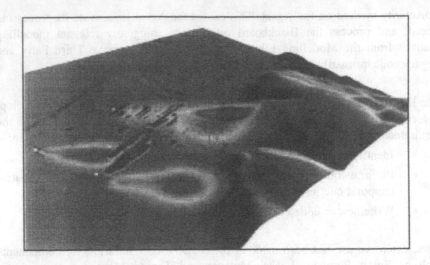

Figure 4: A sample output from the IMPACT dispersion engine, modelling five releases over a real location and using simulated meteorological data.

When interfaced with a WMD Hazard Prediction system, IMPACT's output, dosage and concentration data and additional information (e.g. point concentration estimates at desired locations) are transferred to the host system for risk analysis. A risk engine component considers dosage against human toxicity to determine which units should be warned and to allow alternative courses of action to be considered. This information is presented graphically to the commander, on a map they are familiar with, identifying and prioritising at-risk units in a clear manner.

In addition to the real-time capability of modelling hazards and warning personnel the software will provide decision support tools for the commander.

Decision Support Tools

Decision Support Tools are invaluable for planning against a WMD incident since many decisions a decision-maker may face are non-intuitive, complex and outside their experience set.

During planning, a typical decision-maker's question might be - *where and how should I deploy the biological sensors I have available?* Currently, biological sensors (electronic devices capable of detecting the presence of biological agent) are rare and valuable resources, making it imperative that they are deployed in a manner that maximises their effectiveness. Therefore, Dstl has developed a Sensor Placement Tool (SPT) to provide decision support for optimising the position of biological sensors. This forms an important component of any WMD Hazard Prediction system.

Ideal sensor placement is a problem exhibiting non-linear combinatorial properties since the position of each individual sensor in the set of available sensors will affect the optimal placement of the other members of the set. Thus, given that there are n available sensors and m candidate positions for those sensors, the number of possible sensor configurations approximates to m^n (actually m!-(m-n)! if all sensors in the set have different characteristics). Therefore, for even a small number of sensors it is computationally onerous to exhaustively search all possible solutions for the optimum and the problem becomes one of search-based optimisation.

In order to perform the search, the threat from WMD must be represented. The current threat is represented as a Monte-Carlo like set of releases. This set is produced by sampling (typically 2-5,000 samples) from release density distributions constructed from the parameters in an Intelligence database(a database of Military Intelligence data). The source terms represented by these samples are then run through a fast, terrain enabled, dispersion model (Dstl's Urban Dispersion Model[6] to produce a indexed set of concentration maps, which when combined represent the results of the current threat over the current (and predicted) meteorology and local terrain. The search for optimal sensor placement is performed on this search-space.

Various optimisation techniques were considered including random search, dynamic hill climbing and simulated annealing, but since the surface of the sensor placement search-space is highly uneven/discontinuous due to the many dispersion-modelling runs, Genetic Algorithms (GAs) emerged as the most efficient, typically finding optima with a probability of detection 0.1 higher than their nearest rivals for a given number of generations/iterations.

GAs are computational models inspired by evolution[7]. They encode a potential solution to a problem in a structure (termed a chromosome) amenable to genetic manipulation, so enabling the combination of multiple chromosomes to form new, better chromosomes that build upon the strengths of their parents. As with natural evolution, the population of chromosomes within a GA increases its fitness over successive generations, thus evolving towards an optimal solution.

New solutions form by a process of selection and breeding, and in a further analogy to natural processes, genetic mutation is synthesised. These techniques in combination serve to explore and exploit the search-space in a highly effective manner, rapidly converging toward the optimal solution while evaluating only a small percentage of all possible solutions.

Optimal, of course, requires definition, in this case via the Fitness Function of the GA. This is a monotonically increasing numeric measure of fitness-for-purpose of any chromosome. Careful design of the fitness function is required when encoding a GA to ensure that it meets the objective of the search.

134

For the purposes of biological sensor placement, the definition of "optimal" is the sensor placement which *primarily* gives the best probability of detection of biological airborne contaminant, and *secondarily* gives the best warning time (time between sensor alarm and hazard arrival at the area of protection). A secondary goal is a goal that is sought only when there are multiple solutions with equal primary fitness. This leads to the requirement on the GA that it supports both primary and secondary goals. Therefore, Dstl has designed and produced a GA in C++ which implements a novel method for secondary goal optimisation[8] together with the more conventional primary objective optimisation.

Secondary optimisation in Dstl's GA is achieved by computation of a secondary fitness value, s. The selection operator operates on s where there are multiple chromosomes, n, of the same primary fitness, p. In this case the total fitness $n.p$ is redistributed in proportion to s. In terms of the roulette wheel model, the sector occupied by the chromosomes stays the same, since the value $n.p$ does not change, but the arcs allocated within that sector are adjusted according to the value of s.

Diagrammatically:

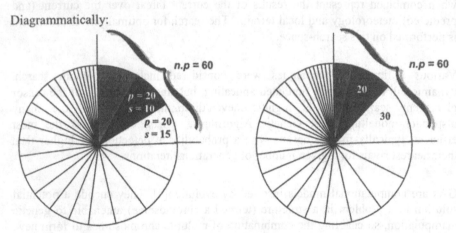

FIGURE 5a: The roulette wheel with   FIGURE 5b: The roulette wheel with
chromosomes partitioned by primary fitness   chromosomes partitioned by secondary fitness

Fitness evaluation, therefore, involves scoring candidate sets of sensor locations, produced by the GA, against the set of concentration maps. The fitness function evaluates the probability of the whole candidate sensor configuration producing an alarm for each of the releases and then combines these to give an average probability over the whole release set. This average probability of detection forms the basis of the primary fitness and the average of, warning time multiplied by probability of detection associated with each sensor, is the secondary fitness.

The GA for sensor placement is currently configured for roulette wheel selection, single point crossover and standard flip-bit mutation[9] but a later tuning phase of the work will involve investigation of different GA operators in order to improve optimisation.

An additional user requirement is that the sensor placement tool gives an indication of the final probability of detection and average warning time for the proposed sensor configuration, and that the user has the ability to modify the configuration and reassess these scores. This enables use of the tool to be an interactive session, allowing the user to iteratively explore the practicality/utility of proposed sensor configurations.

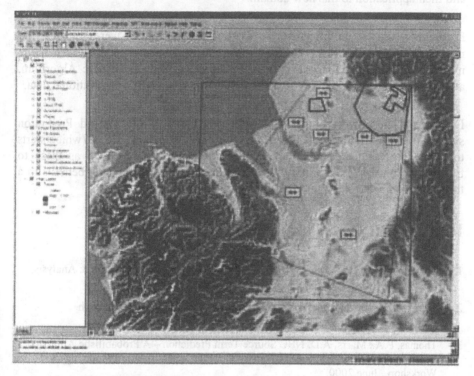

Figure 6: Screen shot from Dstl's sensor placement tool showing optimal placement of sensors (pink icons) for protection of the Protection Areas (blue polygons).

Development experience: The Sensor Placement Tool started as a concept in 2000 with the intention of replacing more manual methods of optimisation. Firstly a simplified computer model of the problem domain was constructed for objective evaluation of the best optimisation technique. It was felt important to capture, in this evaluation harness, the essence of the problem domain sufficiently so that an accurate assessment could be made, while minimising time-consuming detail (both model development time and run time). Striking the right balance between model simplicity and detail at this stage was challenging. Evaluation was performed on simple (low numbers of sensors) scenarios since an exhaustive search was performed for each scenario (taking several years of CPU time for more than 3 sensors) to obtain the absolute optimum sensor placement.

Conclusions

It was found that, in order to develop the capability of operational WMD Hazard Prediction, the contribution of three distinct AI technologies was necessary. Dstl, along with its contractors, has undertaken the integration of these AI technologies and their application to this new domain.

Furthermore, novel modifications to existing AI techniques were found to be necessary in order to fulfil the user requirements in this domain. Such novel modifications include: Secondary goal optimisation using a Genetic Algorithm, and generation of prior probability density function given NBC observational data.

Dstl's work in support of the UK Military's future WMD Hazard Prediction system, the NBC Battlespace Information System Application (BISA) (which starts to come into service from 2004) enables advanced solutions such as these to transition from the AI laboratory to real products, providing tangible benefits in a threat environment.

References:

1. The Strategic Defence Review: A New Chapter, Supporting Information & Analysis, Cm 5566 Vol II. July 2002.

2. Marrs, A.D. NBC hazard assessment using a graphical modelling approach. DERA/S&P/ SPI/TR980109/ 1.0. January 1999.

3. Thomas, P.A., Marrs, A.D. NBC Source Term Prediction – A Probabilistic Approach, Fourth Annual George Mason University Transport and Dispersion Modeling Workshop. June 2000.

4. Gordon, N.J, Salmond, D.J and Smith, A.F.M. A novel approach to non-linear/non-Gaussian Bayesian state estimation. IEE Proceedings on Radar, Sonar & Navigation, 1993.

5. Salmond, D.J. Mixture reduction algorithms for target tracking in clutter. Signal & Data Processing of Small Targets, edited by O. Drummond. 1990.

6. Hall, D.J. et al. The Urban Dispersion Model (UDM) version 2.2 Technical Documentation. DSTL/TR04774. September 2002.

7. Holland, J.H. Adaptation in natural and artificial systems. Ann Arbor, MI: The University of Michigan Press. 1975.

8. Thomas, P.A., et al. "What Should I Do?": Providing decision support in the NCBR environment. The First Joint Conference on Battle Management for Nuclear, Chemical, Biological and Radiological Defense. November 2002.

9. Whitley, D.A. Genetic Algorithm Tutorial, Fort Collins, Colorado, Statistics and Computing. 1994.

Using Domain Knowledge to Boost Case-Based Diagnosis: An Experimental Study in a Domain with Very Poor Data Quality

Lu Zhang, Frans Coenen, and Paul Leng

The Department of Computer Science, The University of Liverpool, Liverpool L69 3BX, UK
{lzhang, frans, phl}@csc.liv.ac.uk

Abstract

The quality of case data can be an important factor for a Case Based Reasoning (CBR) system. In our research, we are facing a diagnostic problem in a product maintenance domain, where a large volume of low quality case data is collected. In this paper, we report an experimental study of whether using domain knowledge can improve the performance of either non-diversified or diversified retrieval in this domain. As each case can be associated with some domain knowledge that can be easily obtained in this domain, we try to use it to assist case matching. Our experimental results show that the domain knowledge can significantly improve the performance of both the non-diversified and the diversified approaches. Furthermore, using the diversified approach seems to be of greater value when also using domain knowledge.

1 Introduction

Case Based Reasoning (CBR) is a multi-disciplinary subject that focuses on the reuse of experiences [1]. In particular, CBR has been applied to solve diagnosis problems (see e.g. [2] and [7]). An obvious advantage of case-based diagnostic systems is that these systems can be built without detailed information about the target domains. In such a case-based diagnosis system, the quality of case data is usually a key factor in the success of the system. However, in many domains there are already a large number of accumulated low quality cases. It therefore is useful to find a way to improve the data quality and thus make them usable for diagnostic purposes.

In our research, we are facing a diagnostic problem in a product maintenance domain, in which cases are mainly described by customers having very little knowledge of their products. Therefore, it cannot achieve a good performance by simply comparing the text description of the new case with those of the previous cases.

137

In this paper, we report our study of using domain knowledge to improve the data quality. Using domain knowledge for text classification has been studied in [8] and [9]. A preliminary report of this approach can be found in [13]. In our study, we use the location information generated for each case by human semi-experts as the domain knowledge, which will be used in the matching process. Our experimental results show that using domain knowledge can substantially increase the overall performance of the diagnostic system.

In a previous study, we found that diversifying retrieved cases (see e.g. [5], [6], [3], and [4]) can enhance the performance in this domain [12]. In this paper, we also use domain knowledge for the diversified approach. Our experimental results show that using domain knowledge can also improve the diversified approach. We also examine the impact of using domain knowledge on diversification. We find that diversification seems more effective when more domain knowledge is involved in the matching process.

The remainder of this paper is organised as follows. Section 2 provides a general description of the background of the domain. Section 3 presents the method of using domain knowledge in our domain. Section 4 describes the setting of our experiment. Section 5 presents the main experimental results. Section 6 concludes this paper.

2 The Stoves Project

2.1 The Diagnostic Problem

The diagnostic problem we are facing originates from the needs of a manufacturer of domestic appliances in a flexible manufacturing context, whose name is Stoves PLC. The company concerned can deliver more than 3000 versions of its cookers to customers, making it possible to satisfy a very wide range of different customer requirements. However, this creates a problem for the after-sale service, because of the difficulty in providing its field engineers with the information necessary to maintain cookers of all these different models. In general, field engineers may need to be able to deal with any problem concerning any of the sold cookers, which may include versions previously unknown to them. Producing conventional service manuals and other product documentation for each model variant clearly imposes unacceptable strains on the production cycle, and the resulting volume of documentation will be unmanageable for field engineers.

The current system used in Stoves employs a large after-sale services department consisting of customer call receivers and field engineers. The product maintenance procedure is depicted in Fig. 1. When a customer calls to report a fault, the customer call receiver will try to solve that case through a telephone dialogue. If he/she cannot do so, he/she will record the case in an after-sale services information system as an unsolved case. The system assigns recorded cases to field engineers each day, and field engineers go to the corresponding customers to solve the assigned cases. After solving a case, the field engineer will phone back to the after-sale services department to report the solved case and that case is recorded as completed in the system. All the data about previous cases is stored in the system for quite a long period of time.

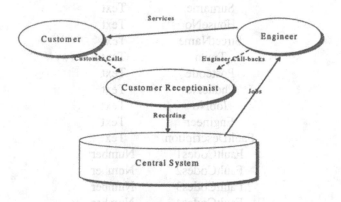

Fig. 1. Stoves' product maintenance procedure

2.2 Case-Based Diagnosis for Stoves

The Stoves Project [10] is a joint project supported by the DTI under the Foresight 'Link' programme, which is carried out in collaboration with Stoves PLC and some other industrial partners. The basic objective of the Stoves Project is to help Stoves PLC to decrease their maintenance costs. As a large maintenance department is managed in Stoves, a little progress may mean saving quite a large amount of money. Ideally our approach should also be generic and easy to be adapted for other manufacturers. To achieve this objective, we exploit a case-based approach [11]. The benefits for us are mainly two-fold. Firstly, none of the researchers really understand the mechanism of cookers, and in a case-based approach we can avoid knowing this in detail. This also makes the approach more generic than would be a method tailored to the product domain. Secondly, this approach allows us to take advantage of all the data recorded in the current system in Stoves. Typically, there will be more than 500 cases in one month.

However, the quality of the case data is a major concern. In fact, all the case descriptions are basically the telephone reports from the customers. As customers typically know very little about cookers, their reports are usually very imprecise. For this reason, our initial diagnostic system failed to achieve a satisfactory performance in some preliminary experiments.

3 Using Domain Knowledge

In Stoves' system, cases are mainly represented as a table in the database. The attributes of the table are listed in Table 1.

Attribute Name	Data Type
ID	AutoNumber
CallDate	Date/Time
Surname	Text
HouseNo	Text
StreetName	Text
Town	Text
Postcode	Text
PhoneNo	Text
JobNo	Text
Engineer	Text
FaultDescription	Text
FaultCodes1	Number
FaultCodes2	Number
FaultCodes3	Number
FaultCodes4	Number

Table 1. Original Case Attributes

A simple coding system is used for recording faults and corresponding actions. A fault and its corresponding action are recorded as four codes. The first fault code is called the *area code*, which denotes the main part of the cooker that the fault is in. For example, the *area code* '6' represents the main oven. The second code is called the *part code*, which denotes the sub-part in the main part. For example, the *part code* '17' represents the door handle. The third code is called the *fault code*, which denotes the actual fault. For example, the *fault code* '55' represents the 'loose wire' fault. The fourth code is called the *action code*, which denotes the action that has been taken to fix the fault. Presently, there are 8 choices for the first code, 194 choices for the second code, 59 choices for the third code, and 26 choices for the fourth code. The four codes are referred to as the four fault codes in Table 1.

From the above case representation, the original diagnostic problem is as follows. Given a text description of a new fault, the diagnosis system should try to find the three fault codes and the action code via matching the text description against previous cases. As the text descriptions are provided by customers who have very little knowledge about cookers, it is understandable that any method would not give a good performance. However, typically a customer call receiver can easily find the rough location of the reported fault, and record the location with the case description. Therefore, we think that using the location information provided by customer call receivers as domain knowledge in case matching may improve the quality of cases.

To evaluate whether and to what extent this case matching strategy using domain knowledge is beneficial, we performed an experimental study. Among the attributes in Table 1, most are for identifying the location of the customers and help field engineers to find their customers. As these attributes are irrelevant to diagnosis, we actually do not use them in our study. As we are interested in diagnosis, we also ignore the *action code*. The attributes used in our study are listed in Table 2.

Attribute Name	Data Type
ID	AutoNumber
FaultDescription	Text
FaultCodes1	Number
FaultCodes2	Number
FaultCodes3	Number

Table 2. Case Attributes in the Study

4 The Experiments

4.1 Experimental Subject: Three Case Matching Strategies

In our experiments, we evaluated three strategies using different amounts of location knowledge in the matching process. The first strategy examined is aiming at the original problem – just matching the text descriptions against previous descriptions. The second strategy is to assume that the correct area code can be provided by the customer call receiver and thus can be used in the matching process. In this strategy, only the cases that share the same area code with the new case are matched against the new case. The third strategy is to assume that both the correct area code and the correct part code can be provided by the customer call receiver and thus can be used in the matching process. In this strategy, only the cases that share both the same area code and the same part code with the new case are matched against the new case. The three strategies are illustrated in Fig 2.

The three strategies share the same similarity measure when determining the similarity between the description of a case in the case base and that of the new case. We exploit a simple method for matching two texts: After eliminating some stop-words (such as articles) in the two texts, we count the number of matched words as the similarity.

4.2 Experimental Objectives

The basic objective was to evaluate the performance of the above three strategies. What we hoped was to see the strategy using most domain knowledge to win the contest, although this seems quite natural. As in our previous study we found that diversification may increase the performance of diagnosis in this domain, we also wished to know what the performance of the three strategies would be when the retrieval set is diversified. We expected the strategy using most domain knowledge to also win in this context. Another interesting point is how the idea of using domain knowledge and the idea of diversification will interplay. Hopefully, they can be bound together to form the best solution.

```
Input: CaseBase, NewCase, k
Output: RetrievalSet
Strategy 1:
    Step 1: RetrievalSet←Φ
    Step 2: for each i in CaseBase
                If (similarity(i.description, NewCase.description)>0)
                    Add(RetrievalSet, i)
    Step 3: sort RetrievalSet according to similarity
    Step 4: delete cases other than most similar k cases in RetrievalSet


Strategy 2:
    Step 1: RetrievalSet←Φ
    Step 2: for each i in CaseBase
                If (i.area=NewCase.area and
                    similarity(i.description, NewCase.description)>0)
                    Add(RetrievalSet, i)
    Step 3: sort RetrievalSet according to similarity
    Step 4: delete cases other than most similar k cases in RetrievalSet


Strategy 3:
    Step 1: RetrievalSet←Φ
    Step 2: for each i in CaseBase
                If (i.area=NewCase.area and and i.part=NewCase.part
and
                    similarity(i.description, NewCase.description)>0)
                    Add(RetrievalSet, i)
    Step 3: sort RetrievalSet according to similarity
    Step 4: delete cases other than most similar k cases in RetrievalSet
```

Fig. 2. Three case matching strategies

4.3 Evaluation Criterion: Retrieval Set and Hit Rate

To increase the probability that the actual fault will be identified correctly, a set of similar cases is retrieved, rather than just the single most similar case. It is hoped that one of the similar cases may have the same fault as the case under diagnosis. Therefore, a well-trained user can analyse the retrieval set to find the fault. To evaluate the success of the retrieval, we use the concept of '*hit rate*'. The *hit rate* is defined as the number of cases under diagnosis whose faults appear in the faults of their *retrieval set*, divided by the total number of cases under diagnosis. If, for example, there are 100 cases under diagnosis, and in 80 cases the corresponding retrieval set includes a case that suggests a correct diagnosis of the fault under consideration, then the *hit rate* is therefore 80%.

Obviously, increasing the size of retrieval sets can usually increase the hit rate. However, as well as the cost of retrieving more cases, a larger retrieval set increases the difficulty in analysing the results to correctly identify the fault. So, in general it is ideal to have a high hit rate when the retrieval set size is still small. In our experiments, we record the hit rates of the three strategies under various retrieval set sizes.

4.4 Experimental Process

To evaluate the performance of the above three case matching strategies, we performed some experiments on some real data obtained from Stoves. We collected 1988 cases recorded in the after-sale services information system during a period in 2001. As the original cases are represented as values in the attributes in Table 1, we extracted only the values in the attributes in Table 2 to form our case base.

We then randomly separated the 1988 cases into a training set containing 1000 cases, used to create the case base, and a test set containing 988 cases. For different values of the retrieval set size k, we recorded the hit rates of the three case matching methods with and without diversification. To avoid occasional results, we performed the experiments three times using different random separations.

5 Experimental Results

5.1 Using Domain Knowledge without Diversification

The results of the first experiment on using domain knowledge without diversification are depicted in Fig. 3. In general, the hit rates of all the three strategies will increase with the increase of the retrieval set sizes. Whatever the retrieval set size is, the third strategy (using both the area code and the part code as domain knowledge) is always significantly higher than the second strategy (using only area code as domain knowledge) and the first (not using any domain knowledge). When the retrieval set size is 4, there is the maximum difference of hit rates between the third strategy and the second strategy – 26.72 percentage points. When the retrieval set size is 7, there is the maximum difference of hit rates between the third strategy and the first strategy – 37.75 percentage points. On average, there is a 25.34 percentage point difference between the third strategy and the second strategy, and a 35.94 percentage point difference between the third strategy and the first strategy, when the retrieval set size is between 3 and 10. From this, it is clear that using domain knowledge for this problem can significantly increase the hit rates.

We can see that highest hit rate of the third strategy is only around 60%, so even using the area code and the part code as domain knowledge gives only moderate success in diagnosis using this poor-quality case data. However, the curve of the third strategy in this figure indicates another merit of using domain knowledge. By using domain knowledge, the highest hit rate is approached when the retrieval set size is still manageable. In this experiment, when the retrieval set size is 13, the hit rate of the third strategy reaches 57.49%, only 2.02 percentage points less than the maximum, and a hit rate of over 50% is achieved with only 6 cases.

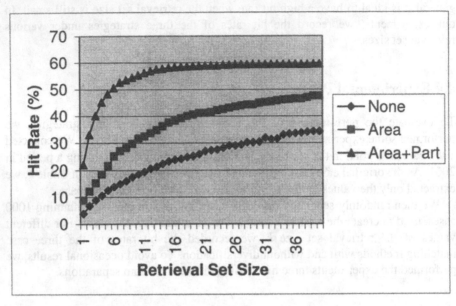

Fig. 3. Using domain knowledge without diversification (experiment 1)

Similar results were obtained in the second and third experiments, depicted in Fig. 4 and Fig. 5. The results of the three experiments are summarised in Table 3.

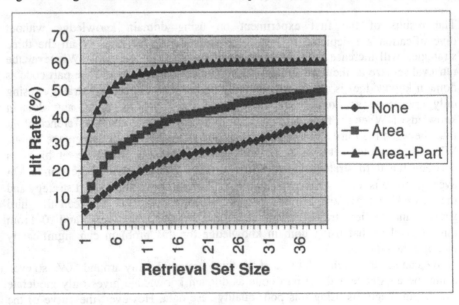

Fig. 4. Using domain knowledge without diversification (experiment 2)

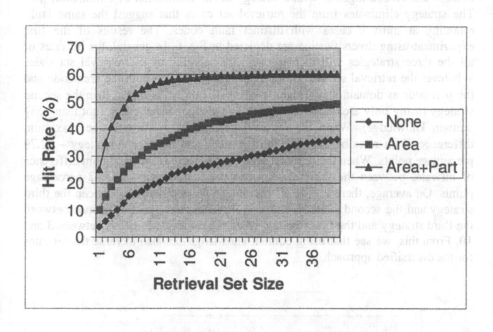

Fig. 5. Using domain knowledge without diversification (experiment 3)

Experiment	1	2	3
Maximum Difference between Strategy 3 and Strategy 2 (Retrieval Set Size)	26.72 (4)	24.60 (5)	25.00 (6)
Maximum Difference between Strategy 3 and Strategy 1 (Retrieval Set Size)	37.75 (7)	37.55 (6)	37.55 (8)
Average Difference between Strategy 3 and Strategy 2 (3-10)	25.34	23.96	23.70
Average Difference between Strategy 3 and Strategy 1 (3-10)	35.94	36.32	35.89
Difference with Highest (Strategy 3 when the Retrieval Set Size is 13)	2.02	2.53	2.23

Table 3. Summary of experiments on using domain knowledge without diversification

5.2 Using Domain Knowledge with Diversification

The second set of experiments we conducted examined the effect of using this domain knowledge together with a strategy of 'diversification by elimination' [4]. The strategy eliminates from the retrieval set cases that suggest the same fault, retaining at most k cases with distinct fault codes. The results of the first experiment using diversification are depicted in Fig. 6. In general, the hit rates of all the three strategies will increase with the increase of the retrieval set sizes. Whatever the retrieval set size is, the third strategy (using both the area code and the part code as domain knowledge) is always significantly higher than the second strategy (using only area code as domain knowledge) and the first (not using any domain knowledge). When the retrieval set size is 4, there is the maximum difference of hit rates between the third strategy and the second strategy – 32.79 percentage points. When the retrieval set size is 6, there is the maximum difference of hit rates between the third strategy and the first strategy – 43.42 percentage points. On average, there is a 29.07 percentage point difference between the third strategy and the second strategy, and a 41.46 percentage point difference between the third strategy and the first strategy, when the retrieval set size is between 3 and 10. From this, we see that using domain knowledge can also increase the hit rates for the diversified approach.

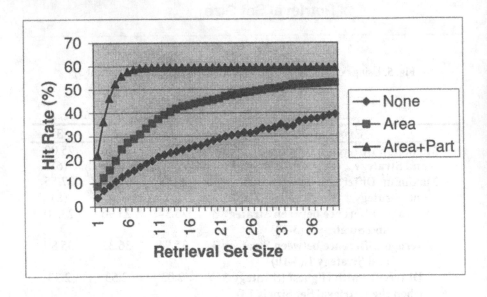

Fig. 6. Using domain knowledge with diversification (experiment 1)

As with the results in the experiments on the non-diversified approach, the curve of the third strategy in this figure indicates that this strategy can nearly reach the highest hit rate when the retrieval set size is still manageable. In this experiment, when the retrieval set size is 7, the hit rate of the third strategy reaches 58.60%, almost the maximum. Similar results were obtained in the second and third experiments, depicted in Fig. 7 and Fig. 8. The results of the three experiments are summarised in Table 4.

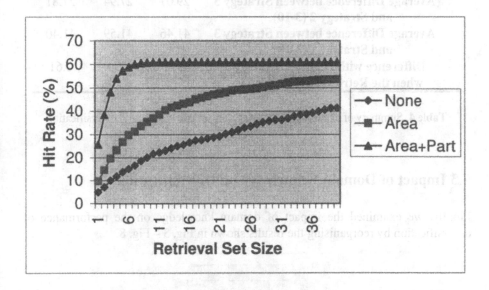

Fig. 7. Using domain knowledge with diversification (experiment 2)

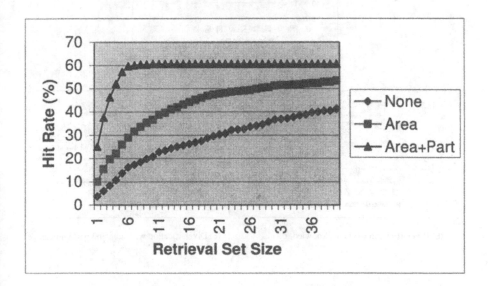

Fig. 8. Using domain knowledge with diversification (experiment 3)

Experiment	1	2	3
Maximum Difference between Strategy 3 and Strategy 2 (Retrieval Set Size)	32.79 (4)	30.36 (5)	31.17 (5)
Maximum Difference between Strategy 3 and Strategy 1 (Retrieval Set Size)	43.42 (6)	43.72 (6)	43.52 (5)
Average Difference between Strategy 3 and Strategy 2 (3-10)	29.07	27.94	27.81
Average Difference between Strategy 3 and Strategy 1 (3-10)	41.46	41.59	41.40
Difference with Highest (Strategy 3 when the Retrieval Set Size is 7)	0.91	0.91	0.61

Table 4. Summary of experiments on using domain knowledge with diversification

5.3 Impact of Domain Knowledge on Diversification

Finally, we examined the impact of domain knowledge on the performance of diversification by reorganising the results shown in Fig. 3 – Fig. 8.

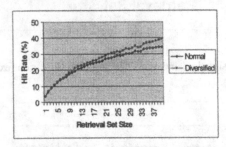

(a) Diversification with no domain knowledge

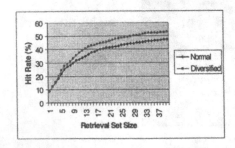

(b) Diversification with area knowledge

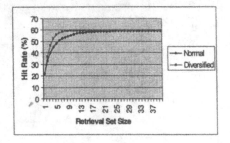

(c) Diversification with area and part knowledge

Fig. 9. Impact of domain knowledge on diversification (experiment 1)

Fig. 9 depicts three line charts reformed from Fig. 3 and Fig. 6 based on the first experiment. In Fig. 9(a) where no domain knowledge is used in case matching, the diversified approach and the normal approach cannot be separated when the retrieval set size is between 1 and 10, and the difference then rises steadily as the set becomes larger. However, in Fig. 9(b) where the area knowledge is used, the two approaches are separable when the retrieval set size is larger than 4, and reaches a maximum when the retrieval set size is 33. In Fig. 9(c) where both area knowledge and part knowledge are used in case matching, the diversified approach and the normal approach can be separated when the retrieval set size is between 2 and 16. The difference between the two approaches is greatest, 7.48 percentage points, when the retrieval set size is only 5.

From the above results, it seems that the more domain knowledge is used, the more the advantage of the diversified approach is over the non-diversified approach. Firstly, the more domain knowledge is used, the more likely it is that the two approaches are separable when the retrieval set size is small. Secondly, the more domain knowledge is used, the smaller the retrieval set size is, when the difference between the two approaches is maximised. Finally, the more domain knowledge is used, the bigger is the maximum difference between the approaches. Similarly, we can find the same impacts in the second experiment and the third experiment, whose results are depicted in Fig. 10 and Fig. 11.

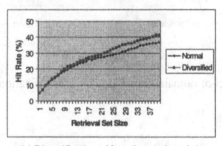

(a) Diversification with no domain knowledge

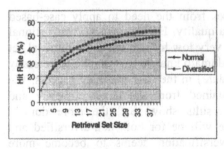

(b) Diversification with area knowledge

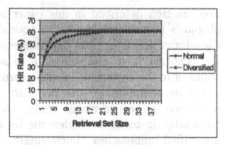

(c) Diversification with area and part knowledge

Fig. 10. Impact of domain knowledge on diversification (experiment 2)

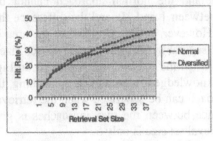

(a) Diversification with no domain knowledge

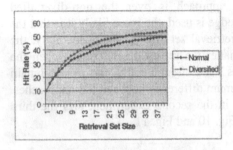

(b) Diversification with area knowledge

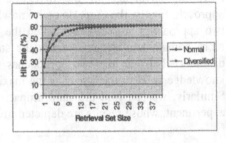

(c) Diversification with area and part knowledge

Fig. 11. Impact of domain knowledge on diversification (experiment 3)

6 Conclusion

The research described in this paper arises from the need to apply case-based diagnosis in a domain with very poor data quality. For this reason, conventional Case-Based Reasoning can only achieve a very low hit rate when the retrieval set size is not too large. Our solution is to use domain knowledge (which can be easily obtained in the current maintenance procedure) in the case matching process. We tested our solution on the real data obtained from the target company and performed an experimental study. Our results show that, the more domain knowledge is used, the higher the hit rate will be for both non-diversified and diversified approaches. Interestingly, diversification seems to become more effective when more domain knowledge is used.

Acknowledgements

The research described in this paper is supported by the Department of Trade and Industry under the Foresight 'Link' programme. We wish to express our thanks to our partners in the project, Stoves PLC and NA Software Ltd, and in particular to Colin Johnson, Prof Mike Delves, and the Project Monitor, Stan Price.

References

1. Aha, D. W.: The Omnipresence of Case-Based Reasoning in Science and Application. Knowledge-Based Systems, 11(5-6), (1998) 261-273
2. Auriol, E., Crowder, R. M., McKendrick, R., Rowe, R.: Integrating Case-Based Reasoning and Hypermedia Documentation: An Application for the Diagnosis of a Welding Robot at Odense Steel Shipyard. Engineering Applications of Artificial Intelligence, Vol. 12, (1999) 691-703
3. Bradley, K., Smyth, B.: Improving Recommendation Diversity. In: Proceedings of the Twelfth Irish Conference on Artificial Intelligence and Cognitive Science, Maynooth, Ireland (2001) 85-94
4. McSherry, D.: Increasing Recommendation Diversity Without Loss of Similarity. In: Proceedings of the Sixth UK CBR Workshop, 10 December (2001) 23-31
5. Smyth, B., Cotter, P.: A Personalised TV Listing Service for the Digital TV Age. Knowledge-Based Systems, 13 (2000) 53-59.
6. Smyth, B., McClave, P.: Similarity vs. Diversity. In: Aha, D.W., Watson, I. (eds) Case-Based Reasoning Research and Development. LNAI, Vol. 2080. Springer-Verlag, Berlin Heidelberg (2001) 347-361
7. Varma, A., Roddy, N.: ICARUS: Design and Deployment of a Case-Based Reasoning System for Locomotive Diagnosis. Engineering Applications of Artificial Intelligence, Vol. 12, (1999) 681-690
8. Zelikovitz, S., Hirsh, H.: Improving Short Text Classification Using Unlabeled Background Knowledge to Assess Document Similarity. In: Proceedings of the Seventeenth International Conference on Machine Learning, (2000) 1183–1190
9. Zelikovitz, S., Hirsh, H.: Using LSI for Text Classification in the Presence of Background Text. In: Proceedings of the Tenth Conference for Information and Knowledge Management (2001) 113-118
10. Zhang, W., Coenen, F., Leng, P.,: On-Line Support for Field Service Engineers in a Flexible Manufacturing Environment: the Stoves Project. In: Proceedings of IeC '2000 Conference, Manchester (2000) 31-40
11. Zhang, L., Coenen, F., Leng, P.,: A Case Based Diagnostic Tool in a Flexible Manufacturing Context. In: Proceedings of the Sixth UK CBR Workshop, 10 December (2001) 61-69
12. Zhang, L., Coenen, F., Leng, P.: An Experimental Study of Increasing Diversity for Case-Based Diagnosis. In: Proceedings of 6th European Conference on Case Based Reasoning (ECCBR), 4-7 September (2002) Advances in Case-Based Reasoning, LNAI 2416, 448-459
13. Zhang, L., Coenen, F., Leng, P.: Can Domain Knowledge Help Case Based Diagnosis? In: Proceedings of the Seventh UK CBR Workshop, 10 December (2002) 1-8

An Environment for the Efficient Analysis of Defining Relationships among Design Entities

Nikolidakis E.A. and Dentsoras A.J.

Dept. of Mech. Eng. & Aeronautics, University Patras,

Patra, Greece

dentsora@mech.upatras.gr

www.mech.upatras.gr/~dentsora

Abstract

An integrated environment is presented that helps a designer to perform efficient dynamic analysis of the defining relationships among the different entities that form the knowledge for a design problem. This environment extends the capabilities and adds new features to a program already used for performing analysis of design relationships.

The formation of the design knowledge is a highly dynamic iterative process that takes place through multiple design cycles. During each cycle, defining relationships among the design entities are established, deleted or modified. The presented environment provides tools for representing these relationships, for analysing them in terms of design information importance and required design effort and, finally, for locating possible inconsistencies among them.

In cases of design problems that involve large numbers of design entities and defining relationships, the time efficiency of the performed analysis is ensured by keeping to a minimum any need for exhaustive search of the design space. This is obtained by storing additional information for every entity and for its relationships to other design entities.

The proposed environment acts as an assistant for the designer by suggesting the optimum order for the instantiation of the independent design entities so that important information is produced with the least effort and relatively early in the design process. It also facilitates the decision-making process at any time during the design process since it provides the possibility of examining multiple design alternatives. An example case of design calculations for a wire rope demonstrates both the functionality and efficiency of the environment.

1.   Introduction

In design, the ultimate goal is the generation of one or more design solutions that should optimally satisfy the stated functional requirements for a product, a machine or a system. The design process is characterized by the intensive exploitation of design knowledge. So, as an activity of knowledge representation and manipulation, design has been the subject of intensive research during the last years. The accumulated design experience and the advances achieved especially in the field of Artificial Intelligence promoted significant progress for issues such as design process representation ([1], [2]), design knowledge representation and handling ([3], [4], [5], [6], [7], [8], [9]), design reuse and machine learning in design ([1], [10], [11]) and for the establishment of a robust, domain-independent design theory ([12], [13]).

In every design problem, there is always the need to establish defining relationships (functional, topological, associative etc.) among the different design entities. These relationships form complicated structures. The ensemble of these structures at any time may be considered as the sum of the currently available design knowledge [7]. The relationships should be tested for their validity through instantiations of the attributes of the interrelated design entities. The designer guides this instantiation process through his general knowledge, skill and expertise.

Design is a data-driven process. The data types used for initiating, preserving and finally completing the design process present an interesting variety. Part of this data plays a decisive role from the very beginning of the design process and affects its evolution. It is usually involved in many design tasks and covers multiple design stages in the sense that it affects value assignment procedures and decision-making processes. In this context, its effects are sometimes traced with difficulty, especially in large-scale design problems. Some other data is less important and its impact is restricted in small design subspaces, searched during the later design phases. In any case, design knowledge always presents itself through dynamic and complicated forms and structures and it is not always easy to establish concise methods and techniques to handle it efficiently.

Among the different factors that affect both the result and the process of the design itself, the experience of the designer plays always a significant role. A. Court [14], in his work, presents a discussion on the relationship between the designer's personal knowledge and the design information during new product development. Concerning the information handled during design, S. B. Shooter et al. [15] present a model for the flow of design information that is sufficiently formal to support eventually a semantics-based approach for developing information exchange standards. Nam P. Suh [12], the founder of the axiomatic design theory, presents a general theory for system design based on axiomatic design [13]. Within this work, the information content of a design is redefined in order to be adapted to the system concept.   D.D. Frey et al. [8] use the axiomatic theory of Suh and consider the case of decoupled designs. They prove that the information content for this type of designs cannot be computed.

Within the context of the effort of differentiating among different types of design information, F. Franceschini and S. Rossetto [9] consider the problem of the "prioritization" of the technical design characteristics of a product and present an interactive algorithm used for a better support of the engineering design process by means of the quality function deployment (QFD).

Considering design knowledge representation issues that could be proved useful for the current approach, Dentsoras [7] and Tsalidis and Dentsoras [4] proposed a design knowledge representation formalism that is based on a separation of the set of design entities in two types: dependents and primaries. The data for the instantiation of these entities, is usually provided by the designer and/or is extracted from other external sources such as databases, previous design cases etc.

In a previous paper by Drakatou and Dentsoras [16], it has been proven that the instantiation of the primary entities is not a random process. It has been also shown that during the instantiation process of the primary entities, some entities must be instantiated prior to some others due to objective reasons that have to do with their significance for the design information generation process. In the aforementioned research work as well as in a newer work that has been submitted for presentation and is currently under review, exhaustive design space search has been used in order to establish the instantiation priorities and to produce relative design information.

During the last years, there have been published some significant papers on the techniques and methods for implementing efficient search of the design space. The reason for that is the fact that there is always a need not only for finding more efficient design solutions but also for decreasing the design cost in terms of time, especially when the designers are faced with large-scale design problems. In a paper by Y.S. Ong and A.J. Keane [17], an automatic and adaptive Domain Knowledge Based (DKB) Search Advisor is proposed. The advisor contains domain knowledge and helps the designers to decrease the cost of design-space search and improve the quality of the resulting designs. W. Y. Zhang et al. [18] present a knowledge-based approach for automating the functional design of mechanical systems. The automated functional reasoning strategy is based on a heuristic method that uses a heuristic evaluation function for searching the design space for behavioral configuration.

A. Gelsey et al. [19] proposed SST, which is a suite of tools for searching continuous design spaces. A. Gelsey et al. [20] proposed also a new design optimization methodology that uses modeling knowledge to guide the design space search. The search is guided by model constraints functions that act as constraint inputs to an optimization numerical method. F.J. Vico et al. [21] presented a new methodology to implement design synthesis that is composed of two different modules: a search method (implemented by genetic algorithms) and a fitness function. Z. Yao and A.L. Johnson [22] considered the variables and the constraints that form the feasible solution space and provided a domain propagation search algorithm that estimates the feasible solution space. Finally, L. Steinberg [23] presented an algorithm called Highest Utility First Search (HUFS) for searching trees that arise in problems which involve candidate designs at several levels of abstraction.

Exhaustive search algorithms are time-consuming and they become even slower as the numbers of the design entities and of the relationships among them increase. It is evident that searching the whole design space is not the most efficient algorithm to be used. This fact becomes more obvious in large-scale design problems where hundreds or even thousands of design entities are involved. In the present paper, an integrated environment is described that is capable of performing the following main design tasks:

- Calculations of the design importance and the required design effort for every design entity used for the design knowledge representation. These calculations are based on the complete dependency matrix (Q-matrix) of the design problem
- Generation of design graphs that relate both the design importance and the required design effort with the design cycles, the latter perceived as a discrete design time measuring unit
- The generation of the instantiation list of primary entities that ensures the production of design information of maximum importance with the least design effort
- The exploration of design entity instantiation alternatives accompanied by the relevant design graphs
- Use of a new search algorithm that is based on a process of storing additional relational information for every design entity used for the design knowledge representation

The environment was developed in C++, a language that fully supports Object-Oriented Programming.

2. The environment and the search algorithm

2.1. The search algorithm

In order for the detailed analysis of the proposed environment and the adopted search algorithm to be fully comprehensible, some basic terms used for the formation of the necessary theoretical background are presented. A more extended analysis on these terms and their interrelations is given in [16].

A *design entity* is a discrete design object of either a qualitative or quantitative nature. A *design descriptor* is any meaningful, identifiable and unique word or phrase that describes an entity [16]. Typical structures for the entities and the descriptors are shown in figure 1.a.

A *primary descriptor* is a descriptor that possesses the unique property to be an independent entity for the design problem under consideration. Once instantiated, the primary descriptor determines (values), through the established defining relationships, the rest, non-primary, *dependent descriptors* (see Figure 1.b). The *importance* of a dependent descriptor is defined as the total number of other, dependent descriptors whose instantiation depends upon it and the *dependence value* for a primary descriptor is defined as the number of dependent descriptors whose instantiation depends upon this primary descriptor.

For the instantiation of a dependent descriptor, a discrete number of non-primary descriptors must be instantiated. This event takes place during the design process and at discrete steps, or in other words, *design cycles*. The total number of primary descriptor instantiations needed for the instantiation of a single dependent descriptor is defined as the *required design effort* for that descriptor.

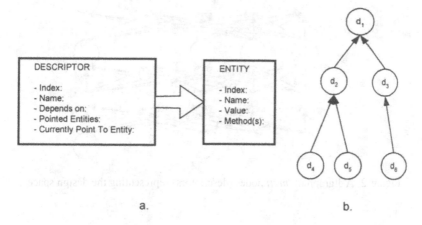

a.   b.

Figure 1. Representation of design Knowledge: a. Typical structures for entities and descriptors, b. Primary and dependent descriptors

Table 1. Information required for a descriptor and the relevant sets

Set	Set description
H	The descriptors on which a descriptor depends directly
C	The descriptors on which a descriptor depends directly or indirectly
A	The descriptors that are directly affected by a descriptor
P	The descriptors that are directly or indirectly affected by a descriptor
D	The primary descriptors on which a descriptor depends

In order to determine the importance, the dependence value and the required design effort, the established associative relationships among the descriptors must be searched [16] and a depth-first method [2] may be used in order to produce the required information (see Table 1). In the present work, a technique of storing additional relevant information for each descriptor and thus avoiding exhaustive space search is used. According to this technique, the information stored within every design descriptor is updated only when a relevant change in the design space (represented as a digraph) occurs. The proposed algorithm does not require large computational power. The only additional cost that has to be paid for the significant reduction of the computational power is a slight increase of the memory needed to store the additional information for each design descriptor.

Consider a design space represented by a digraph of *m* lines of nodes (descriptors) each line containing *n* nodes (descriptors). This digraph of *mxn* nodes (descriptors) represents the design space. Assuming that the design space is very dense in relationships among the descriptors (see Figure 2), then each descriptor is connected to all descriptors of the lower line except of the descriptors of the bottom line.

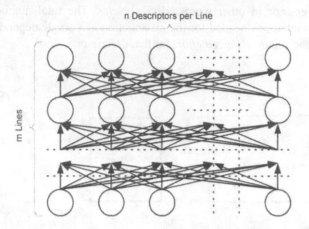

Figure 2. A digraph of $m \times n$ nodes (descriptors) representing the design space

If $d(i, j)$, $i \neq 0, i \neq m$ is the descriptor in the i-line and the j-column, then an exhaustive search method would search two digraphs, namely, the sub-digraph that contains the descriptors on which the specified descriptor depends and the sub-digraph that contains the descriptor that the specified descriptor affects. Then the total number of descriptors that must be visited is equal to:

$$N = n^{(m-i)} + n^{(i-1)}$$

(1)

a number that is much greater than the total number of the descriptors since, during the exhaustive search, each descriptor is visited for more than one time.

Table 2. Sets for descriptor i in the $m \times n$ design space

Set	Set Description	Set cardinality
H	Descriptors on which the descriptor depends directly	n
C	Descriptors on which the descriptor depends directly or indirectly	$(m-1)n$
A	Descriptors directly affected by the descriptor	n
P	All the descriptors that are directly or indirectly affected by a descriptor	$(i-1)n$
D	Primary descriptors on which the descriptor depends	n

The manipulation of the design knowledge includes the following four operations:

1. Adding a new descriptor
2. Removing an existing descriptor
3. Adding a new relationship between two descriptors and
4. Removing a new relationship between two descriptors

The addition of a new descriptor is made without cost since it does not affect any existing relationships and a cost arises as soon as new relationships to the new descriptor are established. Deletion of a descriptor is only allowed when this descriptor is not related to other descriptors. This implies that prior to the descriptor's deletion, the relationships in which it participates must be removed. Finally, the modification of a relationship is considered as equivalent to a deletion of that relationship and then to the addition of a new one.

The addition and the deletion of a relationship are two operations that may modify the stored information for a descriptor. Assume that a new relationship is added to the design space, so that the descriptor d_1 is declared to depend upon the descriptor d_2. The algorithm initially checks whether the relationship to be added already exists. It also checks the possibility of producing a circular reference. If H_i, C_i, A_i, P_i, D_i are the sets for the descriptor d_i, then, for the descriptor d_1, the relationship does not exist if $H_1 \cap \{d_1\} = \varnothing$ and there is no danger of producing a circular reference if $P_1 \cap \{d_2\} = \varnothing$.

Adding a relationship modifies the stored information in some descriptors. For example, the updated sets for the descriptors d_1 and d_2 will be the following:

$$H_1' = H_1 \cup d_2$$

$$C_1' = C_1 \cup d_2 \cup C_2 \qquad\qquad H_2' = H_2$$

$$A_1' = A_1 \qquad\qquad\qquad C_2' = C_2$$

$$P_1' = P_1 \qquad\qquad\qquad A_2' = A_2 \cup d_1 \qquad\qquad\qquad (2)$$

$$D_1' = \begin{cases} D_1 \cup D_2, & if\ D_2 \neq \varnothing \\ D_1 \cup \{d_2\}, & if\ D_2 = \varnothing \end{cases} \qquad \begin{matrix} P_2' = P_2 \cup d_1 \cup P_1 \\ D_2' = D_2 \end{matrix}$$

It must be noticed that the addition of a new relationship between d_1 and d_2 affects all the descriptors affected by d_1 and all the descriptors on which d_2 depends. This implies modifications of the sets of Table 1.

Deleting a relationship modifies the stored information in some descriptors. If:

$h_{1_i}', h_{1_i} \in H_1', i = 1, 2, ..., |H_1'|$ are elements of the H_1' set on which d1 depends

directly and $C_i^{h_{1_i}}, D_i^{h_{1_i}}$ are the C and D sets of the descriptor h_{1_i},

$a_{2_i}', a_{2_i} \in A_2', i = 1, 2, ..., |A_2'|$ are the elements of the A_2' set directly affected by d_2 after

the relationship deletion and $P_i^{a_{2_i}}$ is the P set of the descriptor a_{2_i}', then the updated

sets for the descriptors d_1 and d_2 will be the following:

$$H_1' = H_1 - d_2 \qquad\qquad H_2' = H_2$$

$$C_1' = C_1^{h_{1_i}} \cup C_2^{h_{1_i}} \cup ... \cup C_{|H_1'|}^{h_{1_i}} \qquad C_2' = C_2$$

$$A_1' = A_1 \qquad\qquad A_2' = A_2 - \{d_1\} \qquad\qquad\qquad (3)$$

$$P_1' = P_1 \qquad\qquad P_2' = P_1^{a_{1_i}} \cup P_2^{a_{1_i}} \cup ... \cup P_{|A_2'|}^{a_{1_i}}$$

$$D_1' = D_1^{h_{1_i}} \cup D_2^{h_{1_i}} \cup ... \cup D_{|H_1'|}^{h_{1_i}} \qquad D_2' = D_2$$

The above process must be repeated for every descriptor that belongs to the set P_1 and for every descriptor that belongs to the set C_2.

If $S_1, S_2, ..., S_k$ are k descriptor sets with $n_1, n_2, ..., n_k$ elements each and N is the total number of the design descriptors, then, according to the current algorithm, the set union $S_1 \cup S_2 \cup ... \cup S_k$ requires at maximum $2\sum_{i=1}^{k} n_k + N$ iterations. If each set contains $(N-i)$, $i=1,2,...,k$ elements (so that there is not cyclic references) and $k=N$ then the required iterations in order to form the set union is equal to N^2. During the addition or the deletion of a relation, the descriptors that are affected are already known and for that reason, the maximum number of the descriptors that are visited is equal to the total number of descriptors N.

The worst performance of the algorithm occurs when a relation is deleted, because in that case, the number of the unions between the sets is greater than the corresponding number in the case of the relation addition. The number of unions that has to be calculated is equal to:

$$2(|H_1'| - 1) + (|A_2'| - 1) \qquad\qquad\qquad (4)$$

and since $|H_1'| < N$ and $|A_2'| < N$

this implies that $2(|H_1'| - 1) + (|A_2'| - 1) < 2(N-1) + (N-1) = 3(N-1)$.

Consequently, the total number of iterations needed - in the case that the algorithm has the worst performance - is less than $3N^2(N-1)$.

From the above short analysis it becomes clear that the proposed algorithm:

- Performs much better than the exhaustive search algorithms where the number of iterations increases exponentially with the number of the descriptors

- It does not require any search in order to present additional information for a different descriptor since this information is always available through the sets that are stored with each descriptor

- Search is only required only whenever the designer adds or removes a relationship. This fact gives an important performance benefit over the algorithms that do not store additional information for every descriptor.

2.2. The environment

The user interface of the environment developed is shown in Figure 3. Changes in the design knowledge are made through context menus, while the update of the instantiation list and the checks for cyclical references or duplicated design relationships of the primary descriptors are performed automatically. The environment contains five tabs, each of which gives a different view of the design knowledge. More specific:

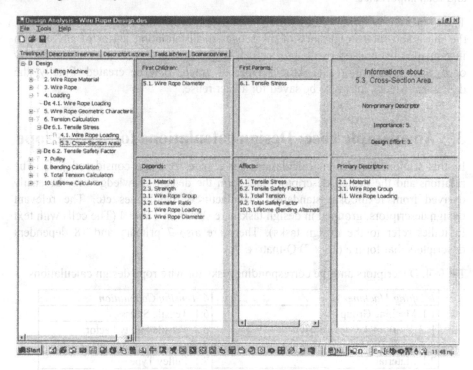

Figure 3: The user interface of the program.

The first tab (Tree Input) is used for working on the design descriptors and for configuring the information on:

- The descriptors on which the currently selected descriptor depends directly and indirectly
- The descriptors that it affects directly and indirectly
- The primary descriptors on which the currently selected descriptor depends directly or indirectly and

- The design importance of this descriptor as well as the design effort required to instantiate it

The second tab (Descriptor Tree View) presents the full trees of the descriptors on which the current descriptor depends and of the descriptors it affects. The third tab (Descriptor List View) presents the sorted Q-matrix.

The fourth tab (Descriptor Task View) presents the primary descriptor instantiation order for a design task to be completed and the design tasks in a completion order corresponding to the suggested instantiation list. Finally, the fifth tab (Scenario View) presents, among other, the mean importance and the total importance for every design cycle. Users are free to create alternative instantiation lists, to view the instantiated descriptors per design cycle as well as the values of the mean importance and total importance.

The Q-matrix, the primary descriptor instantiation order, the task completion order, the mean and total importance of the suggested instantiation list or of any custom instantiation list created by the user can all be exported to Excel either automatically or by user intervention and various types of graphs may be created. Finally, the design knowledge may also be saved for a later reuse.

3. An example case: Design calculations for a wire rope

In this section, the design calculations for a wire rope are considered [24]. The relations and the design descriptors that form the design knowledge may be easily derived from textbooks, standards, manufacturers' catalogues etc. The relevant design descriptors, grouped in design tasks, are shown in Table 4 (The cells with text in italics refer to the design tasks). There are also 7 primary and 18 dependent descriptors that form a (18 x 7) Q-matrix.

Table 4: Descriptors and the corresponding tasks for wire rope design calculations

1. Lifting Machine	*6. Tension Calculation*
1.1. Machine Group	6.1. Tensile Stress
1.2. Working Cycles per Hour	6.2. Tensile Safety Factor
2. Wire Rope Material	*7. Pulley*
2.1. Material	7.1. Pulley Type
2.2. Modulus of Elasticity	7.2. Pulley Diameter
2.3. Strength	7.3. Winding Factor
3. Wire Rope	7.4. C Factor
3.1. Wire Rope Group	7.5. Radius of Pulley Groove
3.2. Diameter Ratio	*8. Bending Calculation*
3.3. Type	8.1. Tension owing to Bending
4. Loading	*9. Total Tension Calculation*
4.1. Wire Rope Loading	9.1. Total Tension
5. Wire Rope Geometric Characteristics	9.2. Total Safety Factor
5.1 . Wire Rope Diameter	*10. Lifetime Calculation*
5.2. Wire Diameter	10.1. Coefficient A

Table 5: The Q-matrix for the wire rope design case

	2.1	3.1	4.1	1.2	7.1	3.3	7.5
2.3	T	F	F	F	F	F	F
3.2	T	T	F	F	F	F	F
1.1	F	F	F	T	F	F	F
5.1	T	T	T	F	F	F	F
7.4	F	F	F	T	T	F	F
2.2	T	F	F	F	F	F	F
5.3	T	T	T	F	F	F	F
7.2	F	F	T	T	T	F	F
6.1	T	T	T	F	F	F	F
5.2	T	T	T	F	F	F	F
10.1	F	F	F	F	F	T	T
10.2	T	T	F	F	F	T	F
6.2	T	T	T	F	F	F	F
8.1	T	T	T	T	T	F	F
9.1	T	T	T	T	T	F	F
9.2	T	T	T	T	T	F	F
7.3	T	T	T	T	T	F	F
10.3	T	T	T	T	T	T	T

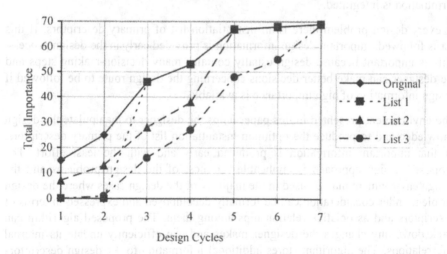

Figure 4: Wire rope design: Total importance of the produced design information vs. the number of completed design cycles for various instantiation list configurations.

The suggested primary instantiation list is formed by the elements of the first row of the Q-matrix and corresponds to the following list:

1. Wire Rope Material - 2. Wire Rope Group - 3. Wire Rope Loading - 4. Working Cycles per Hour- 5. Pulley Type - 6. Type - 7. Radius of Pulley Groove.

The importance of the produced design information may be related to the number of already completed design cycles, as is shown in Figure 4. On the x-axis the number of design cycles is represented and on the y-axis the total importance of the produced design information is shown. The first one corresponds to the original instantiation list suggested by the Q-matrix. The other three correspond to modified lists. It is clear from the figure that the suggested list produces important information early in the design process.

4. Conclusions

Manipulation of design knowledge takes place intensively throughout the design process. In complex design problems that are usually characterized by large number of design entities and relationships among them, this manipulation becomes a difficult task.

The use of an efficient algorithm to update the design knowledge is a very important factor, as design is a dynamic process, during which the designer performs many changes to the design knowledge. This is also true in the initial stages of the design where the user adds new design descriptors and relations. With the algorithm that the environment discussed in the present paper is based on, the analysis of the design knowledge happens gradually, as the user adds new descriptors and relationships, instead of searching the whole design space only when the design knowledge formulation is integrated.

In every design problem there is an instantiation list of primary descriptors. If this list is followed, important design information is provided early in the design process. This is important because design usually contains many decision-making steps and the designer can make better decisions concerning the design route to be followed if design information of high importance is available.

The environment presented in this paper helps the designer to manipulate the design knowledge and to produce the optimum instantiation list of the primary descriptors, so that important information is produced early and with the least effort. The proposed design approach is applicable for most of the design problems and the design environment may be used in the majority of the design cases where the design problem under consideration can be formally decomposed and expressed in terms of descriptors and associative relationships among them. The proposed algorithm can track down any changes the designer makes and can efficiently update its internal interrelations. The algorithm stores additional information to the design descriptors and updates them, without having to search the whole design space. It simply detects the affected descriptors and updates the information for those descriptors.

In its present form the environment may act as a domain-independent, general assisting tool for the designer by providing a platform for keeping track of any changes in the design entities and of the relationships among them. The environment is currently further elaborated in order to add the ability to create, maintain and use libraries of design descriptors and relationships among them that could be exploited in multiple design cases.

References

1. Banares & Alcantara R. Representing the engineering design process: two hypotheses. Computer- Aided design 1991, 23(9): 595 – 603
2. Duffey M. R., Dixon J. R. A program of research in Mechanical Design: Computer - Based Models and Representations. Mechanical Machine Theory 1990, 25(3): 383-395
3. Shaalan, K., Rafea, M., Rafea, A. KROL, A knowledge representation object language on top of Prolog. Expert Systems With Applications 1998, 15(1): 33-46
4. Tsalidis S. S. Dentsoras A. J. Application of Design Parameters Space Search of Belt Conveyor Design. Engineering Application of Artificial Intelligence 1997, 10(6): 617-629
5. Finn, D. Introduction: Preliminary Stages of Engineering Analysis and Modeling. Artificial Intelligence in Engineering, Design, Analysis and Manufacturing 1993, 7(4): 231-237
6. Yagiu, T. A predicate - logical method for modeling design objects. Artificial Intelligence in Engineering 1989, 4(1): 41-53
7. Dentsoras A.J. An Approach of Routine Design Based on Extensive Design Space Search. EXPERSYS-96: Expert Syst. Appl. & AI Proc. of i.i.t.t. - International Conf., Paris, France, 1996
8. Frey D.D., Jahangir E., Engelhardt F. Computing the Information Content of Decoupled Designs. Research in Engineering Design 2000, 12: 90-102
9. Franceschini F., Rossetto S. QFD: an interactive algorithm for the prioritization of product's technical design characteristics. Integrated Manufacturing Systems 2002, 13(1): 69-75
10. Duffy, S. M., Duffy, A. H. B. Sharing the learning activity using intelligent CAD. Artificial Intelligence in Engineering, Design, Analysis and Manufacturing 1996, 10: 83-100
11. Sim, S. K., Duffy, A. H. B. A foundation for machine learning in design. Artificial Intelligence in Engineering, Design, Analysis and Manufacturing 1998, 12: 193-209
12. Suh, N.P. The Principles of Design. Oxford Series in Advanced Manufacturing, New York, 1990
13. Suh N.P. Axiomatic Design Theory for Systems. Research in Engineering Design 1998, 10: 189-209
14. Court A.W. The Relationship between Information and Personal Knowledge in New Product Development. International Journal of Information Management 1997, 17(2): 123-138
15. Shooter S.B., Keirouz W.T., Szykman S., Fenves S.J., A Model for the Flow of Design Information in Product Development. Engineering with Computers 2000, 16: 178-194
16. Drakatou S., Dentsoras A. J. A Method for the Automatic Deduction of Priority Lists of Entities and Tasks form the Design Knowledge. Artificial Intelligence in Engineering, Design, Analysis and Manufacturing 2001, 15 (3): 223-232
17. Ong Y.S., Keane A.J. A domain knowledge based search advisor for design problem solving environments. Engineering Applications of Artificial Intelligence 15 2002, 15:105–116

18. Zhang W. Y., Tor S. B., Britton G. A. A Heuristic State–Space Approach to the Functional Design of Mechanical Systems. Inter. J. Adv. Manufacturing Technology 2002, 19: 235–244

19. Gelsey A., Smith D., Schwabacher M., Rasheed K., Miyake K. A search-space toolkit: SST. Decision Support Systems 1996, 18: 341-356

20. Gelsey A., Schwabacher M., Smith D. Using Modeling Knowledge to guide Design Space Search. Artificial Intelligence 1998, 101: 35-62

21. Vico F.J., Veredas F.J., Bravo J.M., Almaraz J. Automatic design synthesis with artificial intelligence techniques. Artificial Intelligence in Engineering 1999, 13: 251–256

22. Yao Z., Johnson A.L. On Estimating the Feasible Solution Space in Design. Computer-Aided Design 1997, 29(9): 649-656

23. Steinberg L. Searching stochastically generated multi-abstraction-level design spaces. Artificial Intelligence. 2001, 129: 63–90

24 Nikolidakis A., An Environment for Representing and Analysing Structured Design Knowledge, Diploma Thesis, Patra, (in Greek), 2002

SESSION 4:

MEDICAL AND SOCIAL SERVICES

The BUPA 'Decision Engine': An Integrated Case Based Reasoning System at Work in the Private Medical Insurance Industry.

Daniel Kerr

BUPA UK Membership

Staines, TW18 4TL

kerrda@bupa.com

Abstract

The Private Medical Insurance industry has long been an active user of information technology, for instance to assist with the complex task of managing insurance claims, determining conditions for cover and eligibility. In 1997 BUPA developed a 'Decision Engine', a series of interlinked case-bases that consult member and policy data to assist front-line call-centre decision making with regard to pre-treatment authorisation. This business-critical system guarantees a consistent response to member requests with regard to what costs will be indemnified by BUPA. It also enables BUPA to provide information to members to allow them to make informed decisions and encourage specialists to carry out the most appropriate treatments. This paper looks at why the system has been a success and how work is being done to ensure that the system continues to be relevant to business needs and has the flexibility to be compatible with the developing corporate enterprise architecture.

1. Introduction

This paper describes the application of Case-Based Reasoning techniques to a set of real-world problems in a healthcare setting. The domain area is the review of proposed treatment of members covered by medical insurance, and the application described has been successfully employed in BUPA UK Membership for around six years. BUPA UK Membership is the largest UK medical insurance supplier with approximately 40% market share of around 3.7m subscribers [1]. It forms part of the BUPA Group that, as a provident association, is driven by the needs of members (subscribers) rather than shareholders, which means that any profit made is re-invested in better health and care services.

There have been numerous efforts to develop CBR systems for commercial usage and there are examples of projects that have achieved varying degrees of success; some of these were presented at the UK CBR workshop, 2002 [2]. However, anecdotal evidence and the experience of the author suggest that a large proportion of such projects deliver systems that are not adopted by the users and are ultimately abandoned before any business benefits are realised.

The system described here has over 1000 end-users, and it is used around 145,000 times a month. The paper reviews the reasons behind this success and what is being done now to ensure that it continues to deliver value to the business and develops as an integrated part of the business' enterprise architecture.

2. Problem Description

2.1 Background on the Private Medical Insurance Industry

The Private Medical Insurance (PMI) Industry in general works much the same as other insurance areas, and indeed many PMI companies are general insurers with a medical insurance division. A policy is purchased that offers cover for short-term, curable or acute illnesses and injuries. (For a more detailed explanation of what a PMI policy covers see the ABI guide [3]). When treatment has been obtained a claim is submitted and the policy indemnifies the member for an amount dependent upon the detail of the cover and the standard costs of that treatment, and the policyholder covers any other costs.

Whilst BUPA does follow this general process it has a role as a health and care organisation that is more than just being a traditional indemnity insurer; it also offers reassurance on the quality and appropriateness of health care. It reviews consultants and hospitals to ensure they follow best practice, and facilitates quality care networks where groups of hospitals are recognised for a particular specialisation. Additionally BUPA provides more affordable medical insurance solutions with products that limit the choice of hospital, the conditions covered, or the number of additional benefits covered (such as outpatient treatments or post-operative care).

2.2 The Use of Rule-Based and Procedural Systems

The PMI industry, in line with other insurance areas, has been an active user of Information Technology systems for some considerable time to assist in tasks such as determining conditions of cover and eligibility of claims. Since 1988 BUPA have used a procedural system called BASS (BUPA Administration Support System), which has a component for batch processing claims [4]. Contained within this claims component are a number of rule-based systems that handle the tasks involved in checking eligibility. One such system consults data on general exclusions (GEs), which apply for various treatments depending on the product purchased. This GE component assesses whether any GEs apply in a given scenario and if so may reject the claim or suspend it for manual review.

In order to make decisions on claims it is necessary to utilise a great deal of corporate information regarding memberships, policies and providers of treatment. The information required can be modelled by a questioning process that is followed when determining if there is any reason why the treatment may not be covered, and falls into four main categories:

- Membership. E.g. does the member have a paid up policy?

- Condition. E.g. is the condition covered by the member's policy?

- Procedure. E.g. is the treatment procedure recognised for that condition?

- Provider. E.g. are the hospital, specialist and anaesthetist recognised by BUPA?

2.3   Looking After Members

Traditionally the medical insurance industry treated its members in the same way as any other insurance industry. It was taken that members would only make detailed enquiries when they had had treatment that might be covered by their policy and were making a claim. However, given the changing profile of membership and the increase in elective private medical treatments, members were increasingly finding themselves facing a choice prior to treatment. This might be a choice between being treated under the National Health Service (NHS) or 'going private', a choice between treatments or possibly even whether to have the treatment at all. So, increasingly people were telephoning the BUPA call centres prior to treatment to find out if their policies would cover them and whether they would have to meet part of the costs themselves.

2.4   The Manual Process

The BASS claims component is an overnight batch processing system. It requires a lot of information on a claim and does not lend itself to providing quick answers on eligibility. So when members called-in with a specific treatment scenario the call-centre staff were required to provide an answer based on a manual assessment. This meant consulting rulebooks, policy details, tables of information used by the rules-based systems held in BASS, and often policy or medical experts in other areas of the business. The answer the member would get could only be as good as the person they spoke to and the information available. Call centre staff were required to have in-depth knowledge of policies and an expanding product portfolio. Even within a team of experts there will be differing levels of knowledge and the potential for inconsistency. The business risks around offering assurances to members on coverage clearly need to be well handled, there is a need to provide re-assurance to members based on consistent and accurate decisions.

This time-consuming manual eligibility checking process also meant there was less focus on providing relevant information to allow members to make informed choices regarding treatment. It was also very difficult to have any influence over where the treatment was carried out. For example, a hospital may have recently been identified as failing to meet expected standards but treatment that had been carried out there would still have to be covered by the policy even if it would have been preferable for the member to be treated elsewhere.

3. Solution Description

3.1 Selection of Methodology and Development Platform

3.1.1 The Complexity of Alternative Methodologies

Using the claims system as described in 2.2 alleviated a lot of manual processing but around 25% of claims suspend and require manual intervention. Part of the problem is the difficulty in specifying in a procedural way the whole process of checking eligibility. Some parts lend themselves to rule-based solutions but as a whole the process makes for a cumbersome procedural solution. An on-line policy manual has been developed, which resolves some questions of what is considered medically appropriate but it has proved difficult to implement this into the BASS claims system.

The problem is similar to a diagnostic problem in that an appropriate solution is to be searched for by the asking of a series of questions. If a solution is not found then there is default-behaviour, the solutions in this case are reasons to fail the claim and the default is to pass and authorise the claim. This type of task is discussed by Ian Watson [5] as being a typical 'classification' application of Case Based Reasoning.

3.1.2 The Changing Solution Space

Another difficulty is that there are emerging policies with regard to many of the treatments that are covered by the products; this emergence of policy will cause the solution space to change over time. Attempting to reflect these changes in a procedural system has proved time-consuming and expensive. This partly accounts for the high percentage of claims that suspend for manual intervention.

A complex and changing solution space lends itself to a case based reasoning approach and by introducing 'sub-probleming', which is discussed in more detail later, a modular solution that is easily updated can be developed.

3.1.3 Maintainability of the System

A requirement of the solution was that it would be easily maintainable by individuals within the business; the cases needed to be maintainable with a limited amount of technical programming skills. So, an off-the-shelf CBR shell with an intuitive graphical user interface (GUI) was procured. CBR Express from Inference was selected for pragmatic as well as design reasons. It was felt that although there were other offerings in the marketplace (some of the which are compared in Watson '97 [5].), Inference was a sufficiently mature and reputable company that ongoing consultancy and technical support could be relied upon.

3.2 Application Architecture

At the core of the system is CBR Express from Inference, subsequently upgraded to K-Commerce 4 from eGain Communications. This is an off-the-shelf Case Based Reasoning shell normally used for problem resolution in call centres, help desks and for self-service on the web.

In its standard form CBR Express provides the following:

- An intuitive graphical user interface for easy system maintenance without the need for programming skills.

- The Case Based Reasoning paradigm allowing a simple means for specifying individual cases where pre-authorisation must be refused or where there is a requirement for referral.

- A rapid search mechanism using memory resident indexing.

- A Dynamic Link Library (DLL) option to facilitate integration within a custom application.

However the functionality of this tool had to be radically extended to meet BUPA's requirements for the Pre-Authorisation Decision Engine (DE).

The answers to the questions within the eligibility checking process are generally obtained from data, although in exceptional circumstances answers may be required from the user. This data may have been provided in the form of 'input tokens' delivered by the user interface system, for example detail of the member's product and the condition diagnosed and treatment proposed. Alternatively, data may be retrieved from Oracle or BASS tables; for example, policies on treatment and details of what is covered by a product. In order to handle the interaction between the interface and back end systems a wrapper was developed. This wrapper can obtain information through data service calls via an object request broker, running packages on Oracle tables or routines in the BASS. This is shown below in Figure 1.

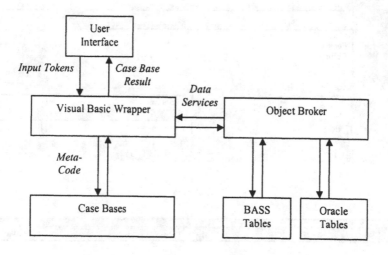

Figure 1 Application Architecture

The wrapper communicates with the case bases by means of a bespoke meta-code language. An example of the meta-code held in the description field of a question is shown in Figure 2. This meta-code is required to communicate how an answer to a question is to be obtained, what the value of an answer is and the result of a case base search.

Given this minimal functionality the wrapper can be very generic requiring very little in the way of updating as the system changes. This reduces the requirements for programming skills in system maintenance.

The example shown is of a question. The Description field holds the metacode instruction explaining how to answer the question, where to find the answer, how to interpret the answer and what to do if no answer is found. 'AskD' means use data to answer this question. An IP prefix refers to an input parameter, in this case the Gender parameter. M or MALE will be interpreted as Male, F or FEMALE as Female. If no answer is found a case called CBError is triggered to acknowledge that a data error has been encountered.

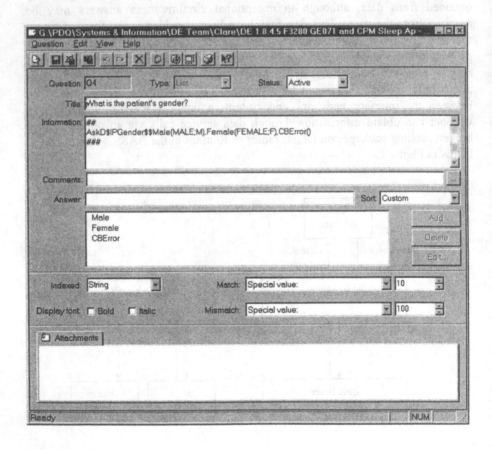

Figure 2 Example of meta-code in a question

3.3 Case Base Architecture

3.3.1 Case base Style

The solution consists of a series of linked case bases that can search for any reasons why the scenario was not acceptable and should be rejected. These case bases use elimination scoring based on the answers to questions that segment the case bases in a similar way one might traverse a decision tree. This exclusive or diagnostic style of case base uses scoring to determine which cases can contribute the next question and whether a case has reached its threshold value, but not to rank the winning cases. This solution falls into the 'retrieve and propose' category as discussed by Leake, '96 [6], with inappropriate solutions being manually identified and adapted.

3.3.2 Sub-Probleming

In order to reduce the complexity and remove repetitive processing a method of sub-probleming has been employed. A question may be answered directly by data from a table or it may call a child case base, which in turn consults tables to answer its questions and provides a search result as the answer to the question in the parent case base. By providing an entry question in a child case base it can effectively represent a whole series of smaller case bases, which has the benefit of allowing the sharing of questions and actions. This sub-probleming or modular approach also makes the maintenance tasks more manageable and provides for greater flexibility, which were key requirements of the solution as mentioned in 3.1.

The wrapper enables a question in one case base to be answered by the results of searching another case base. This permits a modular design whereby every possible reason why Pre-Authorisation should be refused or a referral made will be searched for within a single run of the DE. Each reason for refusal or referral is defined as a single case within one of the case bases. A case is comprised of a number of multiple choice questions each with one or more answers defined as being appropriate to the case and with a message explaining the reason. A case "wins" and becomes the result of a search only when all questions within that case have received answers consistent with those defined in the case. Where multiple winning cases are found, multiple reason messages are displayed. Where no winning cases is found, pre-authorisation is granted. The modular design of this approach allows the authors to maintain each criterion as an individual cluster of cases.

3.3.3 The PEND Case

The system is based on the business assumption that the proposed treatment will be authorised unless there is a case that matches the scenario to FAIL the authorisation. Hence, the system only contains cases relating to circumstances where a claim may not be indemnified and returns a PASS if a matching case is not found. However, there are many areas where it is not clear that a FAIL result is appropriate but a default of PASS may result in an inappropriate commitment to indemnify. So the system design provides a PEND result, which instructs the user on who can make a decision to resolve the query. In this way the system is able to provide a result for the user in 100% of scenarios.

3.3.4 Explaining the Outcome

When a FAIL or PEND case is encountered the system provides an explanatory message for the user. In the PEND case this will provide details of what needs to happen to resolve the authorisation. In the case example in Figure 2 the message code is given in the meta-code and this is mapped to a message narrative to be displayed to the user. Figure 4 shows the relevant excerpt from the message-mapping table.

Code	MSG
0020	The condition is inappropriate for the sex of the patient. Confirm details with the member.

Figure 3 Excerpt of Message Table

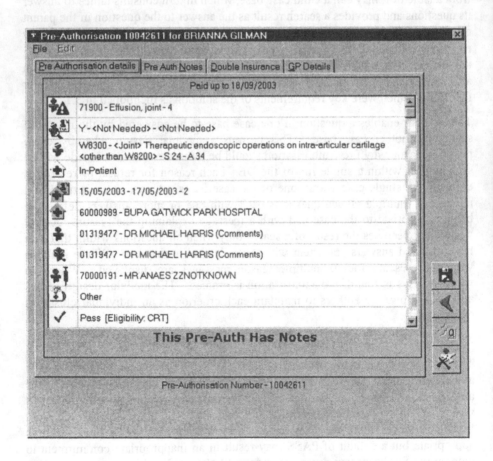

Figure 4 A User View of the System Response for a Test Scenario

The result returned to the user interface in an example scenario is shown in the figure above. A pre-authorisation number is generated, which the member can give to the consultant as an assurance of coverage.

3.4 On-line Access for Treatment Providers

It has been possible to provide access to treatment providers (consultants, hospitals, therapy centres etc.) via an XML web interface. This type of development is discussed by Sengupta et al, 1999 [7]. In this case we use the transfer and parsing functionality of XML to provide a front end to the system, an alternative to the front end used by the call centre staff.

This is supported by the existing system of having a dedicated call centre for providers. Any PEND or FAIL result will return a message asking the user to call in. Thus the result can be checked and full information provided should it be necessary to decline authorisation.

4. Success Factors

4.1 A Result for all Scenarios

A key to the successful adoption of the system was the fact that there is a result returned in every scenario as explained in section 3.3.3. This means that the user can rely on the system to either resolve the authorisation question or provide instructions on where to refer the query to and so usage of the system can be made mandatory. This removes the need for extensive training of new staff and also the temptation for more experienced staff to give a manual assessment that may not be based on the most up to date information.

4.2 Documentation

In order to ensure complete coverage of the problem space, documentation of the checking process was developed in the form of flowcharts as in Figure 6. By thoroughly documenting the design of the system the most efficient set of case-bases can be determined and any conflicts identified. It is often felt that for straightforward case bases simply adding new cases as they are encountered will generate an acceptable solution. However, Kruusmaa and Willemson, 2002 [8] show that even when some measures are taken to ensure reasonable separation of cases an unplanned approach can result in an explosion of cases producing a highly inefficient and unmaintainable case base. In this application, given its complexity, it was felt that mapping out the design was critical.

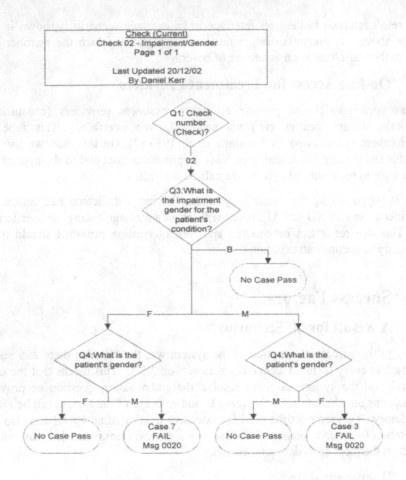

Figure 6 Example of Flowchart Documentation

4.3 Maintenance by a Dedicated Team of Business Users

Over the six years it has been in use there has been a continual cycle of fault identification, enhancements required to support new products and additions to functionality. As discussed in 3.1.3 these changes have had to be authored by business users with limited programming skills. This has been possible thanks to the GUI shell of CBR Express and the Visual Basic wrapper, which is sufficiently generic that it has remained largely unchanged despite these developments.

By having this team with business knowledge it has been possible to ensure the relevance of the system, providing changes to reflect the expansion of the product portfolio and the introduction of new treatments. The importance of being able to assess the effectiveness of the system knowledge and hence implement appropriate maintenance strategies is highlighted by Leake et al, 2001 [9]

4.4 System Integration and Informative Results

The integration of the system with the enterprise architecture has minimised the amount of interaction required from the user. This removes some possible areas of input error and also reduces the amount of user training required, freeing the call centre staff to focus on providing relevant information to the members.

Through careful design of the system and considerable investment in hardware to run this client-based application it had been possible to achieve average result generation times below thirty seconds. This allows the user to continue a conversation with the member. By generating user messages to explain why the authorisation has not been passed and providing some directions as to how to proceed the system removes the need for manual assessment. It gives the user information to support conversations with the member and being integrated with other systems means automatic referrals can happen and the user simply informed it has occurred.

4.5 Business Benefits

All the above factors are about getting people to use the system and maintaining it. In order for the business to continue supporting any system, especially one requiring a dedicated support team, it is necessary to demonstrate that there are sufficient benefits to justify the costs. The large number of users and the high volume of pre-treatment authorisations are key factors in ensuring this is the case.

4.5.1 Internal Benefits

As a result of this system the call centre staff are no longer required to know every variant of every product as discussed in 2.4. This has reduced the training time for staff whilst allowing the product portfolio to grow. Staff satisfaction has improved as well as customer satisfaction as measured by our Service Organisation Profile, which measures employee concerns, and our National Opinion Poll. This has knock-on effects for improved staff retention.

The system has also enabled BUPA to demonstrate consistency of decision making to the Competition Commission and regulatory bodies such as the Financial Services Authority.

4.5.2 Benefits to external users

The web interface gives treatment providers access to relevant member details and details of existing pre-treatment authorisations, as well as allowing pre-treatment authorisations to be requested giving reassurance that developing treatment programmes will be covered by BUPA and they will not be incurring bad debts. It also reduces administration costs as it removes the need to call in every time a new stage of treatment is proposed. Currently 175 out of 200 hospitals that BUPA deal with have access to the web-based interface.

5.   Review

After six years of use the DE looks rather different from its original design. As part of the normal cycle in corporations the majority of people who have had cause to interact with the DE have moved on and new people have filled their roles. This has led to some discontinuity and a diffusion of understanding of the role of the DE. Hence, it would seem time to review how the DE is fulfilling its role and how to ensure its continued success. To facilitate this review a member of the original development team has been brought in.

5.1   Maintaining Success

Reviewing the success factors of section 4 a number of areas present themselves as requiring a re-visit. Flowchart documentation no longer reflects the case bases accurately in some instances. It is necessary to update this and continue to keep it updated in all areas. This will provide the continuity of maintenance that is crucial to all systems. It is easy to feel that changes are minor and not really a change in the design, but over time these accumulated changes can make the system unrecognisable.

How meaningful are the messages? As new cases are added messages are re-used or added to the system. If these are to be useful then they need to be appropriate and informative in the vast majority of cases, so that users have confidence in following the instructions or reporting the detail back to members.

Reducing complexity, removing duplicates and redundant cases. As the case bases grow in functionality they need to be reviewed to maintain the search times currently available. This will also ensure that the system remains flexible and easily maintained.

5.2   Building on Success

5.2.1   Educating the users

Communicating how the DE works and what it does. This will help to ensure business people, system developers and others have a clear view on the role of the DE, that they request relevant changes and that they have realistic expectations. This applies to both internal users and the providers who use the web interface to access the system.

5.2.2   Migration of PENDs

As discussed earlier the policies on treatments change over time and as new treatments are introduced they will need to be handled by the DE. Generally new treatments are introduced to the system with PEND results so that each case can be examined and considered. Emerging policy will be informed by the practice of specialists in the field. Every time the system PENDs the scenario is referred to a policy specialist in the relevant field. There is a finite amount of resource for handling PENDs as the system grows there should not be a requirement for this resource to grow. So from time to time the policy teams may request that certain scenarios do not PEND and give a definition of when they should PASS or FAIL.

Over time emerging policy should be reflected in the migration of PENDs to PASS or FAIL. This may not always be appropriate but it would be reasonable to expect that scenarios can be better delineated to reduce the occurrences of PEND. This would give a trade-off in terms of an increase in the number of cases but a reduction in the number of PENDs.

6.   Concluding Remarks

This paper has presented a case study of a working CBR system which is used to make business critical decisions in the course of a customer conversation. This system has been successfully used for six years. The key reasons for this have been examined in section 4. An extensive review has been carried out to look at which areas need some focus to ensure the system continues to be successful and how to build on this success. This review has resulted in significant optimisation.

In summary, a clear vision shared by all stakeholders combined with continuity of authoring, either through training or good documentation, will ensure the system continues to be utilised. However, the business case needs to be robust enough to support ongoing maintenance and periodical review.

References

1.   Laing and Buisson. *Laing's Healthcare Market Review 2002-2003*. William Clowes Ltd Suffolk, 2002
2.   Lees, B. (ed) *Proceedings of 7th UK Workshop on Case-Based Reasoning*. University of Paisley. 2002.
3.   Association of British Insurers. 'Are you buying private medical insurance?' Available from www.abi.org.uk/Public/Consumer/Medical/
4.   Peter Saunders Associates. 'The BUPA Administration Support System'. Consultants report for BUPA Membership Division. 1992.
5.   Watson I. *Applying Case-Based Reasoning: Techniques for Enterprise Systems*. Morgan Kaufmann Publishers, San Francisco. 1997.
6.   Leake, D. 'CBR in Context: The Present and Future'. In: Leake, D. (ed) *Case-Based Reasoning: Experiences, Lessons and FutureDirections*. AAAI Press / MIT Press, Menlo Park. 1996.
7.   Sengupta, A., Wilson, D. and Leake, D. 'Constructing and Transforming CBR Implementations: Techniques for Corporate Memory Management'. In: *Proceedings of the IJCAI-99 Workshop on Automating the Construction of Case Based Reasoners*. Stockholm, Sweden, 1999.
8.   Kruusmaa, M. and Willemson, J. 'Covering the Path Space: A Casebase Analysis for Mobile Robot Path Planning'. In: Bramer, M., Preece, A. and Coenen, F. (ed) *Proceedings of ES2002*. Springer-Verlag London, 2002, pp3-16
9.   Leake, D., Smyth, B., Yang, Q. and Wilson, D. 'Introduction to the Special Issue on Maintaining Case-Based Reasoning Systems'. *Computational Intelligence*, 2001; 17(2):193-195

Conducting Feasibility Studies for Knowledge Based Systems

John Kingston

Joseph Bell Centre for Forensic Statistics and Legal Reasoning

University of Edinburgh

J.Kingston@ed.ac.uk

www.josephbell.org

Abstract

This paper describes how to carry out a feasibility study for a potential knowledge based system application. It discusses factors to be considered under three headings: the business case, the technical feasibility, and stakeholder issues. It concludes with a case study of a feasibility study for a KBS to guide surgeons in diagnosis and treatment of thyroid conditions.

1. Introduction

Many years of experience have demonstrated that knowledge based systems (KBS) are one of the most effective methods of managing knowledge in organisations – if they are applied in appropriate areas and to appropriate tasks. The identification of appropriate tasks and areas is therefore critical – and yet little has been published on this subject, despite renewed interest in the area from knowledge management practitioners. The purpose of this paper is to outline an approach to conducting feasibility studies for knowledge based systems.[1]

There are three major aspects to consider when carrying out such a feasibility study: the business case; technical feasibility; and project feasibility (i.e. involvement and commitment of the various stakeholders). These will be considered in turn. The paper will then conclude with a case study, illustrating these principles being put into practice.

2. Feasibility Studies: The Business Case

If a KBS is not expected to bring business benefits, then there is no point in an organisation investing in its development, so the business case must be part of any feasibility study. That much is obvious; what is less obvious is the types of business benefit that a knowledge based system can bring to an organisation.

[1] Acknowledgements are due to the following: Ian Filby (for general knowledge engineering contributions), Knox Haggie (for the case study), Robert Inder (who coined the "telephone test"), Ann Macintosh (for managing and marketing the training course that drove the development of these ideas) and Neil Molony (domain expert for the case study). The case study was supported by EPSRC grant number GR/R60348/01, "Master's Training Package in Knowledge Management and Knowledge Engineering".

The most obvious business benefit is increased productivity, which KBS systems may deliver by reducing the time taken to perform a problem solving task. However, this is rarely the initial motivation for building a knowledge based system; the reasons are normally to do with the need for a knowledge management solution – that is, some operation within the organisation requires expertise, and the expertise is either not available often enough, or not exercised fully. The most common problem with expertise is that it is not available widely enough. The experts may be simply too busy to answer all the queries which require their expertise; alternatively, the experts may be frequently employed on routine cases that do not optimise the use of their scarce expertise. A good example of the latter arose within Ferranti several years ago, when Alan Pridder, one of their staff was tasked with analysing core dumps from military software that had crashed. He became so fed up with poring over mountains of printout, only to find out that someone had kicked the plug out again, that he threatened to resign unless Ferranti did something about it. Their solution was to build a knowledge-based system based on his knowledge that could identify the most common causes of core dumps, thus leaving him with the more interesting cases; the process of having his knowledge elicited was also considered to be an interesting diversion. The resulting system, known as APRES (the Alan Pridder Replacement Expert System) was sufficiently successful that he was still working for Ferranti several years later.

There are also situations where the best expertise is not applied to the problem, usually because of time restrictions; a KBS can provide support in making the best decision. A good example of this is American Express' Authorizer's Assistant system [1], which helps to decide whether transactions can be charged to an American Express card. This is necessary because American Express is a charge card, not a credit card, so the effective credit limit varies according to an individual's credit history, use of the card, and several other factors, rather than being a fixed limit. Transactions on the borderline of acceptability are processed by "authorizers" whose task is to discuss the transaction with a retailer by telephone, look up the customer's credit records, and then make a decision, all in about 90 seconds. The transaction may be granted, rejected, or the card may even be destroyed by the retailer. American Express noticed that some of their authorizers performed much better than others, and so decided to implement a KBS to make the knowledge of the best authorizer available to all others. The project was a major undertaking, but when successfully completed, it saved far more money from the improvements in decision making than from the small reduction in the time required to process each authorisation.

Other cases where improvements in decision making are required include cases where 'experts' disagree (in which case the most senior expert or manager may want to use the KBS to enforce the approach s/he considers best), and cases where there is no real expert. An example of the latter can be found in a system developed by a telecommunications company for diagnosing faults in a new switching system; the system did not exist beyond its paper specifications, so there was no-one with any expertise in diagnosing it! The company's solution to this was to build a model-based reasoning system that could reason from first principles.

There are also further business benefits that may arise from developing a KBS. These may include training of users when they ask for explanations of the system's decisions; it has been shown that providing training to someone when they need to know the answer is a very effective training technique. Management information can also be derived from the workings of the KBS. The organisation may obtain a profile as a user of high technology. One advantage that should definitely not be overlooked is that when an expert is getting close to retirement; the KBS can act as an archive of some or all of the expertise. This approach was used by Campbell's when the expert who diagnosed faults in their giant soup cookers came up to retirement; the expert was described as "slightly bemused that his life's experience had been encapsulated in about a hundred rules".

It is sensible to perform a full cost/benefit analysis, taking into account costs of staff training (to develop the KBS and to use it), hardware and software, and KBS maintenance. As an example, consider ICL's Advanced Coating Plant Advisor, a system for diagnosing faults and advising on recovery of a particular manufacturing plant. In a DTI-sponsored study of this system [2], it was determined that the system had cost £30K to develop (6 man months at a notional rate of £50K per man year, plus £5K for hardware and software) plus an annual charge for knowledge base maintenance of about £5K (1 – 3 man days per month). The benefits were in reduced downtime of the plant (the plant was now online for 95% of the time rather than 92.5%), saving £100K per year; there were also far fewer calls on the expert, cutting his workload by about 80% (equivalent to £50K x 0.8 = £40K per year). So the system paid for itself in 3 months – and rolling out the system to other plants would multiply the benefits.

2.1 Organisational feasibility

For a successful feasibility study, it is not sufficient to establish that a KBS could bring benefits to an organisation; it is also important to ensure that the system fits in with the organisation's current or future ways of working. If this criterion is not fulfilled, the system is unlikely to be used after a short period of time.

The most important requirement is to determine how much organisational change will be required in order for the system to be used. It is inevitable that the introduction of a KBS will bring about some organisational changes -- typically some authority will be devolved from the experts to more junior staff. Techniques for handling changes like this are described in the section on Project Feasibility below. However, a KBS that requires major changes in authority or structure is unlikely to be used unless these changes are being carried out independently. A good example of this comes from one of the UK's savings banks, which set up an AI group in the 1980s. The AI group asked for suggested KBS applications from staff, and spent a lot of effort on making a good choice. The final choice was to build a KBS to support the task of mortgage application assessment. Technically and commercially, this was a good decision -- other financial institutions have successfully built KBS to address the same task. However, once the system was built, tested, and demonstrated (successfully), it became clear that the system would be most useful if used by staff in the bank's branches to make good mortgage lending decisions. This would require the bank to devolve its mortgage processing from 6 regional centres to 16,000 branches - a major organisational change which would require considerable redeployment of staff within the regional centres. As a result, the system was quietly shelved.

Another organisational issue is whether the task will continue to be performed. It's reasonably obvious that, if a piece of machinery is obsolete and will soon be phased out, it's pointless to build a KBS to diagnose faults in that machine. However, the longevity of some organisational roles and functions is sometimes less obvious. In practice, it's often easy to spot tasks that *will* continue to be performed, because they deal with the core of the business, or because there will always be a need for these tasks; in other cases, it's worth making enquiries among management if this task is expected to continue for 3-5 years, which is the typical lifetime of an (unmaintained) KBS.

One enquiry that is often useful is "Have you tried any other solutions to this problem? If so, why did they fail?" This is a good way of finding out about any organisational resistance to restructuring or to new technology, which may have a significant effect on the feasibility of the system. It's also possible that other automated solutions have been tried; enquiring about the reasons for the failure of these can provide illuminating technical information. For example, Barclaycard's Fraudwatch system, which monitors Barclaycard transactions to detect spending patterns indicative of possible fraudulent use, was originally implemented using a non-AI computing approach. The reason for failure of this system was that the pattern matching algorithm was not specific enough; with about 100,000 cards being used every day, this system would identify up to 1,000 cards with possible fraudulent transactions, which was far too many for Barclaycard to follow up. The current Fraudwatch system identifies far fewer cards, allowing Barclaycard to telephone many of the card holders and ask if the card is indeed being used fraudulently; if so, the card is cancelled immediately. This system identified 11 frauds in its first 7 days of use, saving Barclaycard an average of £400 per card.

Once a KBS is installed, the effects of *knowledge transfer* and *knowledge seepage* may occur. Knowledge transfer occurs when the KBS has an explanation facility which has a training effect upon the users; the users eventually learn all the knowledge embodied within the system. This effect was observed in the American Express Authorizer's Assistant system, where the use of the explanation facility by new users was monitored. At first, the users accepted the system's recommend-ations with little interest in the explanations. After a while, they began to look at the explanations frequently; after some more time, they ceased to look at the explanations, having presumably learned everything that the explanations could tell them. It's possible that users may cease to use the system at this stage. A solution to this problem (if it is a problem) is to build a KBS that supplies other benefits of automation; the Authorizer's Assistant, for example, performs fast pattern matching on a database of credit records.

Knowledge seepage occurs when all human expertise in the area is gradually lost as the experts and users become dependent upon the system. This is most frequently encountered in AI systems with adaptive capabilities that update their own knowledge (e.g. neural networks), but may also occur with highly complex KBS.

This may be a significant risk to the organisation, particularly in a commercial climate where reorganisations are frequent and far-reaching. Feasibility studies should therefore use the technique of identifying "risk factors" and assessing the impact on the project if these factors should change. For example, the departure of a particular expert who has supplied knowledge for a KBS might be of medium likelihood, but have only a low impact on the project, because knowledge in this domain is very stable. It is wise to build in contingencies to the project plan if there are several risks with both medium/high likelihood and medium/high impact.

3. Technical feasibility

3.1 Task & knowledge

When assessing the technical feasibility of a proposed system there are various issues to consider. The key one – indeed, this is often the first question asked in a good feasibility study – is the type of task being tackled. KBS have been used to perform a variety of knowledge-based tasks, such as classification, monitoring, diagnosis, assessment, prediction, planning, design, configuration and control tasks. If the task type is not in this list, it is worth asking if it is not more suited to being implemented using non-KBS techniques; for example, a task that primarily involves correlation is better suited to a statistical package than to a KBS.

The form of knowledge is also important in technical feasibility. If the reasoning involved is primarily symbolic reasoning based on concepts, objects or states, then a KBS should be suitable. If there is a significant requirement for calculation, based on numerical data; or a requirement for geometric reasoning, based on graphical data; or (worst of all) a requirement for perceptual input, based on textures, shapes, photographs or facial expressions, then it will be difficult to program a KBS to perform all the necessary operations. Alternative approaches to consider might include CAD packages or computer-based training for humans.

It is often obvious to a knowledge engineer when perceptual input is required, because textbooks or training materials will contain many photographs. However, a good heuristic to determine if any non-symbolic knowledge is required is the "telephone test". It requires the knowledge engineer to ask the expert if, in an emergency, the solution to the problem could be described over the telephone. If the answer is "No", or "It would take a very long time", it's likely that non-symbolic knowledge is involved.

There are some types of knowledge that are definitely suitable for a KBS, and less suitable for other approaches. If the knowledge contains procedures, regulations or heuristics in the form of condition-action statements (If A is true then do B), a taxonomic hierarchy, or a set of alternatives which need to be searched through, then knowledge-based systems are probably the most suitable technology for automating this task. Also, if there is any uncertainty about the knowledge (either knowledge which has confidence factors attached to it, or knowledge which is assumed to be true based on continued belief in other knowledge) then KBS technology has techniques for representing this uncertainty that other technologies do not explicitly support.

A feature that KBS are known to provide well is providing explanations. The explicit representation of knowledge in modular units (i.e. rules or objects) allows the knowledge engineer to attach explanations to individual rules or objects. Explanations are useful both for checking the accuracy of the system's decisions and, as described above, for providing on-the-job training. From a commercial viewpoint, the ability to provide good explanations is one of the most useful features of KBS technology.

Another point which should be included in the feasibility study is to make sure that the knowledge in the KBS is verifiable. In other words, there needs to be an agreed way of checking that the knowledge is correct. This can present quite a problem, for if there is only one expert in a task, who is to say whether the knowledge provided is correct or not? In practice, this is rarely a major problem in the commercial world; perhaps this is because of a greater emphasis on knowledge that achieves the correct result than on knowledge that is provably correct. A knowledge engineer should make sure that the manager funding the project either agrees that the expert's opinions should be considered to be correct, or supplies an alternative "knowledge standard" against which checking can take place.

While discussing verifiability of knowledge with the appropriate manager, it's a good idea to continue to determine what proportion of the task the system should tackle. In other words, when is the project considered to be finished? If this is not specified at the outset, then it's common to find all sorts of extra features or knowledge coverage being requested; if it is specified at the beginning, the knowledge engineer has a clear definition of a successful system. The chief difficulty is that early knowledge acquisition often reveals information about the task and its complexity that affects the definition of success considerably. It's therefore wise to do one or two knowledge acquisition sessions before settling down the definition of a successful system.

3.2   Application complexity

Having looked at the task and knowledge to decide whether this problem is feasible for a KBS solution, it's also important to look at how complex the proposed KBS solution would be, for these systems vary widely in levels of complexity; the amount of effort required to implement a commercial KBS can vary from a few weeks to many man years.

A good heuristic for initial estimation of the task complexity is based on the task type. Some task types (principally diagnosis and assessment) are well understood and underlie many KBS applications; others (e.g. planning, design and control) only support a few applications, which are typically complex systems. Task types can be divided into *analytic* tasks such as diagnosis, classification, monitoring and assessment (where there is a finite number of solutions) and *synthetic* tasks such as planning, scheduling, configuration and design (where there is a theoretically infinite number of solutions); the knowledge engineer's heuristic is that analytic tasks are typically less complex than synthetic tasks. This is only a heuristic, however; compare MYCIN, CASNET and INTERNIST, which all have the same task type (diagnosis) and the same general domain (medicine), but have very different levels of complexity.

Another feature worth checking to determine the complexity of the task is the time required by experts to do it. Opinions vary on this, but ideally the expert should take between 3 minutes and 1 hour to solve the problem. If the expert takes less than 3 minutes, then it will be difficult to build a KBS that accepts a meaningful amount of input and solves the problem as quickly as the expert; American Express managed it, but that was a million-dollar project. If the expert takes more than an hour to solve the problem, then it may be that the problem has many sub-components, and it would be better to begin by implementing a KBS to tackle one of the component tasks.

The biggest potential time sinks in any project are the interfaces. Interfaces may take up to 80% of the code for the whole system, and will take up 10-50% of the project time. If the application requires several interfaces to other systems (e.g. databases), or if an impressive-looking user interface is required, then the knowledge engineer should make allowances in the project budget for 30-50% of the effort to be spent on interfaces. If the client will be content with an embedded system or a *simple* mouse-and-menu interface, then 10-15% is more realistic.

Another factor that greatly affects complexity is criticality. If it is critical that the system's answers are always correct and provide 100% coverage of the domain (for reasons of safety, or because there is the risk of significant loss of money, etc.) then the development process will require much more effort. The "80/20" rule states that building a system with 80% coverage (and 100% accuracy) takes 20% of the time required to build a system with 100% coverage, so it's sensible to aim for 80% coverage if that is acceptable.

Looking at the knowledge again, it isn't sufficient to determine if the knowledge is symbolic or not. Certain types of knowledge may be represented as concepts, objects or states, but may still be very complex for a KBS to reason with. These include temporal knowledge (time-based orderings or time restrictions), spatial knowledge (e.g. the location of a desk relative to a door in an office layout problem), cause-effect reasoning at a 'deep' level (e.g. encoding the laws of physics and using them to make predictions), or a requirement to process real-time data inputs. There are existing KBS systems which work with each of these types of knowledge, so none of them make a KBS infeasible, but they do increase the complexity of the task. However, if common-sense reasoning is required, then a KBS is likely to have severe problems. Intelligence and common sense are not the same thing, as many parents of intelligent children will tell you, and without a huge "life knowledge" database, which is beyond the current scope of KBS technology, KBS cannot perform common sense reasoning.

The final factor to consider is validation; that is, judging if the system gives the correct answers based on the knowledge put into it. This can be difficult to do in a live situation, because the correctness of some systems (e.g. loan advisory systems) cannot be judged by their results until years later. The accepted practice is to devise a test suite based on past cases of problem solving, and to make sure that the KBS produces the correct answer for each of these. It's wise to ask the client to agree to the adequacy of this test suite, since conformance to the test suite will be a significant factor in defining a successful system.

Just as with the business feasibility, there will be risk factors that might affect the technical feasibility of the KBS. These should be identified, with high-likelihood high-impact risks being noted in the feasibility study, and contingency plans made.

4.   Stakeholder issues

Stakeholder issues – getting involvement and commitment from all parties involved with the system – is often considered the last important area in a feasibility study. In practice, however, more systems fail to be used because of project factors than for any business or technical reasons. The stakeholders involved will be management, users, developers, and the experts whose knowledge is being used in the system; these will be considered in turn.

4.1 Management

Management must agree that the feasibility study is adequate, must be willing to fund the system and make key personnel available throughout its development, and should support any organisational changes required to introduce the system. Some organisational change is inevitable, but if the organisational changes are small (e.g. devolving authority for routine problem solving from the expert to junior staff or an autonomous system) and well-justified (explanations of the KBS' reasoning can help here), then the changes can be made easier by allowing the expert a monitoring role. If the system is being introduced as part of a deliberate organisational change, it is up to management to ensure an adequate role (and adequate support) for the KBS in the new structure.

4.2 Users

Users must be willing and able to use the system. The ability to use the system can be ensured through training - typically a day's training for one or two people from each user department is sufficient, though training for all users is (of course) ideal. Willingness to use the system is sometimes more difficult to create; giving the users increased authority via the system may be a sufficient incentive, but it's most important that the users understand the justification for the system. An example can be found in a system built for police patrol officers in Ottawa to help with identification of patterns in residential burglaries [3]. The system required patrol officers to spend more time collecting data than they had done previously, so there was a risk that they might not use it. The knowledge engineers handled this by giving the patrol officers slightly more authority (they were permitted to close some cases, rather than referring everything to detectives) and also by giving a 2-hour presentation to all patrol officers in which 90 minutes was spent explaining the justification for the system, and half an hour on how to use the system. The knowledge engineers also demonstrated their own commitment to the project by giving these presentations at 5am, which was the only time when significant numbers of patrol officers could be spared from policing duties!

4.3 Developers

The KBS developers need to know how to do knowledge acquisition, how to build KBS in a structured manner, and how to use the chosen programming tool. The best way to deal with this is to choose a tool that the developers already know well. Any deficiencies in developers' abilities can be remedied by sending them on training courses, which should be built into the cost/benefit analysis of the project.

4.4 Experts

For the expert, the issues that might arise are as follows:

- The expert may be senior to the knowledge engineer;
- The expert may be uncomfortable with describing his job verbally;
- The expert may be too busy to spend time with the knowledge engineer;
- The expert may perceive the system as a threat to his job security;
- The 'expert' is not really an expert at all.

The first two issues can be handled by starting knowledge acquisition with techniques that the expert is comfortable with (e.g. interviews) rather than techniques that are most beneficial to the knowledge engineer (e.g. card sorting). If the expert is very busy, it is important to ensure that knowledge is available from some alternate source, whether it be lesser experts, manuals, previous cases of problem solving, so that meetings with the expert can be kept to a minimum. The 'threat' issue can be handled by building an "80/20" system, thus retaining an active role for the expert; by giving the expert authority over maintenance or knowledge updates to the system; or by choosing an expert who is about to retire, when this is no longer an issue. The issue of non-expert experts is a difficult one, because there is a significant risk that the knowledge engineer will make himself very unpopular by exposing this; some quiet words with an sympathetic senior figure in the client organisation might result in a change of expert, or a change of focus for the KBS.

4.5 Other project issues

An issue that is of great significance for KBS is maintenance. Although the knowledge within KBS is often easier to maintain than the code in many other computing systems, many knowledge-based applications require the knowledge to be updated much more frequently. For this reason, systems that have fast-changing knowledge (such as help desks for rapidly changing products such as computer hardware or software) are often based on case-based reasoning, which combines aspects of knowledge-based and adaptive technologies. For a KBS, the knowledge engineer should ensure that the feasibility study considers knowledge maintenance, and encourages management to select someone capable of knowledge maintenance. A good solution is to give the expert himself enough training that he is able to understand the knowledge base himself; he can then take on responsibility for knowledge maintenance, even if he does not do the actual programming.

5. Case Study: An Internet-based Clinical Protocol

The preparation of a feasibility study will be illustrated by referring to a case study of the development of systems to support doctors in using clinical protocols via the Internet. The protocols are for treatment of thyroid problems, and the system for which this study was prepared has recently been developed to prototype level for New Cross Hospital in Wolverhampton. The technical approach used is similar to that described in [4].

Medicine was one of the earliest application areas for knowledge-based systems: the MYCIN system [5], which recommended antibiotics based on clinical data was the first commercially viable KBS to be produced. Since then, KBS have been introduced throughout the medical field; today, systems can be found in routine use in areas such as managing ventilators in ICUs [6], hepatitis serology [7], clinical event monitoring (based on the Arden syntax) [8; 9], diagnosis of dysmorphic syndromes [10], CSF interpretation [11], and other areas [12].

All these KBS examples are from the practice of medicine or anaesthesia; in many surgical specialties, sharing and re-use of knowledge in many medical fields is still limited to the dissemination of experiences and distilled knowledge by the traditional approaches of seminars, journals, and practical training. However, there is a growing trend to promote "best practice" within a specialised area through the use of *clinical protocols*. The idea is to provide guidelines based on strong scientific evidence. Protocols at present exist as intra-department guidelines for the management of clinical situations; where they exist, it is expected that they will normally be adhered to unless there is a good counter-argument. They are principally used to benefit sub-consultant grades. There are as yet only the beginnings of formalised nationally agreed protocols (e.g. those published by the Scottish Intercollegiate Guidelines Network). They are usually printed sheets rather than computer-based, with copious references to the published clinical studies that justify each recommendation.

This feasibility studies considers development of a system that will assist clinicians in following clinical protocols for the diagnosis and treatment of thyroid-related conditions. The systems will reason about the weight of available evidence (in the form of published clinical trials), and will also provide access to relevant publications if requested. The expected users are surgeons who would normally make use of a written protocol, and who will make the final decision on whether to follow the system's recommendations.

5.1 Business Case

The heart of the business case lies in improving decision making by automating the protocol, making it easier for surgeons to follow (or seek justification of) its recommendations. This can achieved by encoding details of the published clinical studies and reports that justify each step, together with a measure of the reliability (see [13]) of each study. These measures could then be combined to produce qualified recommendations.

The system would also have associated benefits in providing on-the-job training. If the system is regularly updated (and the beauty of an Internet-based system is that it only needs updating on one computer), then all users of the system will be made aware of new studies in the field which support or supersede old studies – or at least, of the effects of those studies on decision making.

The analysis of costs and benefits is an important issue for any IT system. The financial benefits obtained by obtaining *faster* cures can be estimated in terms of savings in salary, time and associated costs. If a new out-patients appointment costs £70, and a review £50, there are huge savings to be made by minimising reviews and reaching a decision at the first clinic visit. To halve the review appointments in a single department would save £600,000 per year; alternatively the routine new patient waiting time for an appointment could reduce from 8-10 weeks to around 2 weeks if referral rate remained steady. The positive effect of this on patient satisfaction should be significant.

There are also possibilities of *more effective cures* or *longer lasting* cures, by reducing erroneous (or, more likely, sub-optimal) decisions made by junior clinicians. The financial benefits of this are hard to quantify, but should manifest in fewer repeat visits, a reduction in exposure to claims for financial damages, and further increases in patient satisfaction. The potential benefits of a system like this are therefore greater than the "bottom line" figure of £600,000 p.a. would suggest.

Balanced against these expected benefits, we must consider the investment required. Based on the experience of similar KBS projects, it is estimated that a fully functional prototype system would take about six months of effort to complete, with a further three months of effort for testing, revision, installation and training. This translates roughly to £45,000 of development costs (at a notional rate of £60,000 per man year). In addition, there will be hardware and software costs to cover. For software, the ideal software package, chosen after a review of available packages (see [14]) is CORVID from Exsys, whose list price is $10,000 for a development version plus $6,000 for a server-based runtime license. Hardware costs and maintenance could be around £3,000, with replacement every three years. Also, there will be maintenance of the knowledge base to read clinical studies and keep them up to date; allowing two or three days per month, this is estimated at £7,500 per year. Altogether, these figures produce an initial required investment of around £55,000 plus a total annual maintenance cost of approximately £9,000. The system would therefore pay for itself in less than 2 months if a 50% reduction in review appointments could be achieved across a whole department; it is sensible, however, to roll out a prototype first to see how achievable this 50% reduction is.

There are some further organisational considerations that should be considered before the business case for this system is declared to be sound. The system doesn't require any change to organisational responsibilities, unlike some pioneering expert systems that aimed to replace doctors rather than supporting them, although it may result in in junior consultants being able to take more responsibility in the decision process. The task of following surgical protocols is highly unlikely to be phased out in the near future. And for a relatively short IT project such as this one, the risk of funding being cut before the end of the project is comparatively low.

5.2 Technical issues

The technical issues affecting these systems are as follows:

- Task type: It is clear that clinical protocols are used to carry out a diagnostic task, so KBS technology looks like a suitable approach.

- Telephone test: Protocols are initially drafted in textual form by a consultant using a specialised vocabulary, and the decision-making process seems to be couched entirely in symbolic terms. This suggests that a KBS approach is appropriate for the task. Some terms do refer to the classification of patterns seen through a microscope, but these descriptions ("sheets", "follicular cells", etc) are manipulated entirely symbolically as far as the protocol is concerned. In other words, the pattern recognition (performed in the hospital's Cytology laboratory) is clearly outside the scope of the system.

- Uncertain knowledge: the knowledge appears to be largely procedural with a need to handle some uncertainty at the decision points.

- Safety-critical: Clearly the task of effective use of protocols is a safety-critical task; however, it is impossible to ensure that an expert system is infallible when agreement amongst surgeons on what is the "best" procedure is still being developed. The aim of this application is to represent the best available knowledge, thus improving on the current situation.

- Verifiability: the knowledge can be verified through clinical trials.

- Complexity: there is little or no requirement for representing temporal or spatial information, cause-effect reasoning or in handling real-time inputs.

- Time required: while the diagnostic process may be spread out over a long period (days or weeks) while test results are awaited, the actual problem-solving time for the vast majority of cases seems to fall into the 3 – 60 minutes range deemed acceptable for a KBS. Very occasionally, consultants will meet together to discuss a more complicated case.

- Interfaces: The aim of this project would be to implement a system that runs within an Internet browser, so that it can be used on an intranet or over the Internet. All interfaces will therefore be written in HTML. Providing links to the studies that provide the evidence for decisions is also required; it is planned that hyperlinks to the Medline online abstracting/publications service will suffice. Links to electronic medical records are not planned since there is no agreed format for these at present.

5.3   Stakeholder issues

- Management: The 'management' for this project are hospital consultants who will also function as domain experts. All the consultants involved seem very keen to pursue the project.

- Users: will initially be junior doctors working for these consultants, so should be enthused and encouraged by management. The development of a prototype, fielded to a limited number of health care professionals for evaluation purposes, will give prospective users a chance to comment on all aspects of the system; its usability, its content, and its decision-making. It is also hoped that a medical evaluation will be possible, in which some patients are treated according to advice given by the system (and approved by the health care professionals), and the results are evaluated

- Developers: University of Edinburgh staff with experience in programming KBS are available to develop the system.

- Experts: see above.

6.   Conclusion

This paper has shown how a feasibility study can be developed for a knowledge-based system, focusing on business, technical, and stakeholder-related issues. In each section, it has highlighted important factors to consider and explained why they are important. A case study was also presented that demonstrated the feasibility – with some caveats regarding interfaces, safety criticality and user acceptance – of a knowledge based system to support the use of clinical protocols in the diagnosis and treatment of thyroid conditions.

Since the task of developing a feasibility study is itself a knowledge-based assessment task, further work in this area might focus on a meta-analysis of these various factors. Issues that might be considered are:

- Priority: which of the factors considered above are showstoppers, and which are merely risk factors that can be managed with contingency plans?

- Tradeoffs: e.g. is it worth making sacrifices in technical feasibility to enhance user acceptance of the system?

- Ideals: what are the features of an ideal KBS application domain?

- Extensibility: how many of these factors apply to approaches similar to KBS: case based reasoning, neural networks, other approaches?

References

1. Feigenbaum, E., McCorduck, P. & Nii, P., The Rise of the Expert Company. McGraw-Hill, 1989.
2. Expert Systems Opportunities Pack, The ICL Advanced Coating Plant Advisor, DTI, 1989.
3. Brahan, J.W., Valcour, L. & Shevel, R., The Investigator's Notebook. In: Milne R. & Montgomery A. (Eds.), Applications and Innovations in Expert Systems II, SGES Publications, Cambridge, 1994; 37–46.
4. Simpson J., Kingston J. & Molony N., Internet-Based Decision Support for Evidence-Based Medicine, *Knowledge-Based Systems*, 1999; 12:247-255.
5. Shortliffe, E.H., Axline, S.G., Buchanan, B.G., Merigan, T.C. & Cohen, S.N., An artificial intelligence program to advise physicians regarding anti-microbial therapy, *Computers and Biomedical Research*, 1973; 6:544-560.
6. Dojat, M., Harf, A., Touchard, D., Laforest, M., Lemaire, F. & Brochard, L., Evaluation of a knowledge-based system providing ventilatory management and decision for extubation, *American Journal of Respiratory and Critical Care Medicine*, 1996.
7. Adlassnig, K.P., Horak, W., & Hepaxpert, I. Automatic interpretation of Tests for Hepatitis A and B, *MD Computing*, 1991; 8(2):118-119.
8. Hripcsak, G., Clayton, P.D., Cimino, J.J., Johnson, S.B. & Friedman C. Medical decision support at Columbia-Presbyterian Medical Center. In: Timmers T. & Blum B.I., editors. *Software Engineering in Medical Informatics*. Amsterdam: North-Holland, 1991:471-9.
9. Hripcsak, G., Ludemann, P., Pryor, T.A., Wigertz, O.B. & Clayton, P.D. Rationale for the Arden Syntax. *Computers and Biomedical Research* 1994; 27:291-324.
10. Gierl, L. & Stengel-Rutkowski, S., Integrating Consultation and Semi-automatic Knowledge Acquisition in a Prototype-based Architecture: Experiences with Dysmorphic Syndromes, *Artificial Intelligence in Medicine*, 1994; 6:29-49.
11. Trendelenburg, C. & Pohl, B. Pro. M. D.: Medical Diagnostics with Expert Systems An introduction to the expert system shell Pro. M. D. Medisoft, 1995.
12. Coiera E. Guide to Medical Informatics, the Internet and Telemedicine, Chapman & Hall Medical, 1997. See also "Artificial Intelligence Systems in Routine Clinical use", *http://www-uk.hpl.hp.com/people/ewc/list.html*.
13. Maran, A.G.D., Molony, N.C., Armstrong, M.W.J. & Ah-See, K., Is there an evidence base for the practice of ENT surgery? *Clinical Otolaryngology* 1997; 22:152-157.
14. Haggie, K. & Kingston, J., KBS Tool Selection for a Medical Protocol Decision Support System for Surgical Treatment of the Thyroid, unpublished report, AIAI/CISA, School of Informatics, University of Edinburgh.

SmartGov: A Knowledge-Based Design Approach to Online Social Service Creation

Nicholas J. Adams[1], Simon Haston[2], Ann Macintosh[1], John Fraser[1], Andy McKay-Hubbard[1], and Andrew Unsworth[2]

[1]International Teledemocracy Centre, Napier University
10 Colinton Road, Edinburgh, EH10 5DT, UK
Telephone: +44 (0) 131 455 2545 Fax: +44 (0) 131 455 2282
www.teledemocracy.org

[2]The City of Edinburgh Council
Wellington Court, 10 Waterloo Place, Edinburgh EH1 3EG, UK

Abstract

This paper covers the work of the SmartGov project [1], a collaborative project funded by the European Commission under their Information Society Technologies (IST) 5th Framework Programme, as it has been piloted in the Social Work Department in the City of Edinburgh Council.

The most significant innovation of the SmartGov platform, which sets it apart from other recent online service implementations for Public Authorities is its use of the e-government ontology [2, 3]. This enables the staff at the Public Authority to record and categorise expert knowledge that they have accrued about service provision so that it can be disseminated among staff, and where applicable selected knowledge can be made available to the users to assist in their completion of online forms and use of the service.

The application described in this paper applies knowledge management techniques using knowledge units and an e-government ontology, to develop and deliver an assessment system for the supply of equipment and adaptations. We describe the building of the SmartGov platform, then detail the deployment in the Equipment and Adaptations service. Finally we consider the performance and evaluation measures for the application.

1. Introduction

The city of Edinburgh in Scotland has one of the fastest growing economies in the UK. To meet this growth it is expected that the number of households in the city will increase by 35,000 by 2016. Correspondingly the demand for public services will increase substantially. To address this pressure for services, the City of Edinburgh Council (CEC) has prepared a 21st Century Action Plan for the development and deployment of e-government transaction services. This is part of the City's "Smart City Strategy" which argues for a radical shift in the delivery of public services over the next five years. Establishing partnerships and harnessing research is fundamental to achieving the strategy. Specifically the City wishes to use leading-edge Information and Communication Technologies (ICT) to re-design its back office processes and support knowledge sharing between the various government departments and external agencies who together provide key services [4], such that by 2005 all appropriate council services will be available electronically [5, 6]. A key requirement is that by 2005 on-line self-assessment in functions such as Social Work will be available. This will mean that intelligent, well-structured assessment tools will support citizens to assess their own and family members' needs for certain Social Work services.

The application described in this paper, applies knowledge management techniques using knowledge units and an e-government ontology, to develop and deliver an assessment system for the supply of equipment and adaptations in Social Work. The work is a part of a large collaborative project called SmartGov, which is part funded by the European Commission under their IST 5th Framework Programme. The overall aim of the SmartGov project is to specify, develop, deploy and evaluate a knowledge-based platform to assist public sector employees to generate online transaction services by simplifying their development, maintenance and integration with already installed IT systems. The overall project has been described previously by [1]. There are five partners from across the European Union; the University of Athens, Napier University in Edinburgh, Indra (Spain), Archetypon (Greece) and TNB (Germany), all providing the technical contribution; and two end-user Government Agencies, The Greek Ministry of Finance and The City of Edinburgh Council.

SmartGov, of course, should not be considered in isolation of other artificial intelligence, and knowledge management related projects being undertaken in the Public Sector, but we hope that it will play its part in increasing understanding as to how state-of-the-art artificial intelligence techniques may best serve Public Authorities. For some recent examples of applications in this area see [7-9].

Here we describe the building and deployment of the initial pilot of the SmartGov application for the Social Works Department in the Council. We start in Section 2 by providing a description of the existing public service and problems related to it, which SmartGov should solve. From this define the set of objectives for the SmartGov Platform. In the following Sections we then describe the application, discuss its implementation, before considering performance and evaluation measures for the pilot application. Finally in Section 6 we conclude and discuss future plans for SmartGov.

2. The Equipment and Adaptations Service

The public service, which is the basis for the intelligent application using SmartGov, is concerned with the provision of any equipment required in the care of the elderly and infirm residents of Edinburgh. This is known locally as the Equipment and Adaptations Service, which is managed by the Social Work department in the Council.

The existing procedure for procuring equipment for a customer involves either a Social Worker, Occupational Therapist (OT) or Healthcare professional assessing the customer's needs and creating a Care Plan. This plan is then agreed with the customer after which their equipment needs, if any, are identified and ordered using paper-based forms. These forms are forwarded to Stores who are responsible for the administration and moving of the equipment to the customer, and reclaiming it when it is no longer required.

For the administration of these services in Edinburgh, the city is divided into four sectors each covered by two Social Work offices. Typically in a four day period one sector may create 250 requests for equipment, each requiring the completion of an A4-sized form (called a 305 form). During this process a Social Worker or Occupational Therapist may have to consult a catalogue to identify the equipment, the client index database to fill in client details, and a variety of other sources. All of these add an overhead, and here electronic service provision holds the potential to contribute much towards streamlining what is currently a very time consuming, but important service. The following Figure describes the steps involved and includes reference to the three legacy databases (Carenap, Social Work Client Index and Midas) currently used to administer the service.

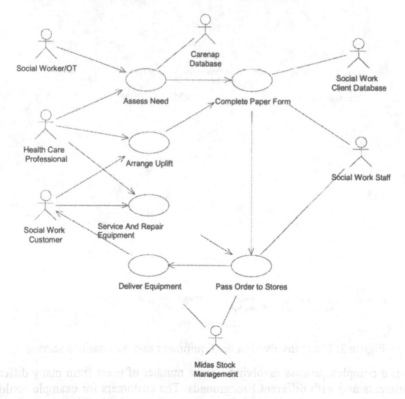

Figure 1: Existing Equipment and Adaptations Service

Assess Need: The qualified professional completes a client assessment form. Through it a client's need for equipment are ascertained. Once completed the client is asked to agree that the assessment is accurate. The result of the assessment is a Care Plan.

Complete Paper Form: A standard paper form is used to apply for all equipment. The need for the equipment is assessed primarily on client's need, but also takes into account budgetary considerations. Each worker has a unique user ID which authorises them to order a specific subset of equipment.

Pass Order to Stores: The order is passed to stores who acquire and ship all equipment.

Deliver Equipment: A team of drivers, each responsible for a particular geographic region of the city, deliver the equipment. The Stores Administrators organise their delivery schedules from data supplied by the Midas stock control system.

Arrange Uplift: Arrange to uplift any unwanted items from a customer's home.

Service And Repair Equipment: Faulty equipment needs to be repaired, and some may require servicing periodically. Either the Customer or a Service Professional can initiate this process.

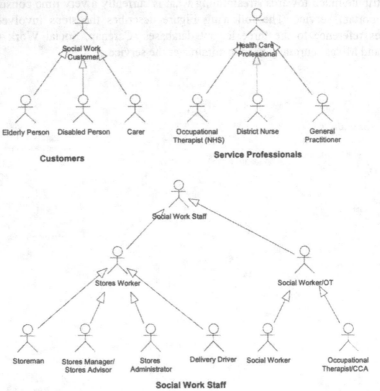

Figure 2: Users involved in the Equipment and Adaptations service

This is a complex process involving a large number of users from many different departments and with different backgrounds. The customers for example could be an elderly person, disabled person or a carer acting on their behalf. Occupational Therapists or Social Workers employed by CEC or external Healthcare Professionals have responsibility for assessing the client and ordering the equipment, and there is a network of stores staff who actually supply it. These user groups are summarised in Figure 2.

The transaction service is further complicated by the existence of three legacy database systems which have to be accommodated in the development of the e-transaction service:

- **Carenap:** A Microsoft Access Database holding the Care Plan details.
- **Social Work Client Database:** Core database used by the Social Work Department to record customer details.
- **Midas Stock Management System:** Stock management database. It is currently independent of the Social Work Core Client Database, and consequently many of the customer details have to be entered twice.

The complexity of the process, the large number of potential users and the requirement to integrate existing software systems highlighted the need to develop an e-transaction service ontology. The large number of users with diverse backgrounds ranging from highly trained NHS nurses to family carers highlighted the need to share knowledge throughout the process and ensure knowledge management techniques were applied in the e-transaction service.

With the current paper-based system there is a very high error rate in the 305 forms used, and a conservative estimate is that in excess of 30% of forms contain at least one error. Many errors stem from omissions, or the handwriting of the applicant being difficult to decipher, which can usually be overcome through the ingenuity and domain knowledge of the Service Professionals in the Joint Equipment Stores. However it can still (and often does) lead to erroneous or duplicate records in the database – if for example an existing client cannot be identified from the information given. More serious errors include the wrong catalogue number being recorded for the equipment, which if undiscovered could lead to a failed delivery. The SmartGov Platform through facilitating checks and lookup of data held electronically will hopefully dramatically reduce such errors, and greatly improve this service.

3. Developing the e-Transaction Service

In this Section we first give a summary of the main features of the overall SmartGov system and then consider in detail the Equipment and Adaptation Service.

3.1. Objectives of SmartGov

SmartGov delivers an intelligent e-forms environment, e-transaction service ontology and an associated knowledge management methods specific to the Public Sector. The development of the SmartGov platform for transaction services has been based on a number of diverse technological areas. It has been necessary to integrate conventional techniques, such as the Internet, XML and user-centred interfaces with AI related techniques such as knowledge based systems and ontologies. Furthermore, knowledge management and process reference models that will enable social acceptance of the system and overcome organisational and cultural barriers support the deployment of the platform.

The key aspects of the SmartGov system are a knowledge base housing the domain knowledge required for e-government services, and a SmartGov agent to allow the system to communicate with other IT systems, operating through an information interchange gateway. The information interchange gateway is the portal through which SmartGov communicates with other IT systems. It publishes an export schema containing the data items that need to be accessed by services running within the SmartGov framework. The schema serves as the vessel for communication but the responsibility for initiating and handling the communication lies with the SmartGov agent. An overview of the platform architecture is given in Figure 3.

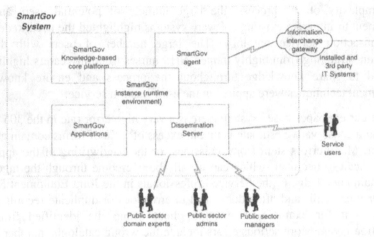

Figure 3: Overview of the SmartGov system

SmartGov is delivering a knowledge-based e-services development environment, together with associated process models, that will facilitate development, deployment, management and maintenance of electronic services. In detail the project deliverables include:

- ❑ a knowledge-based core repository for governmental transaction services. This repository contains the basic Transaction Services. Core elements that can be used to build up the public services and includes domain specific information and knowledge.
- ❑ facilities for specifying and developing the SmartGov services and applications for creating and maintaining e-services, and for communicating with installed IT systems, including:
  - o Services (e.g. SmartGov agent and Information Interchange Gateway) for the communication with other IT systems.
  - o E-services Applications for the different users of the platform (i.e. IT department, managers, service workers and end-users).
  - o An administrative tool for the knowledge-based repository.
  - o The Dissemination Server to support different access channels.
- ❑ a knowledge management methodology specific to the public sector based on process models and relevant social aspects in order to deploy the SmartGov platform and realise its full potential.

SmartGov delivers a development environment that enables public sector employees at different levels to develop and maintain services for both the citizens and for other public authorities. In such an environment an employee with basic IT skills and the necessary domain knowledge is able to use a predefined form template or create a new form in order to implement a new service or to edit an existing service. The knowledge-based development environment supports the employee by offering advice and also automating parts of the development process. At the end of the development procedure the employee is able to activate the service even if the connection to the back-end legacy systems has not been implemented yet. The SmartGov Agent retains all collected data and once the IT staff implement the connection to the back-end the data can be processed.

Since the forms contain not only the objects but also the knowledge and the logic associated with them, the SmartGov system is able to automatically do simple type checking on the form's data and also other more complex validations. Furthermore, if an alteration takes place to the domain knowledge (e.g. change in legislation concerning some of the form elements) the system will either automatically update the validation checks or notify the developer of the possible implications. In the implementation of the SmartGov platform the whole service is encapsulated in a definition called the Transaction Service (TS), containing one or more component elements called Transaction Service Elements (TSEs).

Underpinning the whole SmartGov Platform is a knowledge base that provides the necessary Public Authority specific information required for it to operate. This knowledge base consists of individual items of knowledge – called Knowledge Units (KUs) – organised through an ontology. The use of ontologies is a key principle that is the foundation of this knowledge base, and the entire SmartGov approach. As well as the application domain specific ontologies to support the end-user applications – which will be outlined later – further ontologies have been identified in the context of government online transaction services: process, co-operation and trust. Collectively we have termed these the Government Services Ontology. It consists of a set of over 150 rigorously defined terms, describing the domain of government service provision. The terms were extracted from set of more than 60 interview texts of staff within the City of Edinburgh Council, complimented by other documents published on the internet by government sponsored projects working in this area. This was achieved using term extraction software to find the (meaningful) words most commonly used by the staff working in this arena, and then further developed through a series of workshops involving the PA staff. From the ontology, a set of five taxonomies were extracted for use in the SmartGov platform. They are organised under the following parent terms:

- PA Admin   terms relating to the administration and monitoring of the services provided by the PA
- PA Structure   terms defining organisational structure within the PA
- External environment   terms describing external factors, such as legislation and public-private-partnerships
- Clients   terms describing clients of PA, and their various needs
- Service   terms relating to the different types of services provided by the Public Authority

For further details on this work, please consult [2, 3, 10].

3.2.   Applying SmartGov to the Equipment and Adaptations Service

For requirements capture, we followed the Unified Modelling Method (UML) to identify actors and use cases, returning often to the Social Work department to get feedback on the UML model as we developed it. We developed activity diagrams for the more complex operations in the application.

Extensive interviews were carried out with staff using structured questionnaires, and from their responses user requirements for the various actors in the UML use cases were extracted. For each of these user requirements, we looked at each one in turn to decide whether the previously defined broad functional requirements would support it. Wherever the previous functional requirements were not adequate, we defined new functional requirements.

The following two Figures model the requirements for SmartGov in order to achieve this desired functionality. The first is an update to the current process model shown earlier, and the second details the back-office services within the Stores. For each a description of the use cases is given.

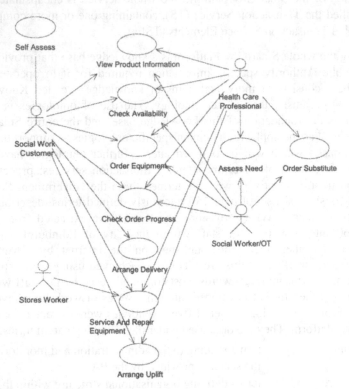

Figure 4: Equipment and Adaptations user requirements

Assess Need: A client assessment form is completed by the qualified professional. Through it a client's need for equipment will be ascertained. Once completed the client is asked to agree that the assessment is accurate. Nurses are employed by the Health Service and use their own system of assessment and application for equipment. The result of the assessment is a Care Plan.

Self Assess: Facility for client to assess their own need for a range of low-cost equipment which does not need healthcare professional involvement.

View Product Information: Browse an online catalogue detailing all equipment held. Visibility of items should be limited depending on the user type who is browsing.

Check Availability: Check availability of items within the Stores. Visibility of items should be limited depending on the user type who is browsing.

Order Equipment: Complete an order for equipment using an online form.

Order Substitute: If desired item is not available then provide a list of alternatives. Certain choices may require advice from specific professionals as to its suitability for the job.

Check Order Progress: The customer or Service Professional can track the status of equipment that they have on order.

Arrange Delivery: Arrange to deliver ordered items to customer's home.

Service And Repair Equipment: Faulty equipment needs to be repaired, and some may require servicing periodically. Either the Customer or a Service Professional can initiate this process.

Arrange Uplift: Arrange to uplift any returning items from a customer's home.

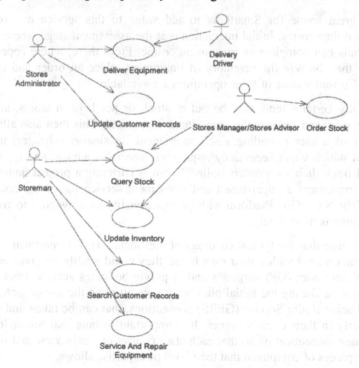

Figure 5: Equipment and Adaptations stores use cases

Deliver Equipment: A team of drivers – each responsible for a particular geographic region of the city – delivers the equipment. The Stores Administrators organise their delivery schedules from data supplied by the Midas stock control system.

Update Customer Records: On receipt of a paper equipment order form, enter the customer details into the database. (We still need to support a paper system.)

Query Stock: Query facilities for monitoring the stock level and performance, and writing reports.

Update Inventory: Whenever an item of equipment is issued or received it is necessary to update the inventory. A facility for stating that some items are in-stock but currently unavailable (e.g. due to repair or cleaning) would provide useful functionality that the current Midas system does not have.

Search Customer Records: Reasons for needing to search customer records include providing information to a customer about equipment they have ordered and for general administrative purposes.

Service And Repair Equipment: Faulty equipment needs to be repaired, and some may require servicing periodically. Either the Customer or a Service Professional can initiate this process.

Order Stock: When stock items fall below set minimum thresholds new items need to be re-ordered. The stores manager/assistant has this responsibility. Most items can be re-ordered from suppliers under standard contracts. Expensive/specialist items need authorisation from Central Purchasing

There is great scope for SmartGov to add value to this service by providing intelligent online forms. Initial interaction is at the assessment stage where service professionals can complete an assessment online. From there, where appropriate, they may then browse the inventory of Equipment, place an order and track its progress. Currently none of these operations are available.

Occasionally certain items may be out of stock or not held in stores, and so a facility to view and order replacement items is required. This then also allows the possibility of a user providing a self assessment for smaller (cheaper) items of equipment which won't necessarily require any specialist advice, and for them to place and track their own orders online. There is currently a project underway to formally implement a paper-based self assessment service for customers, so the arrival of the SmartGov Platform with the functionality to allow staff to create the service online is most timely.

While it is true that the typical customer of the Social Work Department may not have internet access within their own home, they could readily be given access at General Practitioner (GP) surgeries and in public buildings such as libraries and social services. During the initial pilot we are also trialing the use of laptops with General Packet Radio Service (GPRS) connections, that can be taken and used by OTs directly in their client's homes. It is important to note that SmartGov must provide user authentication so that each class of user can only view and order the particular pieces of equipment that their level of expertise allows.

4. Timescales and Resources for SmartGov

The Figure 6 shows the steps undertaken in the implementation of the SmartGov platform, and the configuration and deployment of it in the pilot for the Equipment and Adaptations Service, at the City of Edinburgh Council.

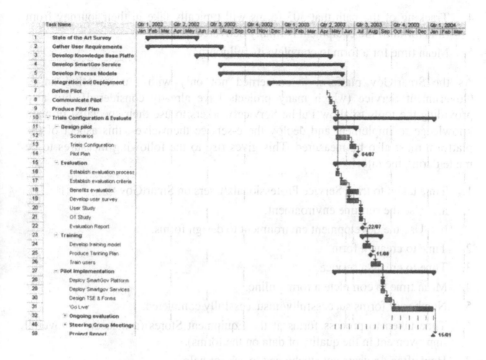

Figure 6: The SmartGov project plan

The total budget for the project was €3,202,328, of which €1,950,000 was provided by the European Commission. It started on 1st February 2002, with an expected duration of 24 months. The consortium consisted of the following seven partners; Dept Informatics and Telecommunications at National and Capodistrian University of Athens; International Teledemocracy Centre at Napier University; T-Systems Nova, Berkom; Indra Sistemas S.A.; Archetypon S.A.; General Secretariat for Information Systems, Greek Ministry of Finance; and City of Edinburgh Council.

5. Evaluation and Potential Benefits of the e-Service

Evaluation of the performance of the SmartGov platform consists of two stages. The first stage consists of measurements of the service prior to deployment of the pilot. The results are then used to provide the baseline for assessing the performance of the SmartGov platform, measured during the second stage.

Measurement of the existing service is primarily focused around the 305 form, as this is the current vehicle for requesting equipment within the CEC.

1. Numbers of errors of various types. These will take form of count boxes for each type of error to be completed by staff over a specified period, to ascertain existing error rates.
2. Number of forms requiring extra information/needing to be returned.
3. Mean time for an OT/Service Professional to complete a paper 305 form.

4. Tracking of the path that 305 forms will typically take in their journey from initiator until the equipment is finally delivered.

5. Mean time for a form to complete its full journey.

As the SmartGov platform is concerned not only with implementing an e-Government Service (which many projects have already considered), but also providing the tools to allow Public Service workers to use their specialist domain knowledge to implement and deploy the e-service themselves, this aspect of the platform must also be measured. This gives rise to the following measures to be made during the pilot:

1. Time taken to train Service Professionals/Users on SmartGov to:
    a. Use the runtime environment.
    b. Use the development environment to design forms.
2. Time to create a form.
3. Time to create a service.
4. Mean time to complete a form online.
5. Number of forms successfully/unsuccessfully completed.
6. Time taken to process forms at the Equipment Stores (a measure of overall improvement in the quality of data on the forms).
7. How often do users get stuck/need to ask for help.
8. Sharing information:
    a. Number of knowledge units created.
    b. Number of accesses to each knowledge unit.
9. Re-usability: amount of re-use of:
    a. Transaction service elements.
    b. Knowledge units.
10. Errors in software.
11. Learnability:
    a. Can the worker repeat the task?
    b. Can the worker teach the task to others?
    c. How often does the worker/user need to ask for help?
12. User Interface:
    a. How often is it that user can't find something?
    b. Does the user interface help or obstruct user in performing a specific task?
13. Memorability: Can the worker/user remember how to perform a task after a time period?
14. Level of acceptance by users.

The user evaluation of the SmartGov Platform on the Equipment and Adaptations Service starts in September 2003. An important component of considering the evaluation is, what constitutes as a definition of success? This is actually quite difficult. Things that will be needed to be taken into account will include:

• User acceptance – involving all types of users. Much of this is achievable through concise structured questionnaires

- Improvements to the delivered service –
  - o Mean time to complete a form/access the service
  - o Processing time improvements in back office (through better quality data)
  - o Reduction in failed deliveries arising from incorrect or incomplete orders
- Sharing of information –
  - o Number of knowledge units (KUs) created by operators of the platform
  - o Degree to which KUs are accessed by Service Professionals/End Users
- Re-usability of components –
  - o Amount of re-use of transaction service elements (TSEs)
  - o Level of re-use of KUs

The overall focus of the evaluation is to quantify the benefits that SmartGov has given to the delivery of the Equipment and Adaptations Service. Among these we hope that the potential benefits will include a significant reduction in erroneous forms, as common errors will be spotted at the form completion stage through intelligence built into the platform, and the knowledge base guiding users through areas that tend to prove difficult to get right. The knock-on effect will be a reduction in time to complete the forms and back-office processing of the order, cleaner and more accurate data on clients and the equipment that they hold, and a higher degree of successful order deliveries[1].

Another potential benefit will be the provision of facilities that hitherto have been unavailable through conventional means, the most notable of which is that of real-time feedback on the status of the orders being made available to OTs. Up until now it has not been viable to achieve this, with the procedure being that on receipt of the equipment the responsibility is given to the customer to inform their OT that it has arrived – which in addition to being highly fallible places upon them an unnecessary burden that is far less than satisfactory. It will also enable OTs to answer direct enquiries from their clients in situations where they may not have received their equipment after some wait, and want to know how things are progressing – such as if the equipment is out of stock and they have been placed on a waiting list.

6. Discussion

This paper has covered the work of the SmartGov project as it has been piloted in the Social Work Department in the City of Edinburgh Council. We have described the building and deployment of the initial pilot of the SmartGov platform, and described in detail the specific Equipment and Adaptations Service. Finally we have considered performance and evaluation measures for the pilot application.

The most significant innovation of the SmartGov platform which sets it apart from other recent online service implementations for Public Authorities is its use of the

---

[1] A very common reason for failed deliveries is that the wrong equipment is ordered, or when the client receives it they decide it is inappropriate for their needs and reject it. Through provision of electronic catalogue facilities within SmartGov users should be better informed about equipment that is ordered, thus reducing the likelihood of such problems.

government services ontology [2, 3].This enables the staff at the Public Authority to record and categorise expert knowledge that they have accrued about service provision, so that it can be disseminated among staff, and where applicable selected knowledge can be made available to the users to assist in their completion of online forms and use of the service.

We see in the Equipment and Adaptations Service a number of examples of co-operation between different agencies (Social Work and Healthcare), and notice that the provision of the service involves many sub-processes, some of which make reference to unconnected legacy IT systems. This service is fairly representative in complexity to other services the City of Edinburgh Council currently provides, and therefore by piloting the SmartGov platform for the Equipment and Adaptations Service we can also appreciate its usefulness for other services.

Acknowledgements

SmartGov is an European Union funded project under IST 5th Framework Programme Key Action Line: On-line support for democratic processes, grant number IST-2001-35399.

References

[1]   Georgiadis, P., Lepouras, G., Vassilakis, C., Boukis, G., Tambouris, T., Gorilas, S., Davenport, E., Macintosh, A., Fraser, J., Lochhead, D.: SmartGov: A Knowledge-Based Platform for Electronic Transactional Services. In: Proc. DEXA 2002, The 1st International Conference on Electronic Government - EGOV 2002 (2002)

[2]   Adams, N. J., Fraser, J., Macintosh, A., McKay-Hubbard, A.: Towards an Ontology for Electronic Transaction Services. International Journal of Intelligent Systems in Accounting, Finance and Management 11 (2002) 173-181

[3]   Fraser, J., Adams, N., Macintosh, A., McKay-Hubbard, A., Lobo, T. P., Pardo, P. F., Martínez, R. C., Vallecillo, J. S.: Knowledge Management Applied to e-Government Services: The Use of an Ontology. In: Proc. Knowledge Management in Electronic Government - KMGov2003 (2003)

[4]   eEurope. Common List of Basic Public Services. eEurope . Available: http://158. 168.149.15/information_society/eeurope/action_plan/pdf/basicpublicservices.pdf

[5]   UK Government E-Envoy's Office. Modernising Government White Paper. Her Majesty's Stationary Office . Available: http://www.e-envoy.gov.uk/oee/oee.nsf/ sections/ukonline-top/$file/related_reps.htm

[6]   European Commission. Public Sector Information: A Key Resource for Europe. Green Paper on Public Sector Information in the Information Society. European Commission . Available: ftp.echo.lu/pub/ info2000/publicsector/ gppublicen.doc

[7]   Palkovits, S., Woitsch, R., Karagiannis, D.: Process-Based Knowledge Management and Modelling in e-Government - An Inevitable Combination. In: Proc. 4th IFIP International Working Conference, Knowledge Management in Electronic Government - KMGOV 2003 (2003) 213-218

[8]   Paralic, J., Sabol, T., Mach, M.: Knowledge Enhanced e-Government Portal. In: Proc. 4th IFIP International Working Conference, Knowledge Management in Electronic Government - KMGOV 2003 (2003) 163-174

[9]   Bouguettaya, A., Ouzzani, M., Medjahed, B., Elmagarmid, A. K.: Supporting Data and Services Access in Digital Government Environments. In: W. J. M. Jr. and A. K. Elmagarmid, (eds.): Advances in Digital Government, Technology, Human Factors, and Policy. Kluwer Academic Publishers (2002) 37-52

[10]   McKay-Hubbard, A., Macintosh, A.: Models of Trust for Knowledge-Based Government Services. In: Proc. DEXA 2003, The 2nd International Conference on Electronic Government - EGOV 2003 (2003)

SESSION 5:

IMAGE RECOGNITION, KNOWLEDGE BASES, ATTRIBUTE SELECTION

Robot Docking with Neural Vision and Reinforcement

Cornelius Weber

and

Stefan Wermter

and

Alexandros Zochios

Centre for Hybrid Intelligent Systems, University of Sunderland
Sunderland, UK   [www.his.sunderland.ac.uk]

July 2003

Abstract

We present a solution for robotic docking, i.e. the approach of a robot toward a table so that it can grasp an object. One constraint is that our PeopleBot robot has a short non-extendable gripper and wide "shoulders". Therefore it must approach the table at a perpendicular angle so that the gripper can reach over it. Another constraint is the use of vision to locate the object. Only the angle is supplied as additional input.

We present a solution based solely on neural networks: object recognition and localisation is trained, motivated by insights from the lower visual system. Based on the hereby obtained perceived location, we train a value function unit and four motor units via reinforcement learning. After training the robot can approach the table at the correct position and in a perpendicular angle. This is to be used as part of a bigger system where the robot acts according to verbal instructions based on multi-modal neuronal representations as found in language and motor cortex (mirror neurons).

1   Introduction

There have been a lot of insights into neural networks and the way the brain works. Also, there have been simulations of how such networks can perform interesting tasks. But when it comes to robotic implementation, traditional artificial intelligence methods are still dominant. One reason for this is that both sophisticated perception and motor skills need to be combined in order to display non-trivial behaviour. However, these cannot be achieved with a single algorithm/network type. Therefore, we propose a hybrid network trained with reinforcement, unsupervised and supervised training to perform a vision-based docking action.

For docking, usually non-trainable models of vision are used such as optic flow from log-polar vision [1], correlation operators on search templates [11] or other devices such as laser range finders [10][14] are used as sensory input. Models of grasping need more sophisticated geometrical information about the

213

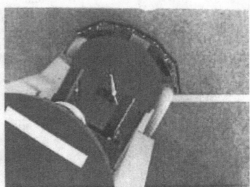

Figure 1: The PeopleBot robot during the docking manoeuvre. On the left are visible the camera pointing downward (mounted underneath the top plate) and the black grippers. Right, the scenario from above. The black grippers are hardly to be seen over the dark robot's base; a fraction of the camera can be seen bright.

object, and use vision algorithms based on graph matching [2], Gabor jets [9] or 3-D geometrical object models [8]. The control scheme employed is usually based on geometrical calculations. Also a reinforcement solution for docking has been presented [6] in which to pre-process the input a neural gas was used for clustering and a neural field for topological action coding. Visual goal recognition was done with colour-based threshold operations.

Many of the docking or grasping scenarios are part of larger projects or goals such as implementing a perceptually guided robot [2] and using hand gestures for robot teaching [9]. Emphasis is put on high-speed performance [8], recharging batteries [10], using embodied representations [1] or addressing top-level control issues [11]. In our case, higher-level mirror neuron behaviour shall be modelled (see discussion). Therefore, we seek a neural network representation of a complex behaviour to obtain realistic input to the envisaged higher level.

Our robot has a single behaviour: in any state it selects the action which leads to the largest expected reward. This makes the action selection network the core part. It consists of four neurons, one of them is "on" at any time, which denote forward, backward, left and right movement of the robot. During training, they are guided by the firing rate of one "value function" unit which assigns a fitness value to any state. Together, these five neurons are trained by reinforcement learning, in which a scalar reinforcement signal is given only at

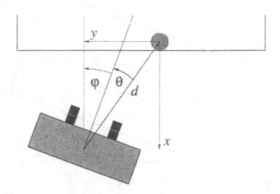

Figure 2: Geometry of the scenario in top view. The figure depicts the table, above, with the orange fruit target on it (filled circle). Below is the robot with its short black grippers. The rectangular field that is visible from the robotic camera facing downward is outlined by a dotted line. Real world coordinates (x, y, φ) specify the position and rotation angle of the robot. The perceived position of the target within the robot's visual field is then defined by the perceived angle θ and distance d.

the end of each training action sequence. The value of the signal is positive, if the robot docks at the object in parallel to the table, or negative, if the robot's shoulders bump into the table at an angle or if the object is lost out of sight (Fig. 2).

The input to the action selection network is the robot's visual perceptual state, defined by its relative position to the target, an orange fruit at the border of a table. The vision module is thus the peripheral part. Vision skills are trained unsupervised as well as supervised. Unsupervised training leads to a sparsely coded hidden representation of an input image. The perceptually important representation of the target object within the image is then trained in a supervised manner: a recurrent associator neural network learns to associate the internal representation of the entire image with the (given) position of the target object. Additional input to the action selection network is the robot rotation angle φ, supplied by the robot's internal odometry.

2 Methods

The peripheral vision module is trained before the action selection network so that it can supply it the necessary visually obtained perception as input. Overall, we have three training phases: first, training the weights W^{td} and W^{bu} between the visual input and the "what" area (see Fig. 3), second, training the lateral weights W^{lat} within and between the "what" and the "where" area,

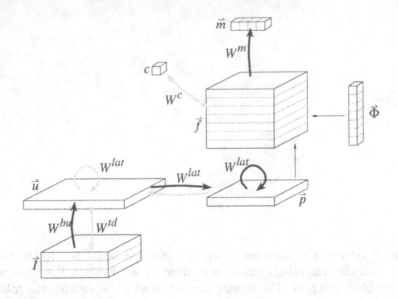

Figure 3: The neural network. Thick arrows denote trained weights W. Only the ones depicted dark are used during performance while those depicted bright are involved in training. Letters other than W denote activations (vectors) on the neural sheets: $\vec{I}$ is the camera image which contains three layers for its red, green and blue colour components. $\vec{u}$ is the hidden representation ("what")of the image. $\vec{p}$ contains the perceived location ("where") of the target within the image. $\vec{\Phi}$ has a Gaussian profile centered on the rotation angle φ of the robot. $\vec{f}$ is the perceptual space, made up by multiplying $\vec{p}$ and $\vec{\Phi}$. c, the critic, holds the value function which is assigned to each perceptual state $\vec{f}$ unit. $\vec{m}$ are the four motor unit activations.

and finally, training the weights W^c and W^m from the conceptual space to the critic of the motor outputs, respectively.

2.1 Training the Vision Module – Feature Detectors

In the first phase, we will obtain feature detector neurons on the "what" area to have a more abstract, higher level representation $\vec{u}$ of the input image $\vec{I}$ (Fig. 3). This is done based on the idea that the model should *generate* the data $\vec{I}$ from a *sparse* representation $\vec{u}$. This is done by the wake-sleep algorithm [7], in which two learning steps are alternatingly repeated until training has completed: *(i)* in the "wake phase", train the top-down, generative weights W^{td} based on the difference between a randomly chosen natural image $\vec{I}^{orig}$ and its reconstruction $\vec{I}^{rec}$ obtained from the internal representation $\vec{u}$ of the picture. *(ii)* in the "sleep phase", train the bottom-up, recognition weights W^{bu} based on the difference between a random hidden code $\vec{u}^{orig}$ and its reconstruction $\vec{u}^{rec}$ obtained from the visual representation $\vec{I}$ of the original hidden code. Training involves only local learning rules and results in localised edge detectors akin to the simple cells of visual area V1. With additional modifications to the learning algorithm the mapping is also topographic.

The following pseudo-code describes the training algorithm in which the wake phase and the sleep phase alternate each other repeatedly. Wake phase:

1. Take a picture $\vec{I}^{orig}$

2. Get a *sparse* hidden representation on the "what" area $\vec{u}$

3. Reconstruct the picture $\vec{I}^{rec}$

4. Top-down weight update: $\quad W^{td} \approx (\vec{I}^{orig} - \vec{I}^{rec}) \cdot \vec{u}$

Sleep phase:

1. Generate a *sparse, topographic* random hidden code $\vec{u}^{orig}$

2. Get the imagined picture $\vec{I}$

3. Reconstruct the hidden code $\vec{u}^{rec}$

4. Bottom-up weight update: $\quad W^{bu} \approx (\vec{u}^{orig} - \vec{u}^{rec}) \cdot \vec{I}$

This algorithm, described in detail in [12], approximates the Helmholtz machine [3]. Fig. 4, left, shows examples of trained weights, most of which have become localised edge detectors, while some neurons are colour selective.

2.2 Training the Vision Module – Object Localisation

The second phase, training the lateral weights W^{lat} between and within the "what" and "where" areas (Fig. 3), requires the first phase to be completed. Intra-area lateral connections within the "where" area (visual area V1) were originally implemented to endow the simple cells with biologically realistic orientation tuning curves: their orientation tuning curves were sharpened via competition, mediated by the lateral weights. In addition, shift invariances were trained and thus V1 complex cells generated [12]. The function of the lateral weights is to memorise the underlying representation over time. As a attractor of a real-valued recurrent network, the representation is thereby simplified. We exploit this for pattern completion where the representation $\vec{u}$ of an image with an object of interest is given on the "what" area while its location $\vec{p}$ on the *where* area is not given – while it has always been given during training.

Training is done by the following procedure: every image $\vec{I}$ now contains a simulated orange fruit at a particular location and this location is reflected – in a supervised manner – as a Gaussian on the "where" area. So the lateral weights are trained to memorise the internal representation $(\vec{u}, \vec{p})$ of the image and the location of the orange. After training, when we have the representation $\vec{u}$ of an image with an orange but don't know the location of the orange. Then pattern completion will give us its location, coded in $\vec{p}$.

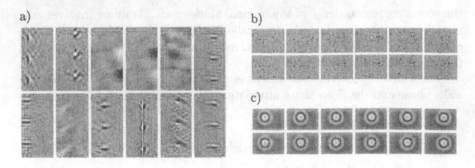

Figure 4: A selection of trained weights of the vision module. Dark shades of grey denote negative; bright, positive weights. **a)** The receptive fields of 12 "what" units, taken from the centre of W^{bu}. Each unit has three sets of weights to the red, green and blue sub-layers of the input. Three of the upper units are colour selective, as the weights are different in different sub-layers. **b)** and **c)** The receptive fields of 12 "where" units, taken from those parts of W^{lat} which are depicted dark in Fig. 3. The weights from the "what" to the "where" area, b), are sparse. The recurrent weights within the "where" area, c), are centre-excitatory and surround inhibitory, because they were trained to maintain a Gaussian activity profile. Self-connections were set to zero.

The following pseudo-code describes a step of the training algorithm, which is repeatedly applied after the "what" network has been trained.

1. Take a natural image with an orange placed at location $\vec{L}$

2. Get the hidden representation on the "what" area $\vec{u}$

3. Initialise $\vec{p}^{L}$ on the "where" area to contain a Gaussian at location $\vec{L}$

4. Initialise activities on "what" and "where" areas as: $\quad \vec{A}^{orig} = \{\vec{u}, \vec{p}^{L}\}$

5. Relaxate activations using W^{lat} for a couple of steps; memorise as $\vec{A}^{attrac}$

6. Weight update: $\quad W^{lat} \approx \underbrace{(\vec{A}^{orig} - \vec{A}^{attrac})} \cdot \vec{A}^{attrac}$

The under-braced term is the association error between the desired state and the one memorised as an attractor. Since $\vec{p}^{L}$ is not naturally contained in the data but produced artificially, training is supervised. Details and parameters are given in [13].

Trained weights are shown in Fig. 4, middle and right, while Fig. 5 demonstrates their performance at object localisation. The representation $\vec{p}$ on the "where" area is at the first time step (third column) purely a result of the feed-forward input from $\vec{u}$ from the "what" area. After relaxation (right column), recurrent connections W^{lat} within the "where" area have cleaned up the representation (while $\vec{u}$ was fixed).

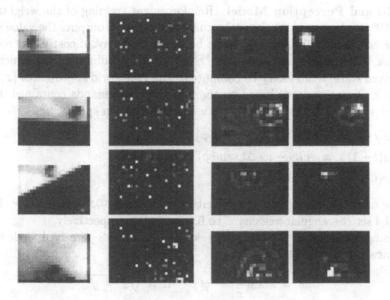

Figure 5: Each row shows, left, the 24 × 16 pixel camera image, which is originally in color. Then its representation $\vec{u}$ on the "what" area. Active units are bright. The third and fourth picture in each row are the representation $\vec{p}$ on the "where" area at the first and the last time step of a 10 iteration relaxation. The last row corresponds to the goal position where the orange is between the tips of the gripper.

2.3 Reinforcement Training of the Action Module

In the last phase, we apply reinforcement learning to the weights W^m of the motor units and the weights W^c of the value function unit. Their common input is the robot's own perceived state $\vec{f}$ which is different for every different visually perceived target location $\vec{p}$ and every different robot rotation angle $\vec{\varphi}$. The representation of $\vec{p}$ is multiplexed over, here seven, layers to obtain $\vec{f}$ (Fig. 3). Each layer corresponds to a rotation angle of the robot. Only the layer(s) nearby the actual angle have non-zero activity (Eq. 2). The weights W^c assign each state $\vec{f}$ a critic value c which is initially positive only at the goal: in our case when the target is perceived in the middle of the lower edge of the visual field **and** when the robot rotation angle φ is zero. During performance, states that lead quickly to the goal will also be assigned a higher value c by strengthening their connections to the critic unit. The weights W^m to the motor units which have been activated simultaneously are also increased, if the corresponding action leads to a better state, i.e. one which is assigned a larger c. The algorithm has been described for a rat navigation task in [4]; in the following, we will give details of our implementation.

World and Perception Model Reinforcement training of the weights W^c and W^m involves as input the perceptual state $\vec{f}$ and as outputs the value c and motor action $\vec{m}$. All these values can be simulated to avoid costly real robotic actions. The simulation runs with "real" world coordinates from which the perceived state $\vec{f}$ can easily be computed. The real world coordinates (x, y, φ) (see Fig. 2) are updated based on the movement commands contained in the output vector $\vec{m}$ for the robot speed v and the rotation speed $\dot{\varphi}$:

$$
\begin{aligned}
x(t+1) &= x(t) - v \cdot \Delta t \cdot \cos(\varphi) \\
y(t+1) &= y(t) - v \cdot \Delta t \cdot \sin(\varphi) \\
\varphi(t+1) &= \varphi(t) + \dot{\varphi} \cdot \Delta t
\end{aligned}
\tag{1}
$$

Motor units $i = 1$ and 2 set the velocity v to 0.9 and -0.9, respectively. Units 3 and 4 set the angular velocity $\dot{\varphi}$ to 0.1 and -0.1, respectively.

Using the relation $\frac{y}{x} = \tan(\varphi + \theta)$, we get the robot's perceived angle θ and distance d to the target (see Fig. 2):

$$
\theta = \operatorname{atan}(\frac{y}{x}) - \varphi , \qquad d = \sqrt{x^2 + y^2}
$$

which is used to draw the perceived target onto the simulated vision input. As a shortcut, instead of drawing a simulated orange fruit to the vision input area, we directly placed a Gaussian onto the "where" area as activation pattern $\vec{p}$.

We expand the representation $(\vec{p}, \varphi)$ so that every different combination of values leads to a different state $\vec{f}$ in the expanded perceptual space. First, φ is transformed into a 7-dimensional vector $\vec{\Phi}$ which represents values of φ between $-45°$ and $45°$ as the center of its Gaussian activity profile. $\vec{\Phi}$ is thus an ensemble of heading direction (robot rotation angle) cells, which contain the information about φ as a population code. The perceptual state vector $\vec{f}$ is a product of the perceived target location $\vec{p}$ and the heading direction vector $\vec{\Phi}$:

$$
f_{ijk} = p_{ij} \cdot \Phi_k , \quad i = 1..24, \ j = 1..16, \ k = 1..7
\tag{2}
$$

which is a Gaussian in a $24 \times 16 \times 7$-dimensional cube. Two examples of $\vec{f}$ are depicted in Fig. 6, right.

The condition whether the robot "shoulders" hit the table is tested in (x, y, φ)-space. If the distance x (of the front middle of the robot) from the table is smaller than the absolute value of $sin(\varphi) \cdot wh$ with wh the half-width of the robot, then one of the robot edges would intrude the table. This constraint in x and φ translates implicitly to the robot's perceptual space $\vec{f}$ and the robot will learn through the negative "reward" to avoid this region.

Reinforcement Algorithm A trial begins by setting the robot to a random initial position (x, y, φ). We have to make sure that the target is visible and, for simplicity, we set the robot in parallel to the table, i.e. $\varphi = 0$. Within one trial, the following steps are performed until a non-zero reward signal R is given. Each step involves one motor action and the reading of perceptions before and after.

1. Compute the perceived target $\vec{p}$ and from this, the perceived state $\vec{f}$.

2. Compute the critic activation: $c = \sum_j w_j^c \cdot f_j$

3. Compute the probability $P(m_i = 1)$ for motor unit i to be active:

$$P(m_i = 1) = \frac{e^{2a_i}}{\sum_{i'} e^{2a_{i'}}}, \qquad \text{with } a_i = \sum_j w_j^m \cdot f_j \qquad (3)$$

The probabilities sum up to 1 over the motor units. One unit is set active.

4. Move the simulated robot according to its motor output, using Eqs. 1.

5. Compute the perceived target location $\vec{p}'$ and state $\vec{f}'$.

6. Compute the critic activation: $c' = \sum_j w_j^c \cdot f_j'$

7. Set the reward signal:

$$R = \begin{cases} 1 & \text{if goal reached } (\varphi = 0 \text{ and target centred at lower} \\ & \text{edge of visual field}), \\ -0.3 & \text{if target at visual field border or robot hits table,} \\ 0 & \text{else.} \end{cases}$$

8. Compute the prediction error: $\delta = R - (c - \gamma \cdot c')$
   between the actual reward R and the critic evaluation $c - \gamma \cdot c'$. The critic evaluation is based on the assumption that the value function increases in time with future values decaying by the discount factor $\gamma = 0.9$:

$$c(t) = R(t) + \gamma \cdot R(t+1) + \gamma^2 \cdot R(t+2); + \dots$$

9. Update the critic's weights: $\Delta w_j^c \propto \delta \cdot f_j$

10. Update the weights of the only active motor unit i: $\Delta w_{ij}^m \propto \delta \cdot m_i \cdot f_j$

Each trial thus constitutes a robot's experience about either reaching the goal or loosing the target or hitting the table. It consists of a sequence of actions and several learning steps. The more trials have been done, the better the robot performs, and the shorter each will be, and the more likely they will end with a *positive* reward.

Note that in order to learn every weight, it is not necessary that every perceptual state has occurred. The state description $\vec{f}$ is made up of a Gaussian covering several state space units simultaneously (see Fig. 6, right, for a visualisation). A critic weight w_j^c is thus updated similar to weight $w_{j'}^c$ if j and j' are neighbours in the perceptual space; analogously motor weights w_{ij}^m and $w_{ij'}^m$. This topological relation exploits the fact that similar states imply similar optimal actions.

3 Results

The weights obtained by reinforcement learning are shown in Fig. 6. The weights W^c to the value function unit are over-trained as can be seen from their wiggly structure around the goal at angle 0. At earlier stages they are smooth

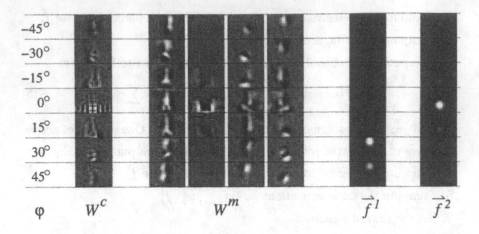

Figure 6: The weights W^c and W^m after reinforcement training, and example activity patterns $\vec{f}$. Positive connections $W^{c,m}$ are white, negative connections dark. Each column shows the connections to one recipient unit from the perceptual space in which $\vec{f}$ resides: it consists of seven 24×16 sized fields, each of which is devoted a target object representation when the robot is at the angle φ, given left. The four units which receive W^m encode motor movements for – from left to right – forward, backward, left turn and right turn. The activation $\vec{f}^1$ corresponds to a situation where the robot is at an angle slightly larger than $30°$ and sees the target at the upper (distant) edge of the visual field (this corresponds roughly to the turning point in Fig. 7, the situation in Fig. 2 or the percept in the third row in Fig. 5). $\vec{f}^2$ is near the goal position, as the robot sees the target right in front and has an angle $\varphi = 0$ (fourth row in Fig. 5).

and positive around the goal position. Nevertheless, training was continued so that the simulated robot has reached its goal thousands of times. The motor weights W^m are seemingly unaffected by over-training – their shape does not change noticeably. However, their absolute values continue to grow. As an effect, the motor unit outputs become more deterministic (cf. Eq. 3).

The structure of the motor weights W^m is complex and only partly obvious. It is obvious in the simple situation where the robot perceives the target in front of him while having a rotation angle of $\varphi = 0$. This corresponds to the perceptual input $\vec{f}^2$ in Fig. 6. The weights to motor unit 1 (left column of W^m in Fig. 6) in this area are positive (white) so to excite the "forward" unit. The "backward" motor unit (second column of W^m) has inhibitory connections (black) originating from this area, thus suppressing its response. The "backward" motor unit, however, has positive (white) connections to the sides of this position, so that the robot moves back if the target is perceived nearby to the left or to the right (only at a rotation angle $\varphi = 0$).

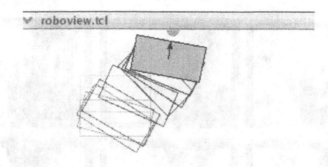

roboview.tcl

Figure 7: The simulated trained robot during the docking manoeuvre. The upper bar corresponds to the table location, the half-circle represents the target. The robot's grippers (not depicted) are near the front of the arrow shown on the robot. Outlines of previous poses are in brighter grey. After start, the robot first moved backward in order to turn and then approach the target.

Simulated Robot Performance A successful example of simulated docking performance is depicted in Fig. 7 which displays a surprisingly complex and successful movement. We have observed the performance limits to be reached, if the offset (y, Fig. 2) to the target is large. This extreme case leads to two possible actions: first, a movement at which the perceived target reaches the border of the visual field or second, a seemingly successful drive toward the target, but in a narrow angle (φ large) so that the robot's "shoulders" eventually touch the table. Success in these cases might be possible with a complex strategy involving small movements forth and back including turning, but is not discovered by the algorithm, possibly because of the rough discretisation of the angle space, in which φ is represented by only seven increments.

Application to the PeopleBot Robot Without having done any training on a real robot, we used the trained network successfully for robotic control. Only a subset of all weights (displayed dark in Fig. 3) are used during performance. The image $\vec{I}$ is now taken from the robotic camera that looks down at a fixed angle to the space in front (Figs. 1, 8). The robot orientation angle φ is taken from a robot-internal proprioceptive update mechanism (the starting angle is always zero). Finally, the outputs are directed to the wheels, the control of which accepts values for speed and rotational speed.

The bottleneck of our application is vision: the recognition of the orange fruit which constitutes the target is brittle and disturbed, for example, by large contrasts in the surrounding. In addition, we have a distortion of vision, because the camera does not point exactly vertically. Thus the physical model, Eqs. 1, is only a rough approximation. This, however, does not matter, first, because in any case the speed values must be adjusted to reasonable values. Secondly, because the concept of assigning one motor output to every state works even,

Figure 8: Snapshots from a docking sequence. The video can be seen at:
http://www.his.sunderland.ac.uk/robotimages/Cap0001.mpg

if the speed is too slow and the state at the next time step remains the same:
then the motor directive will simply remain, until eventually, another state is
reached.

Another restriction is the small size of the visual field, limited by the narrow
position of the camera and its maximal zoom. A narrow table must be used to
increase the visual field – a too large visual field again would lead to problems
in target recognition. Finally, we have not yet implemented the command to
close the gripper at arrival at the target.

4 Discussion

In this paper, we demonstrated that purely neural network based vision and
control algorithms can successfully be applied to a real robotic docking problem.

Currently we are developing a higher-level associative network in which mirror neurons shall emerge (Fig. 9). Mirror neurons have been found in motor and
language cortex and fire either when an action is performed or when it is observed, or both [5]. The network receives information from multiple modalities

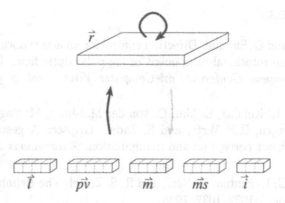

Figure 9: The envisaged mirror neuron network. Mirror neuron properties are expected to evolve among some of the neurons in the top layer. They carry an internal representation $\vec{r}$ of all of the inputs, below. The inputs are from multiple modalities including higher level representations. The vector $\vec{l}$ contains representations from language areas. $\vec{pv}$ contains the visual perception which includes the identity and perceived location of a target to be grasped. $\vec{m}$ are the motor unit activations including wheels, pan-tilt camera and gripper. $\vec{ms}$ denotes motor sensory unit activations and may also include available idiothetic information such as the rotation angle φ of the robot. $\vec{i}$ are other internal states such as the value function of the critic.

and represents them as a hidden code $\vec{r}$. The vertical connections are trained with a sparse coding unsupervised learning scheme similar to the Helmholtz machine described earlier in this paper. The inputs are collected from robotic actions which are performed interactively in the environment. The data contain only instantaneous information, i.e. the whole sequence of actions is not known. Therefore, neurons do not necessarily fire over a sustained period in time as do mirror neurons. However, since $\vec{r}$ is a distributed code, some units may specialise to code for longer sequences. The horizontal recurrent connections (depicted as open circle) are trained as an associator neural network. They are used in a neural activation relaxation procedure which is expected to (i) clear noise of the representation $\vec{r}$, (ii) predict the hidden code of the next time step and (iii) display prolonged firing. As a possible extension, associator recurrent connections may also feed back to the input, acting as a forward model. This would be particularly interesting for the cortical feedback to the motor units, because of implications for motor control: after repetitive exercising this network might be able to perform the action sequence. This would render superfluous the reinforcement trained part with its large perceptual state $\vec{f}$.

Acknowledgements This is part of the MirrorBot project supported by a EU, FET-IST programme, grant IST-2001-35282, coordinated by Prof. Wermter.

References

[1] N. Barnes and G. Sandini. Direction control for an active docking behaviour based on the rotational component of log-polar optic flow. In *ECCV2000 - Proc. European Conference on Computer Vision, Vol. 2*, pages 167–81, 2000.

[2] M. Becker, E. Kefalea, E. Mal, C. von der Malsburg, M. Pagel, J. Triesch, J.C. Vorbrggen, R.P. Wrtz, and S. Zadel. Gripsee: A gesture-controlled robot for object perception and manipulation. *Autonomous Robots*, 6:203–21, 1999.

[3] P. Dayan, G. E. Hinton, R. Neal, and R. S. Zemel. The Helmholtz machine. *Neur. Comp.*, 7:1022–1037, 1995.

[4] D.J. Foster, R.G.M. Morris, and P. Dayan. A model of hippocampally dependent navigation, using the temporal difference learning rule. *Hippocampus*, 10:1–16, 2000.

[5] V. Gallese, L. Fadiga, L. Fogassi, and G. Rizzolatti. Action recognition in the premotor cortex. *Brain*, 119:593–609, 1996.

[6] H.M. Gross, V. Stephan, and M. Krabbes. A neural field approach to topological reinforcement learning in continuous action spaces. In *Proc. of WCCI-IJCNN*, 1998.

[7] G. E. Hinton, P. Dayan, B. J. Frey, and R. Neal. The wake-sleep algorithm for unsupervised neural networks. *Science*, 268:1158–1161, 1995.

[8] A. Namiki, Y. Nakabo, I. Ishii, and M. Ishikawa. High speed grasping using visual and force feedback. In *Proc. IEEE Int. Conf. on Robotics and Automation (Detroit)*, 1999.

[9] H. Ritter, J. Steil, Noelker C., Roethling F., and P. McGuire. Neural architectures for robotic intelligence. *Rev. Neurosci.*, 2003.

[10] M.C. Silverman, D. Nies, B. Jung, and G.S. Sukhatme. Staying alive: A docking station for autonomous robot recharging. In *Proc. IEEE Int. Conf. on Robotics and Automation*, 2002.

[11] J. Spofford, J. Blitch, W. Klarquist, and R. Murphy. Vision-guided heterogeneous mobile robot docking. In *Sensor Fusion and Decentralized Control in Robotic Systems II*, 1999.

[12] C. Weber. Self-organization of orientation maps, lateral connections, and dynamic receptive fields in the primary visual cortex. In G. Dorffner, H. Bischof, and K. Hornik, editors, *Proc. ICANN*, pages 1147–52. Springer-Verlag Berlin Heidelberg, 2001.

[13] C. Weber and S. Wermter. Object localization using laterally connected "what" and "where" associator networks. In *Proc. ICANN*, page in press. Springer-Verlag Berlin Heidelberg, 2003.

[14] M. Williamson, R. Murray-Smith, and V. Hansen. Robot docking using mixtures of gaussians. In *Advances in Neural Information Processing Systems 11*, pages 945–51, 1999.

Combining Wavelets with HMM for Face Recognition

Li Bai and Linlin Shen
School of Computer Science & IT
University of Nottingham
Nottingham NG8 1BB
{bai,lls}@cs.nott.ac.uk

Abstract

This paper describes face recognition algorithms that improve upon the original DCT based HMM face recogniser by using wavelet multi-resolution analysis to extract observation sequences. In this approach a face image is divided into a number of overlapping subimages and wavelet decomposition is performed on each of the subimages. The ORL and our own face databases are used to test the algorithms and it is observed that our algorithms give better performance than the original. The face recognition algorithm is incorporated into a real-time face recognition system developed at the University of Nottingham.

1. Introduction

Automated face recognition systems have a wide range of important applications such as crime prevention and detection. Major approaches to face recognition include Graph Matching, Neural Networks, Hidden Markov Models. An example of graph matching is the Dynamic Link Architecture first proposed by Von der Malsburg [1]. Gabor wavelet responses at the intersection points of a rectangular grid overlaid on the face are taken as image features and represented as a graph structure, with the extracted features as the nodes and topological relationships between the feature locations as the edges of the graph. The face recognition process then becomes an elastic matching process, in which the test face graph is associated with one of the stored model face graphs through an optimisation procedure that maximises the similarities between the test and the corresponding model face graph. More recently the Face Bunch Graph [2] is proposed to cope with variations in face images. Gabor wavelets are applied at manually selected fiducial points (eyes, mouth, nose, etc.) of several images of a face and the results, refereed to as jets, are packed in a graph called the Face Bunch Graph.

Alternatively faces can be recognised by their distinctive features suitable for a certain classifier such as a neural network [3]. Liu described a method that forms feature vectors through convolution of the image with Gabor wavelet kernels at five scales and eight orientations [4]. The rows of each resulting image are concatenated into a single vector and all vectors such obtained are concatenated. This produces a vector of 10240 dimensions and subsequently the eigenface method [5] is used to reduce vector dimension. Eigenfaces are a set of orthogonal eigenvectors arising from applying Principle Component Analysis [6] to a collection of images in a face database and any face image could then be described by its projection coefficients onto the eigenfaces. This reduces the dimension of face vectors before recognition takes place and no longer was there the need of dealing with the potentially difficult problem of locating facial features. Though the most well-known, the eigenface method is by no means perfect. Belhumeur's fisherfaces [7] is motivated by the observation that the eigenfaces corresponding to large eigenvalues often encode variations in illumination rather than the identity of the individual and the eigenface approach projects into a space that captures the most overall variance of all classes without discrimination. The fisherface approach uses within-class and between-class scatter matrices to formulate class separability criteria and it projects into a space that maximises the variance of different classes and minimises the variance of the same class. Other extensions of the eigenface method include McGuire's eigenpixels [8], Etemad's Linear Discriminant Analysis [9], and Pentland's view based and modular eigenspaces [10]. Independent Component Analysis (ICA) is believed to be more effective than PCA [11] as it imposes a much stronger criterion. However, Baek [12] presents a rigorous comparison of PCA and ICA and discovers that, when a proper distance metric is used, PCA outperforms significantly ICA on the FERET face database [13] of more than 1000 face images, even though ICA is computationally more complex and uses PCA for pre-processing.

In the following sections we will describe HMM based face recognition and our experiments in using wavelets to improve the accuracy of Embedded HMM.

2. The Hidden Markov Model

Hidden Markov Models (HMM) see a face image as a sequence of states produced when the face is scanned from top to bottom. More interesting is the Embedded HMM proposed by Nefian [14]. The embedded HMM consists of a set of super states and each super state is associated with a set of embedded states. Super states of such a HMM represent primary facial regions whilst embedded states within each super state describe in more detail the facial regions. States are associated with probabilistic distributions and transitions from states to states can also be predicted from a transition probability matrix but this is not allowed between embedded states of different super states. At a particular state an observation sequence can be generated according to the associated probability distribution. A face image is divided into overlapping subimages. To deal with illumination changes, image shifts and rotation, 2D DCT [15] coefficients of the subimages are extracted to produce observation vectors, but only the coefficients representing low frequencies in the 2D-DCT domain are chosen to further reduce the dimension of observation vectors. Specifically, a HMM can be represented as a triplet $\lambda = \{A, B, \Pi\}$ consisting of

- The number of states N, and the state at time t is given by $q_t, 1 \le t \le T$, where T is the length of the observation sequence.

- The initial state distribution: $\Pi = \{\pi_i\}$, where $\pi_i = p\{q_1 = i\}, 1 \le i \le N$

- The state transition probability matrix $A = \{a_{ij}\}$, where

$$a_{ij} = p\{q_{t+1} = j \mid q_t = i\}, 1 \le i, j \le N, \ 0 \le a_{ij} \le 1, \text{and} \ \sum_{j=1}^{N} a_{ij} = 1.$$

- A probability distribution for each of the states, $B = \{b_j(o_t)\}$, usually probability density function is approximated by the weighted sum of M

Gaussian distributions: $b_j(o_t) = \sum_{m=1}^{M} c_{jm} N(\mu_{jm}, \Sigma_{jm}, o_t)$ where

$N(\mu_{jm}, \Sigma_{jm}, o_t)$ is a Gaussian pdf with mean vector μ_{jm} and covariance

matrix Σ_{jm}, c_{jm} is weight coefficients for the m th mixture in state j with

constraints $c_{jm} \geq 0, 1 \leq j \leq N, 1 \leq m \leq M$ and $\sum_{m=1}^{M} c_{jm} = 1$.

3. Extracting Features for HMM

As described in the last section, the HMM approach to face recognition involves extracting observation vector sequences from subimages. We believe that DCT may not be the best way to describe an image and wavelets may be a better choice so we propose to use wavelet multi-resolution analysis [16].

Wavelets are orthonormal basis functions, which are scaled and translated versions of the ' mother wavelet'. The fundamental idea behind wavelet analysis is to look at a function at different scales and resolutions by spanning the function using wavelets [17][18][19]. In practice this is done by convolving the function with wavelet kernels to obtain wavelet coefficients representing the contributions of wavelets in the function at different scales and orientations. Wavelets have many advantages over other mathematical transforms such as the Fourier Transform or DCT. Functions with discontinuities and functions with sharp spikes usually take substantially fewer wavelet basis functions than sine-cosine functions to achieve a comparable approximation. Mallat started to use wavelets in signal processing in 1985 when he discovered the relationship between wavelet bases and multi-resolution analysis - constructing wavelet bases corresponds to a multi-resolution analysis process [20]. The multi-resolution analysis process is associated with a father wavelet (the scaling function), and a mother wavelet and it is the mother wavelet that forms the basis of discrete wavelet transform. In implementing discrete wavelet transform two filters and their adjoins are used to decompose a signal into a pyramid structure in the form of approximation images and detail images. It is observed that features of the approximation images change smoothly, which is a suitable property for discrimination. The approximation images are also known to be a robust and distortion tolerant feature space for many pattern recognition applications.

In using wavelets to produce observation vectors our algorithms work by scanning the image from left to right and top to bottom using a $P \times L$ sized window and performing wavelet multi-resolution analysis at each subimage using Symmlet 5 wavelet. The subimage is decomp osed to a certain level and the coefficients at the lowest level or the energy of the subbands are selected to form observation vectors for the HMM. 2D J - level wavelet decomposition on an image $I[P, L]$ represents the image by $3J+1$ subimages

$$[a_J, \{d_J^1, d_J^2, d_J^3\}_{j=1,\dots,J}]$$

where a_J is a low resolution approximation of the original image, and d_j^k are detail images containing the details of the image at different scales (2^j) and orientations (k).

Wavelet coefficients in $\mathbf{d}_j^1$, $\mathbf{d}_j^2$ and $\mathbf{d}_j^3$ correspond to vertical high frequencies (horizontal edges), horizontal high frequencies (vertical edges), and high frequencies in both directions, respectively. Figure 1 shows the 2 level wavelet decomposition of a subimage representing an eye. For this 2 level decomposition in total 7 subbands $\{\mathbf{a}_2, \mathbf{d}_1^1, \mathbf{d}_1^2, \mathbf{d}_1^3, \mathbf{d}_2^1, \mathbf{d}_2^2, \mathbf{d}_2^3\}$ are generated.

In the following experiments we produce observation vectors in two different ways:

(i)   Extract wavelet coefficients using $\mathbf{a}_J$.

(ii)   Extract subband energy, i.e., the observation vector is defined as:

$$[\{e_j^1, e_j^2, e_j^3\}_{j=1,\dots,J}]$$

where e_j^k denotes the l_2-norm ($\| \ \|_2$) of the subimage $\mathbf{d}_j^k$.

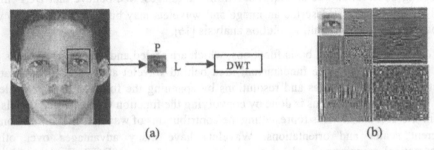

Figure 1 (a) Extracting observation vectors (b) Wavelet decomposition

4. Experimental Results

Two databases, the ORL and the face database created by ourselves are used to test the proposed algorithm. The ORL database contains 400 frontal face images of 40 people whilst our own database consists of 300 images of 30 people. The images in our own database are captured using a Creative webcam in the office environment. These images are more difficult than those in the ORL database due to large lighting and background variations. In the experiments, both P and L are set to 12 and neighbouring subimages are allowed to overlap by 3 in each direction. We first produce observation vectors from approximation images using method (i). 2 level wavelet decomposition is performed on each subimage. We then use method (ii) to extract subband energy by performing 5 level wavelet decomposition on each subimage. The lengths of the observation vectors are 9 for method (i) and 15 for method (ii) respectively.

No.of Training images	1	2	3	4	5
DCT HMM	76.1%	78.1%	85.7%	92.5%	98.5%
DWT HMM i	77.5%	88.1%	95.4%	95.4%	97.5%
DWT HMM ii	80.8%	84.7%	92.5%	95.8%	96.5%

Table 1: Experimental results for ORL database

Table 1 above shows the comparative results of our new algorithm and the original algorithm The number of training images per person varies from 1 to 5. It is clear that when the number of images used for training is less than 5, both of our new methods perform significantly better than the original algorithm. Table 2 below shows the results using our own database when 5 images of each person are used for training. It also shows the computation time required for all of the algorithms. The proposed method (i) performs better and can be applied in real time systems. A Pentium IIII 1.8 GHz PC is used for all the experiments.

	Recognition Rate	Training Time (per person)	Recognition Time (per image)
DCT HMM	92.6%	0.30 seconds	0.48 seconds
DWT HMM I	95.3%	0.68 seconds	1.55 seconds
DWT HMM ii	90.7%	1.27 seconds	2.49 seconds

Table 2: Experimental results for our own database

5. The Face Recognition System

The face recognition algorithm described in previous section is incorporated into a real time face recognition system encompassing two major components: face detection and face recognition. Faces are automatically detected from a video sequence and recognised against a face database. The face detection component is based on that described in [21], which uses Haar-like features to detect facial regions in an image. A tuple $r=(x,y,w,h,a)$ (x, y, w, h = 0 and $a \in \{0, 45^0\}$) denotes a rectangle and its pixel sum is represented by $S(r)$. Given a subimage to be tested for the presence of a face, the feature of the subimage is defined as:

$$feature = w_1 S(r_1) + w_2 S(r_2)$$

where weights $w_1, w_2 \in \Re$ and the pairs of rectangles r_1, r_2 represent one of the 14 feature prototypes shown in Figure 2 - the black and white areas are the two rectangles used to calculate the feature in the equation above. They are four edge features, eight line features, and two centre-surround features. A cascade of classifiers with 13 stages is trained to detect faces while rejecting non-face patterns. At each stage a classifier is trained using the Discrete Adaboost algorithm [22].

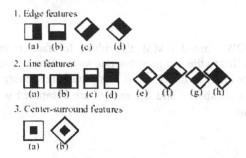

Figure 2 Feature prototypes of simple Haar-like features [21].

Figure 3 below shows an example image captured from a webcam and the detected face image. It is obvious that the detection is not very accurate - too much background information is included in the detected face, which will undoubtedly affect recognition accuracy. Therefore we incorporate to the detection algorithm a skin mask module to refine the detected region. The skin colour module is described in detail in one of our

232

earlier papers [23]. To test the effect of the skin mask on face recognition, we use a Creative webcam to capture pictures of 30 people, 10 pictures are taken automatically when a person stand in front of the camera. Figure 4 shows the flow chart to generate the face databases. Databases B and C are generated with the skin mask on and faces thus captured contain less background. The face detection process takes about 100 ms and the skin masking process takes about 45 ms.

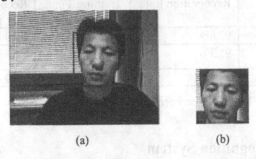

(a)   (b)

Figure 3   (a) Original input image (b) Detected face image

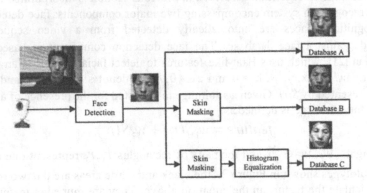

Figure 4 Creating face databases.

6. Conclusion

We have proposed DWT based HMM algorithms for face recognition. 2D wavelet decomposition is applied to the image subwindows to extract observation vectors from low resolution approximation images and from subbands energy. Both methods are tested using two face databases and the results are compared with the original DCT based HMM algorithm.

References

1   von der Malsburg C., Pattern Recognition by Labelled Graph Matching, Neural Networks, vol. 1, 141-148, 1988.
2   Wiskott L., Fellous J.M., Kuiger N., von der Malsburg, C., Face Recognition by Elastic Bunch Graph Matching, Pattern Analysis and Machine Intelligence, IEEE Transactions, VOL. 19, NO 7, July 1997.

3   Bartlett M.S., and Sejnowski T.J., Viewpoint Invariant Face Recognition using Independent Component Analysis and Attractor Networks, Neural Information Processing Systems – Natural and Synthetic, M. Mozer, M. Jordan, and T. Petsche, Editors, 1997, MIT Press.

4   Liu C. and Wechsler H., Gabor Feature Based Classification Using the Enhanced Fisher Linear Discriminant Model, IEEE Transactions on Image Processing, Vol. 11, No. 4, April, 2002.

5   Turk M. and Pentland A., Eigenfaces for Recognition, Journal of Cognitive Neuroscience, 3(1), 1991.

6   Jolliffe I.T., Principal Component Analysis. Springer-Verlag; New York; 1986.

7   Belhumeur P., Hespanhu J. and Kriegman D., Eigenfaces vs. Fisherfaces: Recognition Using Class Specific Linear Projection, IEEE Transactions on Pattern Analysis and Machine Intelligence, Vol. 19, July 1997.

8   McGuire P. and D'Eluteriom M.T, Eigenpaxels and a neural network approach to image classification, IEEE Tansactions on Neural Networks, VOL.12, NO.3, May 2001.

9   Etemad K. and Chellappa R., Discriminant Analysis for Recognition of Human Face Images. In 1st International Conference on Audio and Video Based Biometric Person Authentication, 1997.

10   View-Based and Modular Eigenspaces for Face Recognition, Pentland A., Moghaddam B., Starner T., Proceedings of IEEE Conference on Computer Vision and Pattern Recognition, 1994.

11   Comon P., Independent Component Analysis, A New Concept? Signal Processing, 1994.

12   Baek Kyungim, et al, PCA vs. ICA: A Comparison on the FERET Data Set, International Conference on Computer Vision, Pattern Recognition and Image Processing, Durham, North Carolina, March 8-14, 2002.

13   Phillips P.J., Wechsler, H., Huang J., Rauss P., The FERET Database and evaluation procedure for face recognition algorithms, Image and Vision Computing, 16, 1998.

14   A. Nefian and M. Hayes. An Embedded HMM-based Approach for Face Detection and Recognition, Proc. IEEE Int. Conf. On Acoustics, Speech and Signal Processing, vol. 6, 1999.

15   Ahmed, N., Natarajan, T., and Rao, K. R. Discrete Cosine Transform, IEEE Trans. Computers, vol. C-23, Jan. 1974.

16   C. Garcia, G. Zikos, G. Tziritas, Wavelet Packet Analysis for Face Recognition, Image and Vision Computing, 2000.

17   I. Doubechies, Orthonormal Bases of Compactly Supported Wavelets, Comm. Pure Applied Math, Vol. 41, 1988.

18   Weiss, L. G., Wavelets and Wideband Correlation Processing, IEEE Transactions on Signal Processing, January 1994.

19   Gilbert Strang and Truong Nguyen, Wavelets and Filter Banks, Wellesley-Cambridge Press, 1996.

20   Mallat, S., and Zhong S., Wavelet Transform Maxima and Multiscale Edges. *Wavelets and Their Applications*, 1992.

21   Rainer Lienhart and Jochen Maydt. An Extended Set of Haar-like Features for Rapid Object Detection, *IEEE ICIP 2002*, Vol. 1, pp. 900-903, Sep. 2002.

22   P.Viola and M.Jones, Rapid Object Detection using a Boosted Cascade of Simple Features. *IEEE Conf. on Computer Vision and Pattern Recognition*, Kauai, Hawaii, Dec. 2001.

23   Li Bai and LinLin Shen. Face Detection by Orientation Map Matching. *Proceeding of International Conference on Computational Intelligence for Modelling Control and Automation*, Austria, Feb. 2003.

Characterisation of Knowledge Bases[1]

Derek Sleeman, Yi Zhang, Wamberto Vasconcelos
Department of Computing Science,
University of Aberdeen,
Aberdeen, AB24 3UE, Scotland, UK
Email: {dsleeman, yzhang, wvasconc}@ csd.abdn.ac.uk

Abstract

The process of determining the principal topic of a Knowledge base (KB), and whether it conforms to a set of user-defined constraints, are important steps in the reuse of Knowledge Bases. We refer to these steps as the process of characterization of a Knowledge Base. **Identify-Knowledge-Base (IKB)** is a tool, which suggests the principal topic(s) addressed by the Knowledge Base. It matches concepts extracted from a particular knowledge base against some reference taxonomy, where the taxonomy can be pre-stored or extracted from ontologies which are either stored on the local machine or are assessable through the WWW. The 'most specific' super-concept subsuming these concepts is said to be the principal topic of the knowledge base. Additionally, a series of **filters**, which check if a KB has particular characteristics have been implemented. This paper describes both the Identify-Knowledge Base system and these filters. Some empirical studies of IKB and the filters with a range of problems are also reported.

1. Introduction

Reuse of Knowledge Bases is a promising area in Knowledge Technologies [1]. Nowadays, researchers are focusing on how to reuse existing Knowledge Bases for further applications [2]. Such requests for reuse are often specified as a Knowledge Base (KB) characterisation problem:

Require knowledge base on topic T, conforming to set of constraints C [2].

To respond to such requests we need to:

- Decide what is the principal topic (T) of a given knowledge base.
- Decide whether a KB conforms to certain constraints C.

---

[1] This work is part of the Advanced Knowledge Technology (AKT) project, which is funded by EPSRC, [1]. The IKB system incorporates the ExtrAKT system [3, 4, 5] and interfaces with the Edinburgh Knowledge Broker [6, 7] which were built by the other members of the AKT consortium

In this report, we discuss these two processes in detail. In section 2 to section 5, IKB is introduced. In section 6 and section 7, we discuss the filters that help users find KBs which match their requirements. In section 8, we discuss possible further work.

2. Determining the principal topic of a KB

In order to reuse a Knowledge Base, we need the ability to identify its topic (T). One way to identify the KB's topic is to:

1. Extract concepts from the knowledge base.
2. Match these concepts against a reference taxonomy, which defines a particular domain of interest. The KB's principal topic is given by the 'most specific' super-concept, which subsumes these concepts.
3. If a null result is obtained with a particular taxonomy, then repeat the last 2 steps with other taxonomies thought to be of interest.

The **ExtrAKT** system from Edinburgh [2] can analyse a Prolog knowledge base, and extracts all the KB's predicates. The IKB system then takes the predicates extracted from the Prolog Knowledge base and compares them with a pre-defined reference taxonomy to identify the KB's principal topic. Below we give a simple example using a food taxonomy. Suppose we already have the taxonomy depicted below:

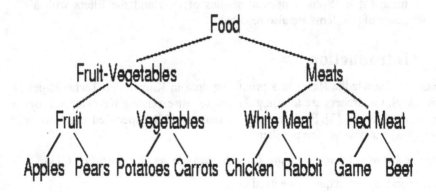

Figure-1 Food Taxonomy showing different kinds of food

If the concepts {Apples, Pears} are extracted (by ExtrAKT) and passed to the IKB system, the system would suggest that {Fruit} might be the focus of the knowledge base. Similarly, if the concepts {Apples, Potatoes, and Carrots} are extracted, {Fruit-vegetables} would be the output. If the set of concepts {Potatoes, Chicken, and Game} is provided, topic {Food} would be returned as the result.

3.   Design of the IKB system

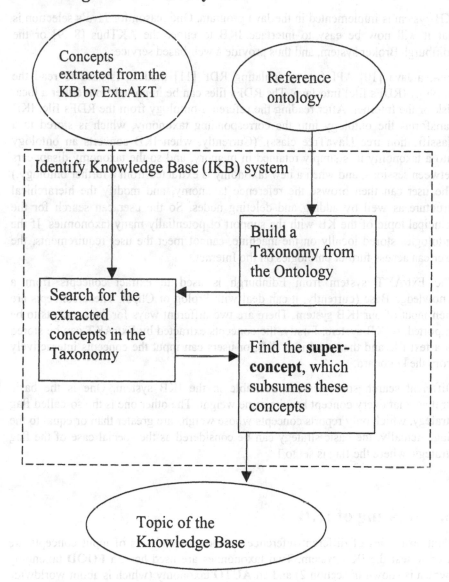

Figure-2 The main components of the IKB system[2]

As shown above, the system includes two important components:

- Taxonomy creator: it builds a taxonomy based on the reference ontology.
- Concepts searcher: it searches the taxonomy to match all the extracted concepts and finds their common parent.

---

[2] The rectangles in the figures represent processes while the ovals represent data or information.

4. Implementation of IKB

IKB system is implemented in the Java program. One reason for Java's selection is that it will now be easy to interface IKB to either the AKTbus [8, 9] or the Edinburgh Broker system, and thus provide a web-based service.

Jena, a Java [10] API for manipulating RDF [11] models, is used to read the ontology (RDFs file) into Java. The RDFs files can be imported from either a local disk or the Internet. After reading the reference ontology from the RDFs file, IKB transforms the ontology into the corresponding taxonomy, which is stored in a classification tree (JavaTree class). (Currently, when IKB converts an ontology into a taxonomy it is simply retained in memory, and so the taxonomy disappears between sessions, and when a new taxonomy is extracted from a further ontology.) The user can then browse the reference taxonomy, and modify the hierarchical structure as well by adding and deleting nodes. So the user can search for the principal topic of the KB with the support of potentially many taxonomies. If the ontologies stored locally on the machine, cannot meet the user requirements, the user can access further ontologies on the Internet.

The ExtrAKT system from Edinburgh is used to extract concepts from a Knowledge Base (currently, it can deal with Prolog or Clips). These concepts are then input of our IKB system. There are two different ways for the concepts to be imported to IKB system. Firstly, the concepts extracted by ExtrAKT can be stored in a text file and then read into IKB, or users can input the concepts interactively from the keyboard.

Different search strategies are available in the IKB system. One is the basic strategy that every concept has the same weight. The other one is the so-called flag strategy, which only reports concepts whose weighs are greater than or equal to the flag. Actually, the basic strategy can be considered as the special case of the flag strategy, where the flag is set to 1.

5. Testing of IKB

Next, examples of different reference taxonomies and sets of input concepts are used to test the IKB system. Two taxonomies are used here: a **FOOD** taxonomy (which is shown in section 2) and an **AUTO** taxonomy (which is about worldwide automobile manufacturers). Different input methods of the concepts and reference taxonomies (as introduced before, such as interactive input or file input, local or internet) are used in these examples. Also different search strategies are applied: the basic strategy and the flag strategy.

Three examples illustrate uses of the IKB system.

5.1 Food ontology with basic searching strategy

As shown in Figure-3, the food ontology is read from the RDFs file: *http://www.csd.abdn.ac.uk/~yzhang/food.rdfs,*

and the extracted taxonomy is subsequently stored, for further use by IKB. In this example, the concepts used are read from the file:

h:/forte/sampledir/work/predicates.txt (the extracted concepts are in fact: Pears Pears Potatoes Potatoes Potatoes Carrots Carrots Carrots Game)

IKB returns **[Food]** as it is the common parent of these concepts.

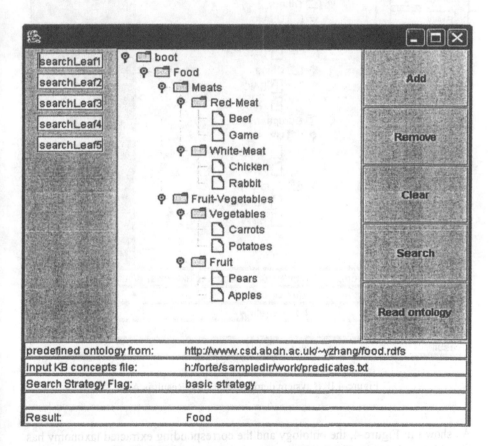

Figure-3 IKB system demonstration 1: Result is Food

5.2 Food ontology with flag searching strategy

The same reference taxonomy, Food, and the same set of concepts were used in this experiment, as were used in the first experiment. However, the search strategy was changed to flag and the value of flag was set to 2, with the result that only some of the concepts are matched, namely:

Pears (occurs twice), Potatoes (occurs 3 times) and Carrots (occurs 3 times). Thus, the search result is **[Fruit-vegetable]** this time.

5.3 Auto ontology with basic searching strategy

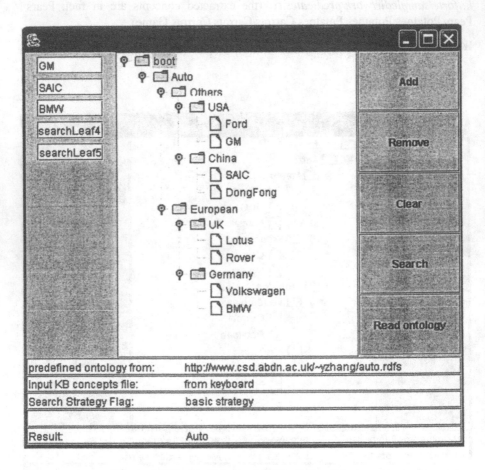

Figure-4 IKB system demmonstration3: Result is Auto

As shown in Figure-4, the ontology and the corresponding extracted taxonomy has been changed to Auto: *http://www.csd.abdn.ac.uk/~yzhang/auto.rdfs*

And this time the user types the concepts himself on the keyboard: (GM, SAIC, BMW). The basic search strategy is used again, and the system reports the highest achieved node, namely **[Auto]**.

To date, IKB has also been used with a number of ontologies, namely [12, 13, 14, 15, 16, 17].

6. Building Filters

Given the existence of IKB, we now discuss a filter which compares the topics of different KBs with the user's interest, T', so that we can find KBs required by the users. Secondly, a further filter, Filter-2, has been developed to determine whether the KB conforms to certain constraints, C (see section 1).

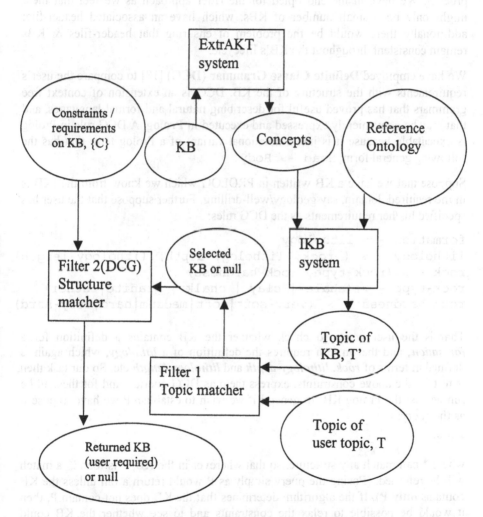

Figure-5 The components of KB Characterisation System

According to our proposed architecture, shown in Figure-5, we need two filters to find KBs, which match the user's requirements. Filter-1 is the **topic filter**. It compares the principal topic of the KB reported by the IKB system with the topic specified by the user. Filter-2 is the **structural filter**. It compares the structure of the KB passed by filter-1 with the user-defined requirements. If a KB satisfied both filters, it is reported to the user.

Filter-1 merely has to compare the required topic, T', provided by the user with the topic, T, returned by IKB for the KB. As filter-1 is trivial to implement, we focus here on the second, more demanding, filter-2.

We considered 2 approaches to checking whether a KB is consistent with the constraints specified by a user. Firstly, if the KB is associated with a header-file, which describes their contents, then it would only be necessary to verify that a header-file satisfies the user's constraints. Secondly, the user's constraints could be applied directly to the KB, which of course would generally be a more expensive process. We have in the end opted for the latter approach as we feel that there might only be a small number of KBs, which have an associated header-file; additionally there would be the problem of ensuring that header-files & KBs remain consistent throughout the KB's lifecycle.

We have employed **Definite Clause Grammar (DCG)** [18] to compare the user's requirements with the structure of the KB. DCG is an extension of context free grammars that has proved useful for describing natural and formal languages, and that may be conveniently expressed and executed in **Prolog**. A DCG rule in Prolog is executable because it is just a notational variant of a Prolog term that has the following general form: Head -> Body.

Suppose that we have a KB written in PROLOG which we know from the IKB is in the required domain, say geology/well-drilling. Further suppose that the user has specified his/her requirements as the DCG rules:

```
formation --> lithology
lithology --> ( rock, lithology-depth, lithology-length)
rock --> (rock-type, rock-hardness)
rock-type --> (shale | clay | chalk | granite| other)
rock-hardness --> (very-soft|soft|medium|hard|very-hard)
```

That is the user wants to check whether the KB contains a definition for a **formation**, and that in turn requires the definition of a **lithology**, which again is defined in terms of **rock**, **lithology-depth** and **lithology-length** etc. So our task then, is to take the above constraints, express them as DCG queries, and for these to be run against the Prolog KB. In general if we wish to establish P we have to pose it as the query:

* P *

where * can match any structure, so that wherever in the KB, P is found, a match will be returned. (Posing the query simply as P would return a fail unless the KB contains **only P**). If the algorithm determines that the KB does not contain P, then it would be possible to relax the constraints and to see whether the KB could satisfy some of the "component" constraints. So in the above example, although the KB might not contain a definition for **formation**, it might contain definitions for **lithology**, **rock**, **rock-type**. The user then has the option to either review further KBs to find one which meets his exact requirements, or to relax his/her requirements given information about which aspects of the user requirements are not satisfied by the current KB.

This approach is likely to be computationally expensive for large KBs; if this becomes a major problem we will introduce a range of heuristics to help control the search space. Further, a more efficient and flexible approach, which supports partial specifications of the problem is being developed [19, 20].

7.   Examples of Filters

Below we give examples of the use of filter-2. In effect, this filter aims to answer

*Is the definition of **Formation** in the KB consistent with the user requirements?*

To answer this question, we have to generate 6 sub-queries, each of which correspond to a component in the requirements, and the algorithm only records a positive result if all sub-queries are answered positively. These sub-queries, their translation into DCG, and the responses obtained are listed below. We shall use predicate **match(DCG, KB, Answer)** to check whether KB (the knowledge base represented as a list of Prolog clauses) contains DCG (the DCG rules stored as a list); and the predicate returns the result (yes or no) in the variable Answer.

```
The initial query concerns the top-level rule, which is
| ?- match([[(formation --> lithology)],
           [...],
           Answer).
Answer = yes
```
That is, for a given knowledge base (shown above as " [...] " to save space) the system returns the **Answer "yes"**, which means the definition of formation (if it exists) in the KB is consistent with the user's requirements.

Similarly, in the query below:
```
| ?- match([[(rock -->(rock-type,rock-hardness))],
           [...],
           Answer).
Answer = yes
```
That is, the knowledge base has the definition of rock conforming to the user requirements as expressed by the DCG rule.

Another interesting example is
```
| ?- match([[(rock-->(rock-type, rock-hardness)),
           (rock-type->(shale|clay|chalk|granite|other)],
           [...],
           Answer).
Answer = yes
```
In this query, we extend the previous query to include another user constraint, (rock-type).

If the KB's structure cannot match the user's requirements, the system will return "No". In this example, the user required rock-type are not found in the KB.

```
| ?- match([[(rock-->(rock-type,rock-hardness))],
            (rock-type-->(hard-clay|soft-chalk|other)],
            [...],
            Answer).
Answer = no
```

8. Further developments

The IKB system is a useful tool to identify the likely topic of a given knowledge base by comparing the extracted concepts against a pre-defined reference taxonomy. The current filters have proven useful. Planned developments include:

- Extend the search strategy

There are two search strategies in our system at this moment: Flag strategy and Basic strategy (the later can be looked on as the Flag strategy with flag as 1). More complex strategy will be developed later, such as a Percentage Strategy, which matches the concepts discussed >P% of times.

- Interface to Edinburgh's Broker system [4]

One can envisaged a future broker service where the broker is asked to use a KB on a particular topic, T and with some structural constraints, C. It is envisaged that this functionality will be provided by linking IKB to the Broker possibly through the **AKTBUS,** [8, 9]. This would then, of course, allow IKB to provide a web-based service.

- More testing with different knowledge base

The usefulness of our system depends critically on the concepts extracted from the knowledge base. More knowledge bases, not only in Prolog, should be used with the ExtrAKT and the IKB systems.

- Creating a "directory" of the Taxonomies

Currently, when IKB converts an ontology into a taxonomy it is simply retained in memory, and so the taxonomy disappears between sessions, and when a new taxonomy is extracted from a further ontology. A further development will allow the user to name and retain the taxonomies on some form of persistent storage (i.e. in a file); the whole set of taxonomies will then be available to users.

- Use IKB with text files

Apply IKB on the words contained in a standard text file to find out the principal topic of that text. Nowadays, researchers in Natural Language Engineering have developed some very good tools to extract important keywords from text files, [21, 22]. We plan to apply the IKB system to these extracted keywords to see how effective the IKB is in detecting the principal focus of textual materials.

- Workbench for characterising KBs

Create a workbench to characterize the KBs, which includes the IKB system and Filters. The workbench will be able to extract taxonomies from pre-defined ontologies. At the same time, it will get concepts (or keywords) from KBs from ExtrAKT-like systems. Finally, the user requirements on the KBs will also be provided as input to the system. Based on this information, our workbench will be able to characterize the KB, both by topic and by structural constraints.

Acknowledgements

This work is supported under the EPSRC's grant number GR/N15764 to the Advanced Knowledge Technologies Interdisciplinary Research Collaboration, http://www.aktors.org/akt/, which comprises the Universities of Aberdeen, Edinburgh, Sheffield, Southampton and the Open University.

References

1. Advanced Knowledge Technology (AKT project)
   http://www.aktors.org/akt/
2. Sleeman D, Potter S, Robertson D, and Schorlemmer W.M. Enabling Services for Distributed Environments: Ontology Extraction and Knowledge Base Characterisation, ECAI-2002 workshop, 2002
3. Schorlemmer M, Potter S, and Robertson D. Automated Support for Composition of Transformational Components in Knowledge Engineering. Informatics Research Report EDI-INF-RR-0137, June, 2002
4. Sleeman D, Potter S, Robertson D, and Schorlemmer W.M. Ontology Extraction for Distributed Environments, In: B.Omelayenko & M.Klein (Eds), Knowledge Transformation for the Semantic Web. publ Amsterdam: IOS press, p80-91, 2003
5. ExtrAKT system: a tool for extracting ontologies from Prolog knowledge bases.
   http://www.aktors.org/technologies/extrakt/
6. Potter S. Broker Description, Technical Document University of Edinburgh, 03/04/2003
7. Knowledge Broker: The knowledge broker addresses the problem of knowledge service location in distributed environments.
   http://www.aktors.org/technologies/kbroker/
8. Hui K.Y. and Preece A. An Infrastructure for Knowledge Communication in AKT Version 1.0. Technical Report, Department of Computing Science, University of Aberdeen. 2001
9. AKT-Bus: An open, lightweight, Web standards-based communication infrastructure to support interoperability among knowledge services
   http://www.aktors.org/technologies/aktbus/

246

10. Jena - A Java API for RDF
    http://www-uk.hpl.hp.com/people/bwm/rdf/jena/
11. Resource Description Framework (RDF)
    http://www.w3.org/RDF/
12. Newspaper ontology
    http://www.dfki.unikl.de/frodo/RDFSViz/newspaper.rdfs
13. People ontology
    http://www.i-u.de/schools/eberhart/ontojava/examples/basic/demo.rdfs
14. wordnet ontology
    http://www.semanticweb.org/library/wordnet/wordnet-20000620.rdfs
15. Food ontology
    http://www.csd.abdn.ac.uk/~yzhang/food.rdfs
16. Auto ontology
    http://www.csd.abdn.ac.uk/~yzhang/auto.rdfs
17. Academic ontology
    http://www.csd.abdn.ac.uk/~qhuo/program/academic.rdfs
18. Bratko I. Prolog Programming for Artificial Intelligence, 3rd Ed,
    Longman. 2000
19. Vasconcelos W.W, and Meneses E.X. A Practical Approach for Logic
    Program Analysis and Transformation. Lecture Notes in Computer
    Science (Advances in Artificial Intelligence), Vol. 1793, Springer-
    Verlag, Berlin, 2000
20. Vasconcelos W. W, Aragao M. A. T, and Fuchs N. E. Automatic Bottom-
    up Analysis and Transformation of Logic Programs. Lecture Notes in
    Computer Science (Advances in Artificial Intelligence), Vol. 1159.
    Springer-Verlag. Berlin. 1996
21. Jones G.J.F. An Introduction to Probabilistic Information Retrieval
    Models, Department of Computer Science, University of Exeter
22. Voothees E.M. and Harman D. Overview of the Seventh Text Retrieval
    Conference (TREC-7), NIST Special Publication 500-242, November
    1998

A Genetic Algorithm Approach to Attribute Selection Utilising the Gamma Test

P. S. Jarvis, I. D. Wilson and J.A. Ware

University of Glamorgan, Treforest, Mid Glamorgan, CF37 1DL

psjarvis@glam.ac.uk

http://www.glam.ac.uk/research/

Abstract

In this paper, we present a methodology that facilitates attribute selection and dependence modelling utilising the Gamma Test and a Genetic Algorithm (GA). The Gamma Test, a non-linear analysis algorithm, forms the basis of an objective function that is utilised within a GA. The GA is applied to a range of multivariate datasets, describing such problems as house price prediction and lymphography classification, in order to select a useful subset of features (or mask). Local Linear Regression is used to contrast the accuracy of models constructed using full masks and suggested masks. Results obtained demonstrate how the presented methodology assists the production of superior models.

1. Introduction

The value of a variable within a dataset may rely upon the impact of several other independent variables. If these variables are appropriately modelled, it is possible to predict the output of the dependent variable if the model is supplied with values for the independent features. Several mathematical modelling techniques are available to assist such prediction, for example Artificial Neural Networks (ANNs) [1] and Local Linear Regression (LLR) [2].

A common difficulty when attempting to predict an output is the selection of inputs with which to construct a model. In real world situations, it is often not immediately apparent which factors are making a significant impact upon the behaviour of the variable to be predicted. Data can be collected for factors assumed to be important, and this data is thrown into the mix of the model, as it were. Some of these factors may in fact have little or no bearing upon the actual result. Furthermore, the data may be incorrectly measured. Functions used to describe the model will rarely be perfectly smooth (i.e. infinitely differentiable) – external factors may result in slight variations in the values of attributes. This variation can be described as noise.

In practice, the inclusion of irrelevant attributes is detrimental to the model created. Even predictively useful attributes may contain a certain level of noise, with the extraneous elements only serving to increase this noise. This is exacerbated if there is relatively little data available with which to construct these models. Therefore, a method that determines which attributes are most predictively useful without *a priori* knowledge would be of great utility. A method that allows only the salient

247

attributes to be selected for inclusion within a model would result in more robust models and improve understanding about the interaction of multivariate data.

In this paper, we describe Genetic Algorithms and the Gamma Test. The Gamma Test guides the selection process upon which the Genetic Algorithm extracts the most important features from genuine datasets. Having selected appropriate features, models are then constructed. Finally, the performance of the methods used is assessed.

Table 1 briefly describes the effectiveness of the techniques at eliminating irrelevant inputs and improving model accuracy.

Experiment	1	2	3	4	5	6
Number of available inputs	14	14	9	18	18	18
Number of inputs used	13	13	2	13	16	11
Percentage reduction in inputs	7	7	78	28	11	39
Percentage improvement in classification accuracy	3.5	12.1	15.4	6	10	20

Table 1 - effectiveness of techniques

Other techniques can be used for feature selection problems. Some of these are described and compared by Hall and Holmes [3].

2. The Genetic Algorithm Overview

This section describes the Genetic Algorithm (GA) [4] techniques adopted to determine those inputs that are most relevant when attempting to predict the output of a particular problem. It explains the basic idea behind the GA process, the genomes used to represent potential solutions, the techniques used to manipulate the genomes into better quality solutions, and the ways of assessing the relative worth of these solutions.

Based upon theories of evolution observed in nature, a GA develops increasingly superior solutions to given problems. A GA makes use of genomes that characterise the structure of the problem, with each one representing a possible solution. In the examples presented, each genome is represented by a string of binary digits. Also referred to as a mask, these binary digits signify whether available attributes are to be included in the creation of a model.

Through the adaptation of these genomes, an optimal (or near optimal) solution can be found. The GA does this by assessing the relative strength of each alternative genome, and combining parts of pairs of genomes (with a tendency to allow superior genomes to be selected for pairing) in order to create new hybrid genomes. In addition to this, a small part of the genome may be randomly 'mutated'. If the GA is successful, these new genomes will be superior to previously created genomes. By following the designated replacement strategy, (typically replacing the weakest genomes) a new population of genomes is created. By repeating the process many times, the overall quality of the solutions provided should continue to improve until a near optimal solution is found. In practice, where there may be many millions (or more) of potential solutions, it may not be practically possible to find an optimal solution (by a GA or by any other method). However, GAs can normally be relied upon to provide a 'good' solution, within reasonable time constraints.

Prior to running a given GA, three factors must be defined. Firstly, the structure of the genome to be used must be formalised. Secondly, the genome operators must be set. Thirdly, an appropriate objective function must be chosen.

In essence, the process the GA follows is relatively simple:

1. Create a population of genomes.

2. Use this population to evolve the genomes according to the set parameters into a superior population.

3. Repeat until pre-specified objective function has been satisfied.

The remainder of this section explains the various aspects of the GA procedure in more detail.

2.1　The Genetic Algorithm

This section outlines the process that the GA follows in order to produce its optimal solution to a particular problem. The steady state GA used in these experiments is similar to that described by DeJong and Sarma [5]. Starting with a user defined initial genome, the GA sets about creating a population full of different genomes, each representing a possible solution to the problem at hand. From this population, the GA picks those genomes that provide the best solutions (using the objective function described in section 2.4) and allows them to 'breed' (according to the rules set down by the crossover operator described in section 2.3). An offspring may undergo a small amount of random mutation (described in section 2.3).

If these new genomes are, as hoped, superior to existing members of the population they will be incorporated into the population at the expense of other genomes. In essence, the population is evolving to create a set of improved genomes. The process is repeated until a pre-specified criterion is satisfied. This can be a certain number of generations, a time limit, the fitness of the best solution, population convergence, or other criterion.

2.2　The Genome

Here, the concept of the Genome is introduced. Genomes contain all information pertaining to the format of a particular solution. They are structured in such a way as to represent the solution in as concise a way as possible. This can include real numbers, integers or binary characteristics. These inputs can be individually assigned to fall within a pre-determined range if need be. It is beneficial to structure the genome using a minimal number of characteristics, i.e. not to incorporate additional unnecessary features. Adding such features, rather than increasing options and hence generating more specific results, detracts from the efficiency of the algorithm. The extra variables increase the search space, increasing the time required to find solutions of acceptable quality.

The relative superiority of these genomes needs to be ranked in order to make progress in finding the best possible solutions. This is done by assigning a 'fitness' score to each genome. The procedure for calculating this fitness score is described in section 2.4. The fitness score calculates the merits of each genome, deeming those genomes with the highest scores worthy of retention within the GA. The creation of subsequent genomes is based upon these retained 'best' solutions.

The various components of the GA can be defined completely independently. The structure of the genome does not necessarily relate exclusively to one particular GA procedure. This structure can be altered without the need to alter other variables in accordance. The reverse is also true – one genome structure can be used in conjunction with different GA procedures.

2.3   Genome Operators

This section summarises the Genome Operators that combine to allow the GA to find an optimal solution. The three distinct operators that can be applied to the genome in order to trigger its evolution are initialisation, mutation and crossover. These can be fine-tuned by the user in a way suitable to the particular problem.

Initialisation involves 'filling' each genome within the population with the genetic material from which all subsequent solutions will be evolved. Typically, in the examples used here, the population consists of a full mask, which incorporates every input, and a set of random masks. Some parts of the genome are randomly mutated at each new generation. The Mutation operator determines how mutation will take place and occurs at a given probability. Such mutations introduce an element of randomness into the equation, which can help the GA escape local optimality on its way towards a globally optimal solution.

Each new genome created (referred to as 'offspring') is formed from the features of previous genomes, (the 'parents'). The Crossover operator is the mating strategy utilised (such as single point crossover). Each of these operators are independent functions that can be adjusted appropriately and separately by the user without any impact upon other components.

2.4   The Objective Function and Fitness Score

This section describes the objective function and the fitness score, which are used by the GA to compare and rank the genomes generated during the evolution process. GA requires only the ability to make direct comparisons in terms of the overall quality of generated solutions, allowing solutions to be ranked relative to one another, to reach a near optimum or optimum solution. From this ranking system, the 'best' solutions are selected and used to generate further solutions. Each genome is ranked according to a score, with this score being obtained using an objective function, which encodes specific instructions for calculating the value of each genome.

The result of the objective function is known as the objective score. This can be transformed by linear scaling to what is referred to as the fitness score. The fitness score is used by the GA to select genomes for mating. The objective function can be modified independently of the GA procedure without necessarily altering the structure of the genome.

3. The Gamma Test

This section outlines the theory behind the Gamma Test that is used to estimate the noise levels a model is likely to face and hence qualify the predictive abilities of potential models.

In experiments such as these, where many potential masks are generated, it would be impractical to implement models for every single mask. The Gamma Test provides a useful guide to the overall quality of any smooth data model (for example Artificial Neural Networks, Local Linear Regression) that can be built using the data provided. By estimating the likely Mean Squared Error (MSE) of these models, only those anticipated to be most accurate need be formally constructed. This section describes the technique in brief, however for greater detail refer to Stefansson *et al.* [6].

In essence, the Gamma Test uses differentiated training and test datasets to build its model. Each dataset consists of a list of M vectors, each containing a series of inputs, x, contributing towards an output, y. Ideally, the input and output variables will relate to one another directly, according to an unknown function, $y=f(x)$. In practice, when models are created using complex data it is highly unlikely that such a simple relationship will present itself. More likely, the model will be of the form $y=f(x)+\varepsilon$. Here, ε is the error of each predicted output compared with the output observed. This occurs when there is noise associated with the data that cannot be incorporated into the function for it to remain true in general. The lower this level of noise is the lower the MSE that can potentially be achieved. In fact, the minimum possible MSE is equal to the variance of the noise. Any attempt to create a model with a lower MSE will be detrimental to results, as such a model will only respond to the vagaries of its particular training set, i.e. it will be overtrained.

So, the Gamma Test uses noise levels as a basis for its prediction of $\Gamma \rightarrow var(\varepsilon)$, proven by Evans *et al.* [7,8]. Γ suggests the minimum value that the MSE is likely to take, and hence the quality of masks can be ranked. The Gamma Test estimates noise levels by creating lists of the k nearest neighbours for each input vector in the dataset. For a vector (x_1, y_1), where x is the list of input vectors $x_{1(1)}, x_{1(2)}, \dots x_{1(n)}$, the nearest neighbour of x is the vector (x_1', y_1'). If the function is continuous, then y' is likely to be a relatively near neighbour of y, if not necessarily its *nearest* neighbour.

The Gamma Test uses the statistic

$$\gamma = \frac{1}{2M} \sum_{i=1}^{M} (y_i' - y_i)^2 \qquad (1)$$

This is repeated for every near neighbour, for every vector in the dataset, to obtain a γ value for each. The algorithm also calculates a δ value using the formula:

$$\delta = \frac{1}{M} \sum_{i=1}^{M} |x_i' - x_i|^2 \qquad (2)$$

|.| denotes Euclidean distance. Again, this is repeated for every near neighbour. Thus there are Mk points considered, each assigned a γ and a δ value. Using these values, the regression line $\gamma = \Gamma + A\delta$ is calculated. The vertical intercept, Γ, is recorded as the estimate of the variance of ε. The gradient, A, is also recorded.

There must be sufficient vectors available to reach a reliable estimate for $Var(\varepsilon)$, which can be determined by applying the GT to an increasing number of the available vectors (known as the M-test) [9]. If the GT reaches an asymptotic level, then it can be assumed that the sample size is sufficiently large to enable an approximately accurate measure to be reached. In this case, the vectors up to the point at which the M-test graph has stabilised are set aside for training (i.e. slightly beyond the point at which the graph first achieves the asymptotic value). Subsequent vectors are set aside for testing.

4. Empirical Analysis

The experiments presented in this section use genuine datasets, obtained from various sources, to demonstrate how subsets of predictively useful attributes can be elicited from a set of features. The data sets were chosen for their mixture of formats- some have many attributes, some have a large number of vectors available. Using this variety demonstrates that Genetic Algorithms and the Gamma Test are able to operate under different conditions.

The primary aim of these experiments was to demonstrate that the Genetic Algorithm is capable of successfully selecting the relevant input attributes required to predict outputs. This relies upon the Gamma Test accurately assessing the likely quality of models that can be constructed.

This section explains decision-making processes that were necessary to initialise the experiments. The format of individual experiments is then briefly described along with results that were obtained.

4.1 Optimising feature selection

As described in Section 3, there are several components of the GA that can be altered in order to increase the likelihood of a good quality model being constructed. This section details the implementation of each of these components.

4.1.1 Objective function

This objective function makes use of three different variables to gauge the relative merits of every particular genome. Applying appropriate weightings to the calculated product of each function will vary the relative importance of these variables. These variables are:

- intercept fitness (referring to the absolute value of the Gamma statistic);

- gradient fitness (referring to the gradient);

- length fitness (referring to the length of the mask under consideration).

Higher weighting for the intercept fitness, f_1, gives more importance to having good model accuracy. A high weighting for gradient fitness, f_2, gives more emphasis to those masks that have low gradients (i.e. have simpler modelling functions). The value of the length fitness, f_3, changes inversely to the length of the mask it is assessing. A high weighting here will give priority to masks containing fewer features. The objective function used to evaluate masks examines the summed, weighted, relationship between these measures of its quality [10]. The general expression of the objective function is:

$$f(mask) = 1-(w_1 f_1(mask) + w_2 f_2(mask) + w_3 f_3(mask)) \tag{3}$$

Where $f_i(mask)$ and w_i represent, respectively, the number of conflicting objects and the weight of that particular measure, with a high value of $f(mask)$ indicating a good solution. These values are then scaled to a positive range.

The first term of the objective function, $f_1(mask)$, returns a measure of the quality of the intercept based upon the V_{ratio}:

$$V_{ratio} = \frac{\Gamma}{Var[y]} \approx \frac{Var[\varepsilon]}{Var[y]} \tag{4}$$

where $Var[]$ is the variance, which is a standardised measure of the Gamma statistic that enables a judgement to be made, independently of the output range, as to how well the output can be modelled by a smooth function. Minimising the intercept by examining different mask combinations provides a means for eliminating noisy attributes, facilitating the extraction of a smooth model from the input data, and is expressed as:

$$f_1(mask) = \begin{cases} 1 - \dfrac{1}{1 - 10 V_{ratio}(mask)} & \text{if } V_{ratio}(mask) < 0 \\[2mm] 2 - \dfrac{2}{1 + V_{ratio}(mask)} & \text{otherwise} \end{cases} \tag{5}$$

The second term of the objective function, f_2, returns a measure of the complexity of any underlying smooth model based upon the gradient determined by the GT. Minimising this complexity is desirable, especially in cases where data points are relatively sparse, and is expressed as where $|.|$ denotes the absolute value:

$$f_2(mask) = 1 - \frac{1}{1 + \left| \dfrac{gradient(mask)}{outputRange} \right|} \tag{6}$$

Lastly, the third term of the objective function, f_3, sums the number of active elements within the input vector and returns this as a percentage of the total number of elements within the input vector. Minimising the number of active genes within our genome encourages the search procedure to find solutions that are less complex, resulting in minimal input vectors.

$$f_3 = \frac{Active(mask)}{Length(mask)} \tag{7}$$

4.1.2   Population

Choosing a population size for the Genetic Algorithm can be problematic. The greater the number of inputs each dataset contains the greater the number of mask permutations that are possible. If the population is too small, the Genetic Algorithm may not have enough genetic material from which to derive a near optimum solution. The heuristic used to determine population sizes for each of the experiments presented in this paper was to multiply the number of inputs by 10, resulting in predictively useful masks in reasonable processing time.

4.1.3   Mutation, replacement and crossover

The number of attributes also effects the value chosen for the Mutation operator. The same value may have a very different effect upon two different datasets. For example, if a 2% chance of mutation is chosen, in a dataset containing 100 inputs, we would reasonably expect approximately two inputs to be mutated. However, in a dataset containing just ten inputs, an input would be mutated typically only every five iterations of the GA. This means that for the Mutation to have the desired effect, it should be increased when using fewer inputs. For these experiments, the heuristic used to calculate the mutation rate, r, for n inputs was: $r=2/n$

The replacement method chosen was to replace the weakest genomes from the population. The crossover rate used was 50%. This value was experimentally determined to be the most useful.

4.1.4   Nearest neighbours

An aspect of the Gamma Test that can be altered is the number of nearest neighbours, p, to be used. The standard value for this is ten, because it has previously been shown to generate good results on a regular basis [*ibid.*]. If the number of data samples is large, then it can be useful to use a larger number of near neighbours. This is because there are more likely to be neighbours close to the point being examined, so the locations of these neighbours will be relevant. If however there are relatively few data samples available, then considering the location of, for example, the thirtieth near neighbour would be detrimental, as it would have little relevance.

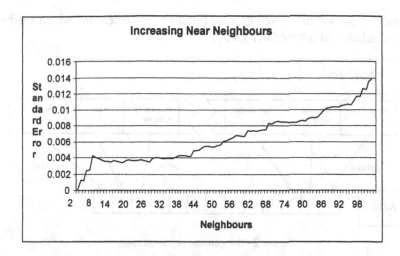

Figure 1 - Increasing near neighbours (*p*)

Using a greater number of near neighbours is also problematical if the unknown function has a high level of local curvature – neighbours that are too far away will not aid the modelling process. An increasing near neighbour test applies the GT to the data for incrementally larger numbers of neighbours, the results from which being easily plotted graphically (illustrated in Figure 1). It is most suitable to choose a point where the standard error (or, the estimated standard deviation) is minimal after stabilising. For example, in the graph in Figure 1, 10 would be a suitable number of near neighbours.

The choice of the number of near neighbours to be used in an experiment can have a significant impact upon the results obtained (although the impact may be negligible). For this reason, experiments are initially performed using full masks and the standard ten neighbours, before altering the number of neighbours and the masks used as appropriate. Following this methodology, the impact of the number of neighbours is made completely transparent. The reasons for any improvements in experimental results can therefore be identified.

The experiments undertaken here often contain many different types of inputs, the format of which can vary considerably. Some may take very large values; some may only have a very small range. Others may consist of a list of discrete options. The Gamma Test and its related modelling techniques cannot handle non-numerical inputs (e.g. spring, summer, autumn, winter). Features that were composed of several options were translated into numerical data by replacing each alternative with a distinct integer.

When one particular attribute can take a value up to several thousand, it may have the effect of 'dwarfing' the other attributes, even if it is not particularly relevant. This can be counteracted by normalising all data so that every input operates over the same scale ($-0.8 < x < 0.8$). Any missing values were replaced by the modal value for that feature.

The genome utilised here consists of a binary string. If an attribute is to be included in the construction of a model, a number 1 is included in the appropriate place in the string. For example, in the case of Boston housing data described in section 4.2, the binary string within a given genome (mask) would determine which attributes are to be included (illustrated in Figure 2).

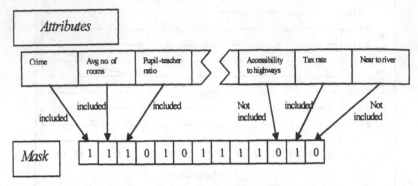

Figure 2 - the genome representation

In the course of these experiments, it was necessary to construct a large number of models for comparison. These models needed to be constructed in a standard way, so as to allow them to be compared fairly. The method chosen to do this was Local Linear Regression (LLR). LLR is a method of estimating a regression line using a multivariate smoothing process. The function is locally fitted, allowing for greater accuracy over a smaller range of the function. For more details on LLR, refer to Cleveland and Devlin [2].

Alternatively, an ANN could have been utilised to construct the models. However, it was decided that Local Linear Regression was a more appropriate technique. This was because it would be difficult to produce a fair comparison between results generated by different ANNs. Local Linear Regression meanwhile cannot be overtrained and any models constructed from the training set are equivalent.

The experiments presented in the following sections (summarised in Section 4.8) were initially carried out using a full mask, with ten nearest neighbours and with the dataset not randomised. The result obtained here is the standard by which all other experiments were judged, to assess whether the suggested changes are beneficial.

Model success was judged according to different criteria. Some experiments were classification tasks. In the case of these, each output was deemed to have been correctly predicted if the prediction was closer to the correct output than to any other classification. Where outputs were of a continuous form, judgements were made according to how many predictions were accurate to within a very small range of the observed output.

4.2 Boston Housing Data

Using housing data originally published by Harrison and Rubinfeld [11], the model attempts to predict the median value of homes within a region, given details of local crime, transport access, number of bedrooms etc. Success was judged according to how many of the 56 pieces of test data were correctly predicted to within a range of 0.04 (i.e. 2.5%), after training on 450 examples.

With a full mask, using ten nearest neighbours, LLR accurately classified 42 examples. In this case, the increasing near neighbour test also suggested ten neighbours should be used ($p=10$). After running the GA and removing inputs relating to accessibility to radial highways and proximity to a river, results were improved. The model correctly classified 44 examples.

4.3   Income

USA census data (containing information relating to age, education standard, race, etc.) was used to predict whether an individual's yearly income was above or below \$50,000. Data was obtained from the UCI KDD archive [12]. This was a classification task, with accuracy measured according to how many of the 46,342 test datasets were correctly assigned as being above or below the threshold.

With a full mask and ten near neighbours, 33,579 were correctly predicted. Using the five neighbours ($p=5$) suggested by the increasing near neighbour test but retaining the full mask improved results to 33,840. However, with five neighbours and the mask deemed to be best according the genetic algorithm (lacking the input relating to marital status), this figure was dramatically increased to 39,197.

4.4   Breast Cancer

Breast Cancer data was obtained from the University Medical Centre of Ljubljana, Yugoslavia. The task here was to ascertain whether individuals suffered a recurrence of breast cancer, based on nine medical variables. Models were trained on 260 examples, tested on 26. Ten near neighbours ($p=10$) were deemed to be most appropriate. With a full mask, 22 cases were correctly classified. With a reduced mask, this value was improved to 26 out of 26.

4.5   Lymphography

This experiment was based upon lymphography records, again obtained from the University Medical Centre of Ljubljana. The model attempted to classify a lymphoma into one of four categories. There were relatively few vectors available, so the model was trained using 130 and tested for eighteen. With a full mask, the model correctly classified the lymphoma on seventeen occasions. Using fifteen near neighbours ($p=15$) and a reduced mask, the model was able to correctly classify all eighteen lymphomas.

4.6   Algae Concentrations

European rivers were tested for water quality over a period of one year. Data was again obtained from the UCI KDD archive [*ibid.*]. Measurements were taken of physical attributes such as flow velocity, as well as the concentrations of certain chemicals within the rivers. These factors were theorised to have an impact upon the concentrations of seven different species of algae within these rivers.

Seven different data sets were created each using the same inputs with one particular alga assigned as the output. Outputs were continuous, accuracy was judged according to the number of times the model was able to predict algae concentration within a certain range. Data was trained using 320 vectors and tested with the remaining 20.

The best results were obtained for the fifth and seventh algae examined. For the fifth algae, with the full mask the model predicted fourteen concentrations to within a range of 0.01 (i.e. 0.625%). After reducing the number of nearest neighbours to nine (p=9) and eliminating inputs relating to season and river size, the model was capable of predicting sixteen concentrations to the same accuracy. For the seventh algae, the full mask was able to predict 16 concentrations accurately. This was improved to nineteen when only four near neighbours (p=4) were used, and improved to twenty with a reduced mask.

4.7 Deliberate noise

In order to establish that the GA was capable of picking out appropriate variables that led to the creation of superior models, noise was deliberately introduced into a dataset. The GA should be able to discard the variables consisting purely of noise. The fifth algae dataset was used to do this, as it was known to be capable of producing useful models. Here, no judgement is made upon the accuracy of models developed, as the aim is merely to ascertain that the GA is capable of picking out irrelevant data.

4.7.1 Introducing Random Data

An additional column was introduced into the dataset, containing random numbers. After reducing the number of near neighbours to three (p=3), the GA correctly suggested the use of a mask that did not contain the random data.

4.7.2 Duplicating Variables

One of the chemical concentrations that had consistently been included in the best masks was copied and repeated in the dataset. This experiment was particularly interesting as the input that was to be discarded *did* contain relevant information, but it was data that was supplied elsewhere (*i.e.* the duplicated attribute) and as such was not necessary for the construction of a good model. With six near neighbours (p=6), the GA removed one of the duplicated inputs.

4.8 Results Summary

This section provides a summary (shown in Table 2) of the experiments described above. These experiments provide empirical evidence that clearly demonstrates the utility of the Gamma Test derived objective function, used in conjunction with a Genetic Algorithm, in terms of determining which attributes are most predictively useful. In addition, it has been shown that the methodology is able to eliminate those duplicated and random attributes that were artificially added to the existing attributes – in other words, those attributes that were *known* to be irrelevant.

Experiment	Accuracy Criteria	Number of inputs in Partial Mask	Suggested number of neighbours (p)	Number of accurate predictions			
				Percentage improvement	Full Mask, 10 neighbours	Full Mask, p neighbours	Partial Mask, p neighbours
1. Boston Housing	Number of examples predicted to within a range of 0.04	13/14	10	3.5	42/56	42/56	44/56
2. Income	Number of examples correctly categorised	13/14	5	12.1	33,579/ 46,342	33,840/ 46,342	39,197/ 46,342
3. Breast Cancer	Number of examples correctly categorised	2/9	10	15.4	22/26	22/26	26/26
4. Lymphography	Number of examples correctly categorised	13/18	15	6	17/18	13/18	18/18
5. Algae 5	Number of examples predicted to within a range of 0.01	16/18	9	10	14/20	15/20	16/20
6. Algae 7	Number of examples predicted to within a range of 0.01	11/18	4	20	16/20	19/20	20/20

Table 2 - Summary of results obtained

The 'Accuracy Criteria' column describes the method of assessing accuracy for that particular experiment. The 'Number of inputs in partial mask' column represents the number of inputs used out of the number available, while the 'Number of accurate predictions' columns represent the number of predictions out of the total number of predictions made.

5. Conclusion

These results demonstrate that the techniques applied to the datasets have improved the accuracy of models that have been constructed. We have shown that the GA has been able to work in conjunction with the GT to appropriately select the relevant inputs within a data set without *a priori* knowledge concerning each application area. This ability to select predictively useful attributes from numerical data sets in a true data driven sense promises to provide knowledge engineers with a formidable tool.

6.   Acknowledgements

The breast cancer and lymphography domain was obtained from the University Medical Centre, Institute of Oncology, Ljubljana, Yugoslavia. Thanks go to M. Zwitter and M. Soklic for providing the data.

7.   References

1.   Zurada. J. M. Introduction to Artificial Neural Systems. West Publishing Company (ISBN 0-314-93391), 1992

2.   Cleveland W.S. & Devlin S.J. Locally Weighted Regression: An Approach to Regression Analysis by Local Fitting. Journal of the American Statistical Association 1988; 83:596-610

3.   Hall, M.A. & Holmes, G. Benchmarking Attribute Selection Techniques For Discrete Class Data Mining. IEEE Transactions On Knowledge And Data Engineering, 2003. 15(3)

4.   Golberg A. Genetic Algorithms in Search, Optimisation and Machine Learning. Addison-Wesley, 1989

5.   DeJong, K. A. & Sarma J. Generation gaps revisited. Foundations of Genetic Algorithms 2, San Mateo, CA: Morgan Kaufmann, 1993.

6.   Stefansson A., Konvcar N. & Jones A. J. A note on the Gamma Test. Neural Computing Applications 1997; 5:131-133

7.   Evans D. & Jones A. J. A proof of the Gamma test, Proceedings of the Royal Society London. 2002; A, 458:1-41

8.   Evans D., Jones A. J. & Schmidt W. M. Asymptotic moments of near neighbour distance distributions, Proceedings of the Royal Society London 2002; A,458:1-11

9.   Evans, D. "Data-derived estimates of noise for known smooth models using near-neighbour asymptotics." Ph.D. dissertation, Department of Computer Science, Cardiff University, Wales, UK, 2002

10. Durrant P.J. "winGamma TM: a non-linear data analysis and modelling tool for the investigation of non-linear and chaotic systems with applied techniques for a flood prediction system." Ph.D. dissertation, Department of Computer Science, Cardiff University, Wales, UK, 2001

11. Harrison D. & Rubinfeld D.L. *Hedonic prices and the demand for clean air*, J. Environ. Economics & Management 1978; 5:81-102

12. Hettich S. & Bay S. D. The UCI KDD Archive [http://kdd.ics.uci.edu]. Irvine, CA: University of California, Department of Information and Computer Science. 1999.

AUTHOR INDEX